QUESTIONS OF VALUE

 **Prentice Hall**

FINANCIAL TIMES

In an increasingly competitive world, we believe it's quality
of thinking that will give you the edge – an idea that opens
new doors, a technique that solves a problem, or an insight
that simply makes sense of it all. The more you know, the
smarter and faster you can go.

That's why we work with the best minds in business and
finance to bring cutting-edge thinking and best learning
practice to a global market.

Under a range of leading imprints, including *Financial Times
Prentice Hall*, we create world-class print publications and
electronic products bringing our readers knowledge, skills
and understanding which can be applied whether studying or
at work.

To find out more about Pearson Education publications,
or tell us about the books you'd like to find, you can visit us at
www.pearsoned.co.uk

CORPORATE FINANCE

QUESTIONS OF VALUE

Master the latest developments in value-based management, investment and regulation

Edited by

Andrew Black

FINANCIAL TIMES

An imprint of Pearson Education

London • New York • Toronto • Sydney • Tokyo • Singapore
Hong Kong • Cape Town • Madrid • Paris • Amsterdam • Munich • Milan

PEARSON EDUCATION LIMITED

Head Office:
Edinburgh Gate
Harlow CM20 2JE
Tel: +44 (0)1279 623623
Fax: +44 (0)1279 431059

Website: www.pearsoned.co.uk

———————————————

First published in Great Britain in 2004

ISBN 0 273 65624 4

British Library Cataloguing in Publication Data
A CIP catalogue record for this book can be obtained from the British Library.

10 9 8 7 6 5 4 3 2 1

Typeset by Land & Unwin (Data Sciences) Ltd
Printed and bound in Great Britain by Bell and Bain Ltd, Glasgow

The Publishers' policy is to use paper manufactured from sustainable forests.

CONTENTS

FOREWORD – Philip Wright

This book was Andrew Black's idea. We first worked together at Pricewaterhouse-Coopers from 1994 to 1997, and amongst the fruits of this was our book *In Search of Shareholder Value* in 1997. Since then, we have been through economic boom and bust and moved in to a new millennium. Andrew has now set up his own value consulting business, and has also correctly identified the continuing thirst to learn about the issues surrounding value. In the view of some, the bubble economy and the accompanying corporate and market excesses have shown how the obsession with shareholder value has misled us, worked to the detriment of other stakeholders and is a false path. However, we have also all learned through the events of the last few years how crucial good governance is to value creation, how crucial value creation is to our future pensions and how crucial quality investment management is to both of these. Andrew's *Questions of Value* are therefore well chosen, and an important contribution to this debate.

In the area of development and regulation of reporting, the last few years have seen a veritable storm of activity in two areas. First, the contents of accounts are under increasing focus as the proportion of intangible assets to total business value grows in importance and compilers and users grapple with how to communicate best the strategy and performance of a business, including how to incorporate and interpret the interaction of earnings, cash flow, share price and value. Second, the role of accountants and auditors in reporting has become the subject of intense scrutiny, debate and new regulation. Again, this book tackles these issues from a variety of interesting angles as to how to improve further communication and reporting.

Finally, the search to improve the understanding of the value creation process goes on. This involves not only new techniques, methodologies and software tools, but also how these can be simply explained, understood and built into the culture of both a continuing business and also into a merger or acquisition. The last section of the book again gives penetrating insights on developments in these areas.

The continuing spread of private capital, the globalization of markets and compound growth in information, means that the fascination with value and how it is best created, managed and distributed will continue. This book makes an important contribution to the debate and understanding of the issues involved.

Philip Wright
Global leader Corporate Finance, PricewaterhouseCoopers

ACKNOWLEDGEMENTS

The editor would firstly like to acknowledge the efforts of the individual authors, without whom this book would not have been possible.

We held an important workshop at the 'Retreat' at Rhos-y-Gilwen in Pembrokeshire in Wales. I would very much like to thank Brenda and Glen Peters for the use of their lovely house. The absence of mobile phone reception there doubtless played a large role in focussing the authors' attention on the task at hand.

Laurie Donaldson from Pearson Educational is also to be thanked for helping keep the project on the road and in seeing it through to a successful conclusion.

I would also like to thank John Davies for his tireless and painstaking work on the detailed editing side. The book is materially the better for his attentions.

Finally, I'd like to thank my wife, Gabi, for supporting me in this endeavour and in reminding me when I got calls from around the world from itinerant authors and contributors!

Andrew Black

ABOUT THE AUTHORS

Jose Arau, a Principal Investment Officer at the California Public Employees' Retirement System (CalPERS), has been a portfolio manager and investment analyst since 1977. He has involved since its beginnings in CalPERS' commitment to corporate governance. He is a chartered financial analyst and president of the Security Analysts of Sacramento – the local society of the Association for Investment Management and Research (AIMR).

J.A. Barbour has been a Director of PA Consulting Group and a partner with Marakon Associates, the US-based strategy consultancy. In 1999, he founded Corporate Value Improvement (CVI) – a specialist managing-for-value consulting practice which works with the leaders of significant businesses to help them to deliver superior returns to shareholders over time. His clients have included the top teams of J Sainsbury plc; Cadbury Schweppes plc; Roche Pharmaceuticals; Royal Philips Electronics NV; and Smith & Nephew plc. John Barbour is also Visiting Professor of Value Based Management at the University of Strathclyde's Graduate School of Business.

Richard Bassett holds a BA in Political Economy and History from the University of Victoria, Toronto, and an MBA from Boston College. Currently Managing Director of Value Analytix, London, he has worked extensively in the area of valuation and shareholder value analysis/value based management implementation since 1988. He has been involved with more than 200 institutions in 35 countries, and with M&A transactions worth a total deal value of over $60 billion. He has also advised extensively on capital structure, debt ratings, strategic planning systems and enterprise wide risk management systems. Prior to co-founding Value Analytix, Bassett was the Managing Director of Alcar International and Managing Director of Corporate Performance Systems. He was a vice-President at Security Pacific Merchant Bank in London and New York and he has also served on the personal staff of several Canadian cabinet ministers.

Andrew Black has a PhD and MSc in economics from Birkbeck College, and a BA in economics from Sussex University. Currently Managing Director of Building Value Associates Ltd, a financial consulting company, he has previously worked at PricewaterhouseCoopers as a director, where he set up and managed a group working in the shareholder value area. During this time he helped develop the software tool 'ValueBuilder' and co-authored *In Search of Shareholder Value* (1998, 2nd edition 2001). Earlier he worked for several banks on both the sell side as an economist and equity analyst, and as a global investment strategist. He has earlier experience with large corporations at Unilever and as a UK government economist at the DTI.

Colin Clubb is Reader in Accounting and Head of the Accounting Section at the Business School, Imperial College London, where he teaches on the MBA and MSc in Finance programmes. His main research interests are in the area of accounting information and equity valuation and his work has been published in major international research journals. He also has research and consultancy interests in the area of shareholder value analysis and reporting.

David Gee has a degree in mathematics from Cambridge University. After qualifying as a chartered accountant he worked first for Aston Martin Lagonda and then for the British Leyland Motor Corporation. In 1974 he joined the corporation that is the subject of his chapter, working in its regional and central finance and planning departments. his last position before retirement in 2002 was as Corporate Planning Controller. Since retirement he has set up his own business as a strategic and financial consultant. In May 2003, David Gee was elected as a Liberal Democrat member of Redditch Borough Council and has become a member of its executive committee. David welcomes enquiries by e-mail to david_gee@talk21.com.

Paul Lee is a Shareholder Engagement Manager at Hermes Investment Management in London. Having graduated with a first in law from Oxford University, he spent a decade as a journalist on various specialist journals, including five years as editor of *International Financial Law Review* and then as managing editor of *CFO Europe*. He now applies shareholder engagement disciplines to discussions with companies in the Hermes core index-tracking portfolios and also in the two Hermes Focus Funds in the UK. He continues to write, including chapters for various corporate governance and strategy books and winning the second PricewaterhouseCoopers European Shareholder Value Award for his article 'Not badly paid but paid badly'.

Elizabeth Legge has an honours degree in econometrics from the London School of Economics and a master's degree from Birkbeck College, London. Upon graduating she went to the National Institute of Economic and Social Research. Her career has taken her from academic research to computer programming with Lufthansa in Germany and then into the banking world. As an economist and financial markets analyst she has worked in the City since the 'Big Bang', setting up the economic research facility in the London branches of Dresdner Bank and Bankgesellschaft Berlin. Since 2001 she has worked for Building Value Associates and Weavering Capital. She has done extensive research into Europe's impending pensions crisis, writing and lecturing on the subject, and appears frequently as a speaker on global financial TV channels.

Erik Ottosson has a Master of Science degree in Industrial Engineering and Management from Linköping University, Institute of Technology. Previously Strategic Controller at the Swedish company SCA, where he was mainly involved in questions concerning acquisitions, strategy and management control and was the driving force behind SCA's successful shift towards a strong cash flow and growth focus. He is chairman of Anelda, the company that he co-founded with Fredrik Weissenrieder in 1998 to develop and market solutions for financial management control based on cash flow.

Mark L. Sirower holds a PhD in Competitive Strategy and Finance from the Columbia University Graduate School of Business and an MBA in Finance and Statistics from Indiana University. Currently, he is a Senior Advisor with the Boston Consulting Group and is the global leader of BCG's Mergers and Acquisitions practice, products and thinking. Before joining BCG in 1999, he taught M&A at the Wharton School of the University of Pennsylvania and consulted extensively on strategy and valuations issues in M&A transactions. He was a professor at Columbia University and has also held positions with KPMG, Burroughs Corporation and Price Waterhouse. He maintains a Visiting Professor appointment at New York University's Stern School of Business. Mark Sirower is author of the classic *The Synergy Trap: How Companies Lose the Acquisition Game*, and his research and articles on best practice in acquisition performance have been featured in major business periodicals.

Mark Storrie is Chief Technology Officer and co-founder of Value Analytix and is the chief designer of the software products produced by Value Analytix, blending over ten years' experience of work with financial institutions, valuation, risk identification and value-based planning with a solid grounding in IT. He has worked as an analyst with the Alcar Group International, and as a software developer for Software AG.

Alison Thomas has a bachelor's degree from Oxford University, a master's in finance and accounting from the London School of Economics and a doctorate in intangible asset evaluation. She started her career as a North American equities fund manager, working for a variety of blue-chip investment houses, including Baring Asset Management, where she was Director of Global Research. Frustrated with the paucity of information available on potential investments, she left the investment world and spent a few years examining, in an academic setting, the economic content of non-financial information, complementing her detailed empirical analyses through her own consultancy practice. This combination of empirical enquiry and client activity led Alison Thomas to PricewaterhouseCooper's ValueReporting team. Within PwC she works with clients across the world in the quest to add economic value through the improved quality of corporate reporting.

Fredrik Weissenrieder has a Master of Science in Economics from Gothenburg School of Economics and Commercial Law. He has worked as a consultant within cash flow based financial management in the European capital intensive industry since the early 1990s and has taught at Gothenburg School of Economics and Commercial Law. Together with Erik Ottosson, he developed CVA®, which is a system that supplements traditional accounting and provides companies with the capability to link strategic planning and strategic decisions with feedback from financial outcome.

LIST OF TABLES

LIST OF FIGURES

INTRODUCTION – Andrew Black

The value of corporations is of great importance to everyone in our society. Our future depends on it, since a lot of our money is invested in the equity market in the form of pensions and other savings. Society feels better off when equity prices are soaring, and is correspondingly depressed when they plunge. This in turn can affect consumption and investment decisions by all the major participants in the economy. While there has been considerable discussion about what drives value in the equity market, and also what determines the intrinsic value of an enterprise, the assumption that these two things are the same is frequently unfounded. A firm's equity market value can differ sharply from other more internally and retrospective views.

This book looks at a number of topical issues affecting the value of companies and how it is determined. They are in three areas closely associated with determining corporate value: we see

> This book looks at a number of topical issues affecting the value of companies and how it is determined.

them as *questions of investing*, *questions of financial reporting* and *technical questions about the delivery of value*.

Our first section deals with *Questions of investing*: we explore how another breed of institutional investors has developed alternative approaches to companies. This involves considering longer-term investment horizons and focuses on getting good shareholder value creation and good corporate governance. There is a very clear association between the two in their eyes. This approach requires a greater degree of shareholder activism aimed at raising corporate performance.

And corporate performance is going to have to be raised, if the onerous requirements of funding future pension needs are to be met. With longer-term demographic changes placing ever larger burdens on pension funds, it is essential for funded pension systems that equities continue to perform well.

In the second section, *Questions of financial reporting*, we look at ways of re-configuring the current system of financial reports. These have been found wanting in several respects. A regular feature of commercial and financial life is the sensation of a scandal, followed by a flurry of regulatory activity, followed by a period of somnolence as business gets back to 'normal'. In this book we

A regular feature of commercial and financial life is the sensation of a scandal, followed by a flurry of regulatory activity, followed by a period of somnolence as business gets back to 'normal'.

present some reasons why we think the latest set of scandals is not just a storm in a teacup, but perhaps marks an important watershed in the way society reacts to the implosion and annihilation of large corporates. Clearly the enormous social and economic consequences involved in getting it wrong point to a greater involvement of non-accounting people in determining future regulatory environments.

In the last section, *Questions of delivery*, we look at some of the outstanding technical issues relating to valuation and to the delivery of value. We consider the experience and activities of the practitioners of value-based management both from the client's and the consultant's point of view. We also look at some of the technical issues that have arisen as a result of the Enron case, investigate how investment decisions often fail to produce the desired results and consider why so many mergers and acquisitions also fail the value-creation test.

During the process of collecting these articles much was changing in the world. The book could also have been called 'The Trouble with Enron' or 'Cash Flow Valuation Techniques Come of Age'. We will necessarily be touching on such matters. Yet the main purpose of the book is to assemble a number of disparate strands of thinking that rarely come together. It is as if a river has divided a town into two communities leading separate and distinct lives. On one shore is the financial market community, used to looking through its telescope at the inhabitants on the other side of the river. These are the corporate managers, who spend most of their time on their side, often suspicious of what their counterparts on the other shore get up to. This book aims to provide a bridge connecting the two sides of the river, with the traffic of various arguments flowing across it. There are tolls on this bridge, made up of fees to accountants, auditors, lawyers and consultants – which might explain why the traffic is sometimes scarce. There are also surges of traffic in one direction or the other, as happens when the interests of one group appear to be ignored by the other. (Recently a lot of traffic has crossed from the financial side to the managerial side, and traffic jams are in evidence.)

This book is also an effort to understand how successful the cash flow and DCF-based view of company valuations have been over the past few years, and whether it forms an useful point of view, different and separate from others based on earnings or other more arcane measures.

So in the following chapters investment managers, economists, consultants, corporate managers, former bankers, academics and IT experts write about how they see developments in value-based management, corporate strategies, investment decisions, IT investment, financial reporting and the future shape of accounting. All of this is connected through a common understanding that the cash flow value-based approach to companies and financial assets offers insights that are being developed further. The views expressed here are far from uniform; some authors take quite different positions regarding recent developments. But this is very much a subject area still unfolding, and it is important to try to understand the likely course of further developments in this area.

It would be over-optimistic to suggest that the difficulties and problems have been identified, let alone resolved. Yet, as this book was being written, many of the initial critiques from the cash flow 'school' seemed to have been borne out by events, and today it looks as if the financial markets and the accounting profession are having to grapple with some very real issues.

> As this book was being written, many of the initial critiques from the cash flow 'school' seemed to have been borne out by events.

The structure of this book

This book begins by looking at the financial markets. Shareholder value theory and practice means trying to align the interests of the shareholders with those of corporate management more closely than used to be the case. One of the outcomes for this has been the rise of what can be called 'shareholder activism'. We have two contributions from two leading proponents: Paul Lee from Hermes Investments in the UK and Joe Arau from CalPERS in the USA. Lee spells out the view that most institutional investors' main goal should be the development of long-term shareholder value – which is by no means the same as the sum of a series of short-term 'maximized' positions. Achieving better shareholder returns, he argues, ensures along the way that the other stakeholders involved in the process come out better off too. He also provides evidence that good corporate governance can also be good for the pocket. Institutional investors can indeed intervene to change the direction and components of management, and in so doing enhance shareholder returns.

In Chapter 2, Joe Arau details the approach taken by CalPERS over the years, and documents how an investor that is fully committed and following a largely indexed approach benefits from intervening to pep up the performance of underperforming companies by the judicious replacement of failing executives. Arau cites several examples where CalPERS intervention has been timely and effective, including with companies as large as General Motors. He also quotes studies showing that companies in their portfolio that had previously underperformed before CalPERS intervention went on to outperform the national average substantially in the subsequent five years.

Both chapters provide ammunition for the argument that more direct involvement by investors – the owners of publicly quoted companies – can be beneficial, helping to reduce the gap between ownership and control that some argue has been responsible for much substandard corporate financial performance. All of which is relevant to proposals in the UK (by the Higgs Committee, which reported in the summer of 2003) that a senior independent director (SID) should be empowered as a non-executive director to talk directly with a company's major shareholders once a year, or more often if required. We believe this reflects the thinking represented by groups such as Hermes and CalPERS.

This is followed by a chapter, by Elizabeth Legge of Weaving Capital, exposing the dire problems facing the European pensions industry. It is a sorry litany of missed opportunities and botched reforms, and also delineates the demographic time bomb that will be the source of much political friction in the future. Already there has been major discontent in France on the pensions issue, and in the UK educational system as additional government grants to schools have been entirely consumed by increased pension contributions for teachers. She suggests that retirement ages will have to rise to the mid-70s later this century if the pension system is to survive.

The underlying issue, of course, is that it is essential that pensions are provided for, and in a funded system the only asset that can provide the required capital growth are equities. Here the search for better investment returns must heighten interest from the financial side of the city in management performance.

The chapter identifies a number of conundrums affecting policy-makers. All pension schemes require there to be more contributors than pensioners: demographic factors make this increasingly unlikely in the OECD area. Legge raises the question of whom is ultimately responsible for providing pensions, since state involvement has been driven by a deep distrust that individuals would save the required amount for their future needs. This scepticism is by no means misplaced, but the highly interventionist stance by many continental European countries is probably raising expectations to an unsustainable degree. Alas, UK policy has hardly performed better; indeed, arguably it has done rather worse. Poor decisions by the management of Equitable Life, for instance, have already left many elderly people disappointed. The Maxwell scandal, involving the pillaging of a corporate pension fund, was not even technically illegal, and underlines how fragile the entire system of privately funded pensions in the UK is. So if ordinary investors are seeking higher returns, the pensions industry is crying out for them, if only to escape an imminent breakdown.

We then turn to some issues around the whole area of *financial reporting*. Clearly if there is a need for financial performance, it is important to know if we can actually measure it properly without too many biases and difficulties. The first of four chapters in this section is by Alison Thomas from Oxford University and PwC, who looks at the questions raised by the growth in intangibles, and the related issue of how to report on non-financial factors that clearly have a bearing on the overall success of a company. Intangibles are a bit like the 'dark matter' in the universe; they are there but no one can really see them, let alone value them properly.

Thomas also considers a number of alternative measures of performance from economic, environmental and social points of view, the so called 'triple bottom line'. Some of this can be subsumed under the idea of value-based reporting that gives a more rounded view of corporate performance. She argues that increasing the extent of non-financial disclosures will help investors and others understand the nature of the longer-term relationships needed to maintain prosperity for the company.

Such requirements could be seen as intrusive by companies seeking to avoid more 'red tape', and be treated with suspicion by the financial community, who might argue that there are few controls over the nature, quality and reliability of the information. This may suggest a need for a different kind of audit in the future, one that might well be performed by a rather different kind of auditor.

The specific issue of intangibles is clouded by confusion in the accounting treatment of goodwill (should it be depreciated or shouldn't it?) and in judging when the value of the intangibles and goodwill can be 'realized'. At the moment there is a clear problem: endogenously produced goodwill doesn't feature on the balance sheet – it is 'dark matter' – until it is crystallized out as part of a transaction. Which may help explain why so many mergers and acquisitions happen in industries where valuing intellectual property is both difficult and essential.

> The specific issue of intangibles is clouded by confusion in the accounting treatment of goodwill (should it be depreciated or shouldn't it?) and in judging when the value of the intangibles and goodwill can be 'realized'.

In Chapter 5 Andrew Black from Building Value Associates Ltd takes on the challenging task of trying to identify systemic problems in the world of accounting, and what can be done about them. Among these problems are the issues of revenue recognition and special purpose vehicles (SPVs). These affect all accounting systems. He then goes on to catalogue a rather sorry sequence of scandals and issues related to 'faulty audits', developing this in more detail with reference to recent events in the USA, where the Sarbanes-Oxley Act is likely to lead to major changes in the accounting and auditing profession, both in the USA and elsewhere, with lay opinion playing a far greater role in setting standards. Other leading OECD countries, too, will take further steps to regulate auditors, in particular with respect to their independence and standards of professional conduct.

While the intent to emphasize content over form is a good one, the complexities of international financial reporting are likely to lead to further efforts to codify and standardize accounting practice worldwide. While the idea of moving over to the IAS (International Accounting Standards) system in 2005 is desirable, one standard for financial reporting to the markets is only likely to be achieved if major compromises are made. Given the importance of financial reporting for the completion of the internal European Capital Market, there is likely to be pressure on the European Commission to introduce measures to standardize and harmonize corporate tax structures – going much further than most politicians and their desire for national 'fiscal independence' are likely to want to go. Already lawsuits are pending over the recognition of tax losses in one EU country by the tax authorities in another.

Black's view is that the backwash from Enron and other cases has weakened the accountancy profession and could open up the field of financial and non-financial auditing and analysis to a wider group of advisors. The accountants may be about to lose their monopoly.

Drawing on the insights of the cash flow approach, Colin Clubb from Imperial College Business School proposes a new approach to financial reporting. He suggests that more explicit recognition be given to looking at corporate valuation as being the sum of both operating cash flows and an assessment of the future cash flows a company might earn. He argues that adopting this approach would enhance the social visibility of total shareholder return and shareholder value objectives, and would encourage companies to explain or challenge the capital market's assessment of their opportunities and performance – perhaps leading to more traffic between the two parts of the city. It would accelerate the decline in the use of the profit and loss account and would focus attention on valuing assets. Finally, it would place even more emphasis on the derivation and reporting of cash flows, which would then move centre stage and become a core part of the financial reporting system – a point also made in Chapter 5.

Continuing in this vein, we then have a chapter from Richard Bassett and Mark Storrie from Risktoolz in the USA, who take a very close look at the demise of Enron. They think that the root problem was that too little attention was paid to the cash flow analysis. If this had been done more assiduously, it is likely that the misdeeds of the Enron management would have become more widely understood more quickly. They make the point that the retrospective financial reporting of the company was still racking up growing earnings even as the share price was plummeting, thus highlighting what happens when the bridge between the two parts of the city (financial and managerial) is closed for a while. They identify several factors that led to the company's downfall, but suggest that this is not so much a systemic crisis as the result of a misapplication of the US GAAP rules. But, they then go on to argue, this too is not appropriate since the company would still have failed even if the rules had been correctly applied. This they think gives further weight to the importance of cash flow, forward-looking statements that are essential for the proper working of the US capital markets. In their view, the Sarbanes-Oxley Act will make the provision of such statements from auditors virtually impossible, which in turn could increase volatility in the financial markets.

We then move onto a different complex of issues, this time *technical questions about the delivery of value*. Has the application of cash flow methods of valuation and value-based management (VBM) so far been worthwhile? David Gee presents an interesting case study documenting the detailed issues that have to be resolved if a VBM project is really going to work well. He concludes that from a client's point of view, VBM exercises really can make an important difference – perhaps most notably in the way they contribute to a change in corporate culture and get managers asking similar questions to those being asked on the other side of the 'bridge'. Although the exercise can be time-consuming and expensive, with the right backing from the senior management team, VBM can achieve useful outcomes, not the least a rise in shareholder value and the attainment of improved performance.

> The Sarbanes-Oxley Act will make the provision of such statements from auditors virtually impossible, which in turn could increase volatility in the financial markets.

So if it is all right for the client, how was it for the consultant? Professor John Barbour provides a concise view of the dos and don'ts of VBM or 'managing for value' from the consultant's viewpoint. He argues that it is essential to see VBM as more than just a set of spreadsheets; it has to involve understanding and changing the strategy at a company's highest levels. This is not always popular, especially if it involves the slaughter of one or several shibboleths held dear by management. He also points out that successful VBM projects do require top management support, and will also involve changes to the company's internal IT systems.

Another consultant, Mark Sirower of BCG, provides us with a detailed view on how to achieve valuable growth through mergers and acquisition. A long-time critic of much M&A activity, Sirower tells us that the initial market view of a merger or takeover is almost always correct. If the initial market reaction is to mark down the price of the acquiring firm, then it is highly probable that the share will subsequently underperform the market. If the initial market reaction is more upbeat, an initial rise in the acquiring company's share price following the announcement of a merger will continue. So if nothing else, investors and managers alike should be glued to their screens and their copies of the *FT* and *Wall Street Journal* when following mergers. Sirower shows that companies that overpay for their targets tend to do badly subsequently, and that cash deals tend to perform better than deals financed by share offerings.

If all of this sounds like a shaft of light in what is sometimes a very murky area, readers will be pleased to know that he also outlines a 'road map' for capturing the benefits of mergers and for avoiding the more obvious pitfalls, and looks at what he calls 'always on' company and its successful M&A strategies. He develops his ideas with a list of successful post merger integration (PMI) exercises.

We then move still deeper into the world of corporate management. Eric Ottosson and Fredrik Weissenrieder from Anelda explain why so much of current financial reporting is fundamentally flawed. They pick up on the often observed phenomenon that despite the best of intentions, individual investment projects often fail to deliver the promised results. This is despite the often impressive ratings the projects and the companies can achieve when return on investment indicators are used. They provide a framework for getting to grips with this dilemma, using cash-flow-based methodologies that provide a superior framework for judging and valuing the impact of individual investment projects. They also make a sly dig at the efforts of the Sarbanes-Oxley reforms by suggesting that the average CEO and CFO would be ill advised to sign off on their financial reports, riddled as they are with inconsistencies.

We hope that after this rich diet, the reader will have crossed the 'bridge' several times and have begun to comprehend some of the serious issues currently exercising the minds of the more thoughtful financial analysts and commentators. Policies are evolving, and these affect both shareholders and the major stakeholders in companies. This book is a small contribution to throwing more light on these developments, with the hope that previously obscure elements are now better understood within the context of trying to increase shareholder value.

section I:

QUESTIONS OF INVESTING

1

INVESTORS AND LONG-TERM SHAREHOLDER VALUE

PAUL LEE
Hermes Pensions Management

The late 1990s and early 2000s saw a remarkable stock market boom and bust, with theoretical billions added to the value of companies only to be wiped off again. This, in a conventional view, was a tremendous creation and then destruction of shareholder value.

But this mistakes short-term pricing for long-term value. From 1998 to 2000, Vivendi Universal made acquisitions worth more than €60 billion, leading to its economic return falling from about its cost of capital to nearly 10% below. Was this worthy of a share price increase of €60, from €35 to €95? In the summer of 2002, Vivendi Universal flirted with bankruptcy, and the share price at the time of writing remains resolutely under €20. In 2000, at the peak of the telecoms hardware boom, Cisco's share price was $82 – which meant that in net present value terms it had to grow by 30–50% a year, and maintain its already high returns. Unsurprisingly, its share price went down over 80% from its peak. Of course, the dot-com companies were never worth the absurd valuations the markets put on them; and it does not take the accounting irregularities of an Enron or WorldCom to show that market price can get divorced from real value.

Imperfect market

That this was a price, not value, issue should be plain even to doubters when you think about the supply and demand factors. Some stocks – the otherwise unattractive Wanadoo for example – got overheated because of a limited supply of shares even though they were given full weighting in indices. The move by all the index providers to change the weightings they give to stocks with limited free float played its part in deflating demand for those stocks, and bringing the price down. The level of free float, of course, is irrelevant to the underlying value of the company.

Everyone knows that the market gets things wrong. Few have the temerity still to cling to the perfect-market hypothesis. Those of us who have experienced stock-market sentiment from the inside know that often there is no explanation other than psychology for apparent failures to recognize value – until some external event changes the mood and makes it impossible to ignore – or for overvaluations going unquestioned until the destruction of value becomes so great it cannot be ignored.

> It is daft simply to think of shareholder value as the price at any given time put on a company's shares by the market.

In this light, it is daft simply to think of shareholder value as the price at any given time put on a company's shares by the market. Sometimes that price will indeed be an accurate one – certainly, over time, movements in it will come close to an accurate reflection of changes in a company's value – but market sentiment is a supertanker, slow in altering its course to reflect change. What's more, short-term supply and demand factors within the market can have skewed impacts. The dot-com debacle also showed that the sentiment supertanker often sets off at high speed in entirely the wrong direction. Turning it around then is still harder than usual.

The long view

It should not be a radical view that shareholder value is something longer-term than the market's short-term price fluctuations. The bulk of investment is long-term in any case. In the UK, for example, pension funds and life assurers, which both have investment horizons of 20 years or more, hold more than 60% of the market as a whole, and much retail investment will be for the longer term too. Similar proportions apply to the majority of developed markets.

And these investors genuinely are long-term in their outlook. A survey a couple of years ago by the UK's National Association of Pension Funds found that pension funds held stocks for an average of eight years. When you remember that many shares will not have been sold per se by the funds but that a number of the companies will have been subject to takeover or to bankruptcy – so that the pension funds intended holding period would have been still longer – it is clear that the investment policies of funds are not short-termist in the way often alleged.

So why do share prices in the short term not always reflect the intrinsic value of a company? There are a number of reasons.

First, as well as the long-term investors, there are many shorter-term investors. By their nature, these shorter-term investors will be more active in the marketplace and have more of an influence on day-to-day share prices. Hedge funds are just one example of these fleet-of-foot, often momentum-driven investors who may drive valuations beyond where logic would suggest – indeed, some may benefit from prices overshooting in either direction. The analyst community favours this sort of behaviour, and tailors its advice to the market to suit such traders. This is partly at least because the sell-side analysts are part of brokerage institutions that benefit from high volumes of trading. Because of these economic drivers, analysts' discussions, both with companies and in their reports, tend to focus on the short-term factors that influence trading strategies. No wonder companies think the City is obsessed with the short term.

What gets measured gets done, and where fund managers feel themselves to be judged on their three- or six-month performance figures compared with a benchmark, it is difficult for them to look beyond such short-term performance and think about long-term value.

Second, the agents acting for long-term investors may not work to the long-term timescales that would benefit their clients. The UK's Myners Report[1] pointed to the various conflicts of interest, and differences in attitude that can arise, between the long-term beneficial owner and the fund manager who acts as its investing agent. What gets measured gets done, and where fund managers feel themselves to be judged on their three- or six-month performance figures compared with a benchmark, it is difficult for them to look beyond such short-term performance and think about long-term value. Risk management becomes focused on hugging the benchmark – closet index-tracking (but with active management fees) – rather than managing client risk. The evidence that, after fees, active fund management does not add value above passive index-tracking tends to get ignored. Proposals for increasing the professionalism of pension fund trustees and other more structural reforms within the industry may go some way to addressing this.

Third, it is clear that not all long-term investors are equally long-term in their outlook. A study published in 2000 by Shaker Zahra of Georgia State University and two colleagues[2] is informative. Not only did the authors find that certain investors – such as insurance companies and banks – tend to be sensitive to pressure because of the conflicts of interest they face, while other institutions – generally pension funds – are more resistant to pressure from companies. They also found that companies with more shareholders who are resistant to pressure tend to perform better.

The logic of this finding is that the sensitivity or resistance to pressure on the part of investors tends to imply a lesser or greater willingness to be robust in confronting underperforming companies. If companies with a predominance of pressure-sensitive investors are less entrepreneurial than those with a predominance of those that are pressure-resistant, they are liable to have poorer financial performance.

Fourth, most funds have strict rules about the type of companies in which they can invest, in terms of location, industries, relevant weightings and so on. So if a company delisted from the UK to, say, France, then despite no change in intrinsic value, there would be downward pressure on the share price as all the UK funds sold out.

Notwithstanding these factors, the fact remains that the majority of investors in stock markets are involved for the long run. Were this more widely understood, and instilled in market practice, a number of positives would follow.

The cynicism about investors among investee companies would begin to dissolve; a more mature dialogue would be possible between investors and investees, on issues that genuinely generate value for

> The majority of investors in stock markets are involved for the long run.

the long term, rather than the current focus on short-term numbers to update spreadsheets. This ought to lead to more efficient allocation of capital and better long-term investment strategies, driving GDP and employment growth.

Were we to achieve this, it ought to defuse criticism of the weight companies give to the concept of shareholder value. For example, in mainland Europe, in many emerging markets and among unions and protest groups in various developed economies, there is a fear that an emphasis on shareholder value implies, and international investors require, a focus on short-term cash returns to shareholders, often to the detriment of the interests of other stakeholders, such as employees and local people dependent on environmental quality.

Where it is clear that shareholder value is more focused on the long term and not on immediate cash returns, international investment, and the growth and development that it can bring, may be more welcome. Many investors are now explicit about the need to protect the interests of all stakeholders in order to preserve shareholder value for the long term. We at Hermes have been asked by our owner and principal client, the British Telecom Pension Scheme, to apply the following to all our investments:

> A company run in the long-term interests of its shareholders will need to manage effectively relationships with its employees, suppliers and customers, to behave ethically and to have regard for the environment and society as a whole.

Furthermore, focusing on long-term shareholder value does indeed benefit all stakeholders over the long term. Customers benefit because in a competitive market the company will strive to provide them with a superior offering. By driving for cost efficiencies, more people are employed and paid better. Even the environment should benefit. Compare the dilapidation of cities and the wider environment in failed Communist societies with those in capitalist economies. We engage with companies to encourage them to be aware of our clients' interests in this regard.

The benefits of good governance

Having referred to the increasingly explicit nature of the emphasis on the long term, there are nevertheless good intellectual reasons why investors focus more strongly on short-term cash returns from their investments in less developed markets. This is the bird-in-the-hand theory of investment: it is more valuable to have cash dividends returned to shareholders than to see them reinvested in the business. This will generally be the case where investors do not trust management, and do not trust that value will be created by any reinvestment. Generally, it requires greater disclosure and better corporate governance to drive trust and so reduce the pressure for high dividends and little reinvestment.

> It is more valuable to have cash dividends returned to shareholders than to see them reinvested in the business. This will generally be the case where investors do not trust management.

Unless shareholders believe that the cash that could otherwise be used for dividends is going to be reinvested wisely, and is likely to earn a return in excess of the cost of capital, they will demand that dividends be paid. Certainly, if investors fear that funds are liable to be appropriated from the business, they will want a high yield to compensate them for that risk. Thus investors' calls for good corporate governance – such things as genuinely independent outside directors and remuneration schemes that align the interests of executives with shareholders – should be heeded by companies looking for long-term investment. If they do so, they will attract further investment, will lower their cost of capital and will be put under less pressure to pay out the bulk of their earnings in dividends. Freed to reinvest in the business, they will be creating value for long-term shareholders and for themselves as well.

There is substantial and growing evidence that good corporate governance practices do lead to outperformance by companies. As well as the more anecdotal surveys by McKinsey, that indicate valuations companies with good governance may be 15% more higher than less well-governed peers, some studies have produced hard numbers based on past total shareholder return performance. A 1998 study by Ira Millstein and Paul MacAvoy of the Yale School of Management[3] found that well-governed companies produced better returns. Using CalPERS[4] ratings for companies, they found that top-rated companies produced a return 7.3% above the cost of capital in excess of the return above the cost of capital achieved by the lowest-rated companies. More recently, Paul Gompers and Joy Ishii of Harvard and Andrew Metrick of Wharton[5] ranked companies using their own sophisticated governance index, and found that a portfolio which bought the top-rated stocks and sold (went short of) the bottom-rated would have earned abnormal returns of 8.5% a year throughout the 1990s.

> There is substantial and growing evidence that good corporate governance practices do lead to outperformance by companies.

Value from renewal

We believe that companies with well-structured and properly functioning boards are best able to develop successful strategies and to adapt quickly to changing circumstances. Time and again, in the companies we invest in, we see that a board can become entrenched in its views, slowly allowing a strong competitive position to erode – and with it financial returns. We also find that revitalizing boards with new independent outside directors and better governance structures in general inspires new thinking and a stronger focus on core competencies.

Take Tomkins. We worked with the company from mid-1999, cajoling then chair and CEO Greg Hutchings to reshape the business he had built and turn it from a sprawling conglomerate into a focused company once again. We were helped by the fact that the company had recently added a fully independent non-executive director (NED) in former GEC finance director David Newlands. After some encouragement, the board also added a further heavyweight independent director in the form of Sir Brian Pitman, widely respected for having revitalized Lloyds Bank.

Over this period, Tomkins was reshaped, starting with the sale of RHM, the baking and foods division, soon after we became involved. Subsequent deals saw the piecemeal disposal of the so-called gardening and leisure division, which included both Smith & Wesson handguns (then subject to US litigation) and Hayter lawnmowers, as well as a further eclectic range of businesses.

Tomkins was already a much tidier company by the time scandal broke at the 2000 AGM and Hutchings was forced to resign in November of that year. At that stage, the presence of respected outside directors became vital not just to the reshaping of the business but to its continuing survival. If Newlands had not been able to step up to executive chair and take control of the company, Tomkins might well have been broken up in a fire-sale which would have enriched purchasers and not helped shareholders at all; a still worse possibility was bankruptcy.

The principles of engagement

Our engagement with Tomkins is typical. We seek to ensure that there are sufficient independent outside directors on boards properly to consider long-term strategic issues. We then ask questions relating to their strategy and help them to challenge the status quo. Only through such challenge are strategies renewed and improved. Hermes has recently published a document, the *Hermes Principles*,[6] which lays out our expectations of companies in which our clients invest, in strategic, capital structure and social, environmental and ethical terms.

The principles set out various standards in the communication, financial, strategic and social, ethical and environmental fields. On the communication side, we expect companies to be transparent and open in their communications with shareholders, particularly on strategic and forward-looking matters. On the financial side, we expect companies to be able to identify and measure where they create most value; to test and evaluate any investments in detail; to seek to fully exploit opportunities within their core business and grow organically there before seeking diversification; to evaluate and incentivize executive performance to create shareholder value; to be cost-effective; and to have an efficient capital structure that will minimize the cost of capital.

On strategy, we expect companies to identify their competitive advantages and design their strategies fully to exploit those advantages; and to explain why they are the best parent of any of their businesses. On social, ethical and environmental matters, companies will need to manage their relationships with employees, suppliers, customers and any others with a legitimate interest. They should also support voluntary, regulatory and statutory measures that minimize the externalization of the costs of their activities.

Principles into practice

These principles will perhaps be best understood by looking at some of our engagements with companies. We seek to explore ways in which we can encourage companies to live up to our principles. In the real world, engagements tend to touch on several principles at once, but we attempt here to distil a few lessons from each. We deal with strategic issues first.

Companies should seek to earn, and ensure that they will continue to earn, a return over and above their cost of capital and demonstrate they have sustainable competitive advantage in the businesses they operate. They need to exploit their opportunities to grow profitably; long-term investment is valuable, provided that there is the potential for financial returns in the future that fully compensate for the upfront costs. The strategy most likely to deliver returns to shareholders will be a focus on core competencies that enable a company to protect and enhance its competitive advantage in its chosen market. Boards should be able to explain what their company's core competencies are and how those are being exploited to the full; they should also be prepared to explain why their company is the 'best parent' of all the businesses it operates.

With this principle in view, we involved ourselves at Rank when it was a sprawling conglomerate, with operations ranging from caravan parks to the Hard Rock Café, from video reproduction to bingo halls. The lack of logic or synergies between these businesses, and the impossibility of managing them all effectively, was reflected in a share price that undervalued the company and set it at a discount to the sum of its parts.

Throughout our discussions with the executives and chairman of the company, we repeatedly emphasized the need for focus and to discover a core for the company. We argued that those businesses that were already readily separable should be sold, and work should be done to make it possible to sell off other segments in due course. Over a period of a couple of years, Mike Smith, the new CEO, slimmed down the business drastically, offloading the holiday operations, the cinemas and the pubs business. He recognized the video duplication business as non-core, but was unable to complete the sale of that unit. Instead, it was retained but with minimum reinvestment. New Rank became a relatively focused company, with the Hard Rock business and gambling interests – in which the UK's deregulation offers a substantial opportunity. We look forward to Smith demonstrating the synergies that he believes exist between these two segments.

Cutting the cost of capital

To ensure the highest possible return to shareholders, companies need to minimize their cost of capital. Usually, this will involve increasing gearing because the tax benefits to the company of gearing feed through to a lower cost of debt capital. Most companies have too low gearing, thereby dissipating shareholder value. Our engagement with Six Continents, the hotelier/pub landlord company (also, at the start of our engagement, a brewing business), focused on the inefficient capital structure of the company, alongside the need to split the company into its different business units.[7]

> To ensure the highest possible return to shareholders, companies need to minimize their cost of capital.

In the same sort of category as capital structure is dividend policy. This formed a small part of our engagement with healthcare company Smith & Nephew. A conglomerate which spanned tampons, Elastoplast and some impressive high-technology wound treatments and artificial joints, Smith & Nephew's earnings had stagnated for over a decade. It appeared to us that its lack of focus was stifling its advanced technology units' potential for rapid growth.

With our encouragement, its new CEO revamped the company, exiting from consumer operations and focusing on the areas where the company had technological leadership and strong market positions. The market was slow to recognize the change until the company announced a change to its dividend policy, retaining the bulk of it to fuel growth. This triggered a reassessment of the stock as a growth rather than value one.

Solving the Premier Oil riddle

The best example of our work on social, environmental and ethical (SEE) issues was at Premier Oil, a company with strategic, capital structure and governance problems as well as a huge ethical dilemma. On the strategic side, along with much of the UK exploration and production sector, Premier had moved a long way from the most freewheeling end of the upstream segment of the oil market, and now was involved in consortia on relatively mature oil and gas fields. It was therefore competing with much larger companies in markets where it would appear to have little competitive advantage.

On the governance side, it had two 25% shareholders, Petronas and Amerada Hess, which as well as effectively insulating the company from takeover appointed two board members each. With other NEDs failing our criteria for independence for other reasons, we at Hermes had been encouraging board change for a number of years.

In addition to this issue, Premier faced regular campaigns from pressure groups over the company's status as the second largest foreign investor in Myanmar (Burma), where a military junta had refused to accept the results of a democratic election. While Premier was involved in many positive schemes in Myanmar, it was not clear to us as investor representatives that the company was fully managing the reputational and other risks which its involvement in the country implied.

Not surprisingly, Premier's share price had dramatically underperformed for several years. We became more actively involved in 2000, upping the level of our discussions and engagement with the company, with other investors (both in the UK and overseas) and with the pressure groups campaigning about Myanmar. We helped reduce the public campaigning spotlight on the company, giving it more space to find a solution to its problems, and believe that our interventions helped the company reach a resolution with its 25% shareholders more rapidly than might otherwise have been the case.

In September 2002, the company announced a deal paying for the exit of the major shareholders with assets, including those it held in Myanmar and also providing cash to cut Premier's debt. The deal led to the departure of those NEDs representing the major shareholders, making the board better able to take into account the interests of all shareholders. The deal also solved the company's strategic problems by removing all its mature production assets, freeing it to compete as a small exploration company fleet-footed enough to exploit opportunities the major oil companies might miss. Unsurprisingly, the news of this deal led to a substantial share price bounce.

Intervening to assist

We believe that these sorts of intervention assist companies to solve their problems. Too often, managers and boards are led to believe that their sources of finance are short-term and that quick fixes are desired, not reinvestment for the long term. Hermes acts to make clear that the genuine interests of most beneficial owners of companies are for long-term success, not short-term returns. We believe that this assists companies to find the right long-term solutions to their problems.

How might the story of Marconi have turned out if shareholders had asked tougher questions about the cash purchases of US companies Reltec and Fore at what was in retrospect the peak of the market? The short-term market reaction was favourable, but long-term investors could have done a better job of challenging and questioning the thinking behind those deals. Shareholders can often offer companies a useful perspective from an external and hopefully independent viewpoint.

> How might the story of Marconi have turned out if shareholders had asked tougher questions about the cash purchases of US companies Reltec and Fore at what was in retrospect the peak of the market?

We do not claim unique insights – rarely do we say things that have not already been discussed around the boardroom table – but we will often help the board level debate move forwards, demonstrating that investors are prepared to see radical change and accept perhaps some short term reduction in financial return in the short term. The realization that the majority of shareholders are responsible long-term owners, not short-term traders, can often help companies find the right solutions to their problems. Which is why we believe that companies with involved and interested shareholders will tend to perform better.

Paying (only) for performance

We have stiff expectations of companies, not least in the area of executive pay. We expect executives to be remunerated well (but cost-effectively) where they deserve it, and not where they do not. This means rigorous performance targets should be set, tailored to the likely performance of the company and to its medium-term strategic aims. It also means that pay-offs for failure are kept to a minimum.

We have seen many structures in recent years that do not incentivize executives to do the right thing. The mere assertion that pay is linked to share price performance through the award of options is meaningless: as the bubble and bust have shown, a share price of itself may have little link to good performance. Unless remuneration committees attach stiff performance hurdles designed around the company's strategic aims, options – and indeed any other executive reward scheme – are next to useless.

> The all-or-nothing nature of the reward being dependent on share price is one of the reasons that options seem to us an unsatisfactory incentive system.

Our preference is not only for hurdles that fit snugly into the board's strategy for the company, but also for a scheme that should include several tiers of award, making the incentivization bite in a smooth manner rather than in a binary way which can act as much as a disincentive as an incentive. The all-or-nothing nature of the reward being dependent on share price is one of the reasons that options seem to us an unsatisfactory incentive system.

We have seen many occasions where individuals have felt cheated because of a share price fall (as we've discussed, it may not be right to lay such a fall entirely at the door of executives) and are then demotivated. Such situations increase the pressure for a repricing of options, a practice that just emphasizes the one-sided nature of such incentivization schemes. As Hermes made clear at the time of our public stance on the Marconi repricing call, we will not support repricing except in exceptional circumstances, for instance at small companies with growth potential where technical staff need to be compensated for their lower salaries. Even in such cases, we will not support repricing at the board level.

This consideration on options is just one example of our views on pay. The key is that pay should cost-effectively incentivize executives to carry through a board's strategic plan. Too often we have seen executives receive substantial awards that are not obviously justified by their company's performance. Awards may nonetheless be needed and individuals may deserve to be rewarded for their performance in hitting the company's strategic aims. But if so, remuneration committees must explain much more clearly why the pay is justified and demonstrate that shareholders do receive full value for the sums they give out in executive pay. That is part of the transparency obligation.

Value for the long term

It is the role of companies to create shareholder value. That does not mean the inexorable rise of the share price, because many factors feed into short-term stock market volatilities. But in the long term, positive work by boards should feed through to long-term share price performance. That is only possible in the long term if boards do not just consider shareholder interests but also bear in mind the need to maintain good relations with other stakeholder interests such as employees, customers, suppliers, local communities and the public as a whole. If they fail to, the business model is not sustainable in the long term.

In other words, companies need to focus on strategy that will deliver value in the long term and seek to minimize their cost of capital so that financial returns are maximized. If they can do this, they can expect our long-term support as shareholders – and once investors as a whole recognize the long-term value being created, a much higher stock-market rating.

Notes

1   For the Myners Report, see www.hm-treasury.gov.uk/Documents/Financial_Services/securities_and_investments/fin_sec_myfinal.cfm

2   Zahra, Shaker, Neubaum, Donald and Huse, Morten (2000) 'Entrepreneurship in Medium-Size Companies: Exploring the Effects of Ownership and Governance Systems', *Journal of Management*, Vol. 26, No. 5, pp. 947–76.

3   Millstein, Ira and MacAvoy, Paul (1998) 'The Active Board of Directors and Performance of the Large Publicly Traded Corporation', *Columbia Law Review*, Vol. 98, No. 5.

4   On CalPERS, see Chapter 2.

5   Gompers, Paul and Ishii, Joy (2001) *Corporate Governance and Equity Prices*, (US) National Bureau of Economic Research Working Paper 8449.

6   For the principles see www.hermes.co.uk

7   This engagement has become public not through our actions.

2

CalPERS' ROLE IN CORPORATE GOVERNANCE[1]

JOSE ARAU
California Public Employees Retirement System

I

I started working at the California Public Employees' Retirement System (CalPERS) as an investment analyst/portfolio manager in 1977. In the following five years, considerable value could be found in strategic and financial mergers. It was cheaper to buy a division of a company, or a company itself, than to build a business from the ground up. Many companies were merged with others and many divisions were sold to financial acquirers whose job was to streamline the business operation and sell it for a profit to some strategic buyer.

The late 1970s and early 1980s also saw a proliferation of shareholder proposals. Many socially or politically committed individual shareholders, holding only a few shares of a company, decided to spur change not just by lobbying the political seats of power but also by asking companies to change the way they conducted business in order to promote environmental, public policy or labour agendas.

These two business trends forced CalPERS to develop internal expertise to deal with them. Was it more advantageous to keep a business or division with the current company or should we sell it? Was it beneficial for CalPERS to support shareholder proposals espoused by civic-minded shareholders?

The CalPERS board developed a set of proxy voting principles that addressed these issues. As well as drawing on investment consultants Citicorp and Scudder Stevens and Clark for merger issues, the board turned to the Investor Responsibility Research Center (IRRC) for social shareholder proposals. Importantly, CalPERS fiduciary consultant, Ian Lanoff, advised that the purpose of the fund was to invest for the sole benefit of the fund members. This basic pronouncement became a guiding light for CalPERS' proxy voting principles, which basically stated that shareholder proposals on sociopolitical issues could only be supported if they resulted in a stronger company and a more robust long-term outlook. Thus fortified, CalPERS' board did not support – though it was forced to comply with – California legislation ordering it to divest securities of US firms with operations in South Africa.

II

Our deeper involvement in corporate governance was triggered by a confluence of events. CalPERS' board became incensed when it found out that Texaco had offered to buy at a premium ('greenmail') the company stock held by a hostile raider. In addition, CalPERS disagreed with the 1984 Delaware court finding that Household International was right in having had its shareholder rights plan ('poison pill') instituted without prior shareholder approval. With Delaware court's blessing and with corporate raiders extremely active, poison pills became the most popular takeover defence.

> CalPERS' board became incensed when it found out that Texaco had offered to buy at a premium ('greenmail') the company stock held by a hostile raider.

These two events led the IRRC to publish an influential booklet about conflicts of interest. It focused on the need for directors to represent shareholders and to protect them from the entrenchment actions of managements.[2]

At the same time, another consultant on proxy matters opened shop. This was the former Labor Department Commissioner, Bob Monks. Imbued with a strong desire to force companies to behave as responsible citizens and to treat shareholders as owners of the corporation rather than holders of certificates, Monks started Institutional Shareholder Services (ISS), a firm that provided voting recommendations on management proposals and shareholder proposals.

An internal event at CalPERS led also to a stronger interest in proxy voting and corporate governance in general. This was the 1985 conversion of the active domestic equity portfolio to a passive (indexed) portfolio. Securities were no longer bought and sold according to their relative attractiveness. Now securities were being bought and held for a long time. This decisive structural change made the exercise of voting rights and the defence of shareholder interests a paramount objective.

III

Texaco's 1984 'greenmail' payment was such a climactic event that Jesse Unruh, a California political heavyweight who had been the head of the California Democratic Party, and was at the time the State Treasurer and a member of the board of the CalPERS and CalSTRS (California State Teachers' Retirement System), took the corporate governance banner and convinced the New York City and New Jersey pension funds to join CalPERS and CalSTRS in the formation of a Council of Institutional Investors (CII).

The CII became a clearing house for ideas on how to protect shareholders from unscrupulous boards and managements. Most public pension funds joined the CII shortly thereafter, but corporate pension funds and mutual funds to this day are meagrely represented.

The CII's first order of business was to prepare a set of general principles. In an abridged form they are:

1. Each share of common stock, regardless of class, should have one vote.

2. Individual voting issues should not be bundled.

3. A majority vote of common shares outstanding should be sufficient to amend company by-laws or take other action requiring or receiving a shareholder vote.

4. Broker non-votes and abstentions should be counted only for purposes of a quorum.

5. A majority vote of common shares outstanding should be required to approve major corporate decisions including:
   (a)   the corporation's acquiring, other than by tender offer to all share-holders, 5% or more of its common shares at above-market prices;
   (b)   the implementation of a shareholder rights plan ('poison pill');
   (c)   limiting the rights of shareholders to vote, to make nominations for directors, to call special meetings of shareholders or take action by written consent;
   (d)   granting any executive upon termination of employment any amount in excess of two times that person's average annual compensation for the previous three years; and
   (e)   provisions resulting in the issuance of debt to a degree that would excessively leverage the company and imperil the long-term viability of the corporation.

6. Shareholders should have the opportunity to vote on all equity-based compensation plans that include any director or executive officer of the company.

7. Shareholders should have better access to the proxy for corporate governance issues.

IV

In 1987, CalPERS realized that in order to be able to force companies to change their ways it had to introduce shareholder proposals. Some 22 shareholder proposals were filed on subjects such as the prohibition of greenmail, the institution of confidential voting, the repeal of anti-takeover provisions and to redeem the poison pill or put it to a shareholder vote.

Of the 22 targets, 16 companies were able to get the proposals thrown out at the Securities and Exchange Commission (SEC) on technicalities, but six proposals were accepted by the SEC. Those six were fought aggressively until voting day. However, the proposals had widespread shareholder support. Two proposals passed. They were the 'prohibit greenmail' proposal at Gillette and the 'repeal anti-takeover provisions' proposal at Texaco. The proposal to redeem the poison pill or put it to a shareholder vote received 48% of the vote at US Air Group, 42% of the vote at Consolidated Freightways and 28% of the vote at Great Northern Nekoosa. The proposal to institute confidential voting received 22% of the vote at Ryder System.

> In 1987, CalPERS realized that in order to be able to force companies to change their ways it had to introduce shareholder proposals.

In 1988, CalPERS came back armed with better weapons. It had hired outside legal counsel to guide it through the minefield of shareholder proposal introduction. This time the large majority of shareholder proposals introduced were accepted by the SEC. Gratifyingly, the repeat proposals from the prior year received substantial increases in their approval votes and the new proposals received a substantial vote. This strong shareholder response was very encouraging and showed that institutional investors were a force to be reckoned with.

In 1989, CalPERS realized that in order to effect change it had to do more than introduce shareholder proposals that, after all, were not binding. It had to actively engage the CEOs and boards of the targeted companies. So the cover letter of the shareholder proposal that went out to each CEO of a targeted company said that the proposal would be withdrawn if the company agreed to meet with us. That year, not too many CEOs responded. Managements and boards believed shareholders were not important enough to pay attention to them. CalPERS was dismissed as another gadfly.

Managements' haughty attitude persisted until 1991, when CalPERS introduced a 'majority independent directors' proposal at General Motors. American automobile manufacturers had spent two decades fighting the onslaught of Japanese car producers, spending billions of dollars on modernizing their operations and trying to stay competitive with Japan's high-quality, economical vehicles. General Motors' Chairman and CEO, Roger Smith, realized that for GM to return value to its shareholders it had to become a twenty-first century company. He thought that by acquiring EDS and Hughes Electronics the company would get a new-technology injection that would turn General Motors into a hard-driving company in the forefront of technological developments.

By investing time and money on these two large acquisitions, GM got distracted from its fundamental business of producing cars. The stock market priced GM as a very mature company without exciting prospects. In the meantime, where was GM's board? It had only one really independent director, Ross Perot, the CEO of the recently acquired EDS, a software solutions company. He was the only one to question Roger Smith's actions. On 1 December 1986, with Perot having become too belligerent, Roger Smith asked the board to approve the purchase of Perot's stake at a substantial premium. Scandalized, Perot gave the board two weeks to cancel its offer. At Smith's insistence, the board maintained the offer, which was too good to be refused.

This event and the general mismanagement by Roger Smith led a coalition of pension funds, of which CalPERS was a member, to engage Roger Smith in conversations and in asking to remove Smith from the board after his retirement from the CEO post.

V

In 1989 CalPERS began investing in international equities. At that time voting in international proxies was a hit-and-miss affair. Poor communication between issuers and subcustodians, and between subcustodians and US custodians, made it very hard for the average US beneficiary to receive proxies in time for the vote or to receive them at all. Fortunately for us, a small firm – Global Proxy Voting Advisors – saw the need to improve the process and met our needs.

With its help, CalPERS was able to vote proxies in most of its international equities. CalPERS made a conscientious effort to vote all proxies and to express dissatisfaction whenever a management proposal was not to our liking. In the case of the German electric utility, RWE, for example, CalPERS sent a representative to the shareholders' meeting to complain about the favourable voting treatment given to local authorities, which redounded negatively for the rest of the shareholders. More recently, CalPERS has exhorted the board of Ericsson to eliminate dual-class voting rights, which favour inordinately the Wallenberg family.

CalPERS' international corporate governance policy has been restrained in comparison with our US corporate governance policy. It has been our policy to proceed slowly in the belief that the cultural, sociological and structural differences between the Anglo-Saxon world (the USA, the UK, Canada, Australia and New Zealand) and the rest of the world are so large that to promote

> CalPERS' international corporate governance policy has been restrained in comparison with our US corporate governance policy.

indiscriminately what is accepted practice in the Anglo-Saxon world might produce an undesirable backlash. For instance, directors in the USA are usually a mix of insiders and outsiders. In Japan, all directors are company employees. In the USA, drastic company restructurings are generally accepted. In Japan, France or Germany they are not.

If CalPERS had gone abroad pushing for a US-style corporate activism, the result would have been a circling of the wagons and outright opposition to an

> CalPERS adopted a set of global corporate governance principles in 1997.

improvement in corporate governance. Instead, the route CalPERS has taken is to create a set of global corporate governance principles and specific codes for the four largest countries in our portfolio – Japan, the UK, Germany and France.

CalPERS adopted a set of global corporate governance principles in 1997. Since then, many other investors and organizations have considered their own governance standards, leading to the approval by the International Corporate Governance Network (ICGN) in July 1999 of a set of global corporate governance principles, which were fully accepted by CalPERS. Sensing that the compilation of corporate governance principles was a noble endeavour, the OECD approved in May 1999 the OECD Principles of Corporate Governance. These principles were negotiated in consultation with key players in the market including the ICGN, which considers the OECD principles to be the minimum acceptable standards for companies and investors around the world. The ICGN and CalPERS believe that it is in companies' best interest to adhere to the OECD recommendations, even without any domestic legal requirements.

The ICGN has produced a 'working kit' Statement of Corporate Governance Criteria based on the OECD principles. They refer to corporate objectives, communications and reporting, voting rights, corporate boards, corporate remuneration policies, strategic focus, operating performance, shareholder returns, corporate citizenship and corporate governance implementation.

In an abridged form, the 'working kit' states as follows:

- The main goal of a corporation should be to optimize over time the returns to its shareowners. To achieve this objective, the corporation should endeavour to ensure the long-term viability of its business, and to manage effectively its relationships with stakeholders.

- Corporations should disclose accurate, adequate and timely information so as to allow investors to make informed decisions.

- Ordinary shares should feature one vote for each share. Corporations should act to ensure the owners' rights to vote. Fiduciary investors have a responsibility to vote.

- Directors should be accountable to the shareowner body as a whole. Independent non-executives should comprise no fewer than three members and as much as a substantial majority.

- Remuneration policies should be aligned with the interests of shareowners.

- Major strategic modifications to the core business(es) of a corporation should not be made without prior shareholder approval of the proposed modification.

- Corporate governance practices should focus board attention on optimizing over time the company's operating performance and the return to shareowners in comparison with its peers.

- Active cooperation between corporations and stakeholders (employees, customers, suppliers, creditors and the communities in which the company operates) will be most likely to create wealth, employment and sustainable economies.

VI

Beginning in 1993, CalPERS turned its focus towards companies considered, by virtually every measure, to be 'poor' financial performers. Every year, CalPERS reviews the performance of the US companies in its stock portfolio and identifies which are among the lowest long-term relative performers. The screening process identifies those companies that are both poor economic performers and have deficient corporate governance structures. CalPERS selects ten to twelve companies each year as 'Focus List' companies, and invests time and resources to engage in dialogue with the companies' CEOs and directors in order to improve their economic performance and corporate governance structure. The Focus List companies are monitored for at least three years.

> Beginning in 1993, CalPERS turned its focus towards companies considered, by virtually every measure, to be 'poor' financial performers.

To date, CalPERS has engaged over 100 public US companies, so there are sufficient data to conduct statistical analyses of the effectiveness of corporate activism. A well-known study by Wilshire Associates has found that from 1987 to 2000 the collective returns of 95 CalPERS Focus List companies under-performed the S&P 500 Index by 95.4 percentage points in the five years before engagement by CalPERS, but outperformed the same index by 14.7% for the five years following CalPERS' intervention.[3]

In its engagement with portfolio companies, CalPERS at times relies on litigation to obtain redress. For instance, CalPERS as co-lead plaintiff helped to obtain more than $2.8 billion for shareholders in a settlement of a lawsuit against Cendant Corporation for financial statements falsification.

VII

In April 1998, CalPERS released its US Corporate Governance Core Principles and Guidelines.[4] The result of many years' experience in the battlefield of engagement with boards and top management at many US companies, they are set out below (in an abridged form):

Core principles

A. Board independence and leadership

Independence is the cornerstone of accountability. It is now widely recognized throughout the USA that independent boards are essential to a sound governance structure. Therefore, CalPERS suggests:

1. A substantial majority of the board consists of directors who are independent.

2. Independent directors meet periodically (at least once a year) alone, without the CEO or other non-independent directors.

To instil independent leadership, CalPERS suggests:

3. When the chair of the board also serves as the company's chief executive officer, the board designates – formally or informally – an independent director who acts in a lead capacity to coordinate the other independent directors.

4. Certain board committees consist entirely of independent directors. These include the committees that perform the following functions: audit, director nomination, board evaluation and governance, CEO evaluation and management compensation, compliance and ethics.

Lastly, independence also requires a lack of conflict between the director's personal, financial, or professional interests, and the interests of shareowners. Accordingly, CalPERS recommends that:

5. No director may also serve as a consultant or service provider to the company.

6. Director compensation is a combination of cash and stock in the company. The stock component is a significant portion of the total compensation.

B. Board processes and evaluation

No board can truly perform its overriding functions of establishing a company's strategic direction and then monitoring management's success without a system of evaluating itself. CalPERS views this self-evaluation to have several elements, including:

1. The board has adopted a written statement of its own governance principles, and regularly re-evaluates them.

2. With each director nomination recommendation, the board considers the mix of director characteristics, experiences, diverse perspectives and skills that is most appropriate for the company.

3. The board establishes performance criteria for itself, and periodically reviews board performance against those criteria.

4. The independent directors establish performance criteria and compensation incentives for the CEO, and regularly review the CEO's performance against those criteria. The independent directors have access to advisers on this subject, who are independent of management. Minimally, the criteria ensure that the CEO's interests are aligned with the long-term interests of shareowners, that the CEO is evaluated against comparable peer groups and that a significant portion of the CEO's total compensation is at risk.

C. Individual director's characteristics

In CalPERS' view, each director should add something unique and valuable to the board as a whole. Each director should fit within the skill sets identified by the board (see B.2, above). No director, however, can fulfil his or her potential as an effective board member without a personal dedication of time and energy and an ability to bring new and different perspectives to the board.

1. The board has adopted guidelines that address the competing time commitments that are faced when director candidates serve on multiple boards. These guidelines are published annually in the company's proxy statement.

Governance guidelines

The section above represents CalPERS' view of elements of corporate governance that form the foundation of accountability between a corporation's managers and its owners. Many additional features are important in the continuing evolution of corporate governance. The importance of these issues often varies from company to company, depending upon the unique composition of each board, and the special challenges that each company faces. CalPERS offers the following guidelines as additional topics for discussion in the governance dialogue.

A. Board independence and leadership

1. Corporate directors, managers and shareowners should come together to agree upon a uniform definition of 'independence'. Until this uniformity is achieved, each corporation should publish in its proxy statement the definition adopted or relied upon by its board.[5]

2. With each director nomination recommendation, the board should consider the issue of continuing director tenure and take steps as may be appropriate to ensure that the board maintains an openness to new ideas and a willingness to critically re-examine the status quo.

3. When selecting a new chief executive officer, boards should re-examine the traditional combination of the chief executive and chairman positions.

B. Board processes and evaluation

In addition to the processes described in the Core Principles above, CalPERS recommends that boards consider the following:

1. The board should have in place an effective CEO succession plan, and receive periodic reports from management on the development of other members of senior management.

2. All directors should have access to senior management. However, the CEO, chair, or independent lead director may be designated as liaison between management and directors to ensure that the role between board oversight and management operations is respected.

3. The board should periodically review its own size, and determine the size that is most effective towards future operations.

C. Individual director characteristics

Many of the Core Principles and Guidelines in this document would not be necessary if corporate boards had an effective means of evaluating individual director performance. It is this seeming inability to promptly replace directors who are not fully contributing towards overall board success that has led shareowners to question many concepts that would, under a true delegation of management responsibility to boards, otherwise be unnecessary. With this in mind, CalPERS recommends that:

1. Each board should establish performance criteria, not only for itself (acting as a collective body) but also individual behavioural expectations for its directors. Minimally, these criteria should address the level of director attendance, preparedness, participation and candour.

2. To be renominated, directors must satisfactorily perform based on the established criteria. Renomination on any other basis should neither be expected nor guaranteed.

3. Generally, a company's retiring CEO should not continue to serve as a director on the board.

4. The board should establish and make available to shareowners the skill sets which it seeks from director candidates. Minimally, these core competencies should address accounting or finance, international markets, business or management experience, industry knowledge, customer-base experience or perspective, crisis response, leadership or strategic planning.

D. Shareowner rights

Shareowner rights – or those structural devices that define the formal relationship between shareowners and the directors to whom they delegate corporate control – are not typically featured in the governance principles adopted by corporate boards. CalPERS generally believes that, if the principles and guidelines described above are internalized and become part of the way in which American corporations operate, then shareowners should trust that independent boards will make the decisions that promote long-term shareowner interests – whether those decisions concern shareholder rights or other issues. But we are not yet at that point. Therefore, to help build tomorrow's corporate governance structure, CalPERS offers today's corporate boards the following views on issues affecting shareowner rights:

1. A majority of shareowners should be able to amend the company's by-laws by shareowner proposal.

2. A majority of shareowners should be able to call special meetings.

3. A majority of shareowners should be able to act by written consent.

4. Every company should prohibit 'greenmail'.

5. No board should enact or amend a 'poison pill' except with shareowner approval.

6. Every director should be elected annually.

7. Proxies should be kept confidential from the company, except at the express request of shareowners.

8. Broker non-votes should be counted for quorum purposes only.

9. Any shareowner proposal that is approved by a majority of proxies cast should be implemented by the board; if it is not, the next annual proxy statement should contain a detailed explanation of the board's reasons for not doing so.

10. Shareowners should have effective access to the director nomination process.

VIII

After 20 years of domestic proxy voting and 12 years of international proxy voting, and intense dialogue with domestic and international institutions and regulators in different countries, in March 2001, the CalPERS Board approved the CalPERS Global Proxy Voting Principles, which are summarized below.[6] The main principles are:

> In March 2001, the CalPERS Board approved the CalPERS Global Proxy Voting Principles.

- CalPERS' board members should exercise duties of care, loyalty, and in monitoring investment performance. They should try to maximize returns while minimizing risk.

- While financial and economic considerations take priority, attention can also be paid to ensuring that those companies CalPERS invests in adhere to principles of Corporate Social Responsibility, the Sullivan Principles of Corporate Responsibility, and the MacBride Principles.

- CalPERS maintains an active global corporate governance programme and encourages companies to adopt the best corporate governance practices in their own territories.

IX

On 19 August 2002, CalPERS accepted the Investor Protection Principles adopted on 31 July that year by the state treasurers of California, New York and North Carolina. These principles are modelled on the settlement agreed earlier in 2002 between New York Attorney General, Eliot Spitzer, and Merrill Lynch & Co.

The main Investor Protection Principles are summarized below: An invest-ment bank that wants to provide banking services to CalPERS would need to:

- sever the link between compensation for analysts and investment banking;
- prohibit investment banking input into analyst compensation;
- create a review committee to approve all research recommendations;
- require that upon discontinuation of research coverage of a company, firms will disclose the coverage termination and the rationale for such termination;
- disclose in research reports whether a firm has received or is entitled to receive any compensation from a covered company over the past 12 months; and
- establish a monitoring process to ensure compliance with the principles.

When retaining active equity managers, CalPERS will give significant consideration to the following:

- Equity (money) managers have to disclose whether they are investing CalPERS' funds in any of their own clients.
- Money management firms must disclose annually the manner in which their portfolio managers and research analysts are compensated.
- Money management firms shall report quarterly the amount of commission paid related to CalPERS' assets to broker-dealers, and the percentage of commissions paid to broker-dealers that have publicly announced they have adopted the Investment Protection Principles.
- Money management firms affiliated with banks, investment banks, insurance companies or other financial services shall show how they maintain their independence from other parts of their respective groups.
- Fund managers shall consider the quality of the audit used to assess the performance of companies the fund invests in.

X

In February 2002, in response to the US financial crisis, the CalPERS' board adopted a Financial Reform Program. Of the 25 specific issues approved in the programme, 19 have been addressed in part by a combination of the Sarbanes-Oxley Act and the proposed listing standard changes by the NYSE and the NASDAQ.[7] A summary of the programme (as of September 2002) is given in Table 2.1, alongside a

> In February 2002, in response to the US financial crisis, the CalPERS' board adopted a Financial Reform Program.

comparison with the Act's provisions and the proposed stock exchange amendments.

TABLE 2.1
CalPERS' Financial Reform Programme

Issue	Status	Commentary
Audit committees		
1. Increase the number of members required to be 'financially literate' (at least two, or a majority).	Indirectly addressed in Sarbanes-Oxley. Provisions in NYSE proposal apply to Audit Committee Chair.	The Sarbanes-Oxley Act requires the SEC to issue rules requiring each public company to disclose whether its audit committee has at least one member who is a 'financial expert'. The Act gives the SEC 90 days from the date of enactment to propose rules to implement this provision. The proposed listing standard changes by the NYSE include a requirement that the chair of the audit committee have accounting or financial management experience.
2. Provide guidelines on what 'financial literacy' means.	The Sarbanes-Oxley Act provides suggested criteria for 'financial expert'.	General agreement, though whether 'financial literacy' equates to 'audit expertise' is a matter of debate. Should audit comm. members be experts, or simply have the skills to competently question the experts? Need market guidance (perhaps from NACD?) on the types of questions/scope of inquiry that an audit committee should undertake.
3. Impose minimum training require-ments on audit committee members.	Not addressed in Sarbanes-Oxley. Partially addressed in NYSE proposed listing standards.	Proposed NYSE listing standards will require listed companies to adopt and disclose corporate governance guide-lines. Director qualification standards and director orientation and continuing education are required elements in the corporate governance guidelines.
4. Require audit committee approval of any non-audit services by the auditor, and disclosure of the reasons in the proxy.	Addressed in Sarbanes-Oxley. Addressed in NYSE proposed listing standards.	The Sarbanes-Oxley Act prohibits most forms of non-audit services by the external auditor. However, for services that are not prohibited by the Act, or by the Oversight Board,* the audit committee must pre-approve the service.

TABLE 2.1 *continued*

Issue	Status	Commentary
(This applies only to the extent non-audit services are permitted, which has been CalPERS' preferred approach; see 'Auditor Independence' 1, below.)		The proposed NYSE listing standards require that the Audit Committee approve any significant non-audit relationship with the independent auditor or any affiliates.
5. Provide that audit committees have the power to hire and fire the auditor.	Addressed in Sarbanes-Oxley. Addressed in NYSE proposed listing standards.	The Sarbanes-Oxley Act makes audit committee directly responsible for the appointment, compensation and oversight of the independent auditor. The proposed NYSE listing standards require that the audit committee have the sole authority to hire and fire the independent auditor.
6. Require that audit committees meet at least once per quarter, review the company's internal audit functions at least annually, and have at least one meeting per year with the external auditor and without any company employees present.	Not addressed in Sarbanes-Oxley. Addressed in NYSE proposed listing standards.	The proposed NYSE listing standards require minimum duties and responsibilities of the audit committee, which includes that it should meet separately, at least quarterly, with management, with internal auditors, and with independent auditors. The standards also require the audit committee to obtain and review a report at least annually from the independent auditor describing, among other areas, the firm's internal quality control procedures.
7. Require that audit committees have access to their own resources (e.g. dedicated staff).	Addressed in Sarbanes-Oxley. Addressed in NYSE proposed listing standards.	The Sarbanes-Oxley Act grants audit committees the authority to engage independent counsel and other advisers necessary to carry out their duties. Further, the Act requires each public company to provide for appropriate funding, as determined by the audit committee, to pay for any advisers retained by the audit committee to assist in carrying out its duties.

TABLE 2.1 *continued*

Issue	Status	Commentary
		The proposed NYSE listing standards require minimum duties and responsibilities of the audit committee, which include, as appropriate, obtaining advice and assistance from outside legal, accounting, or other advisers.
8. Require that audit committees have full access to company books and records.	Not specifically addressed in either Sarbanes-Oxley or proposed NYSE listing standards.	While this item is not specifically addressed in either the Sarbanes-Oxley Act or the NYSE standards, the level of authority, and responsibility placed upon the audit committee is completely consistent with this item.

Auditor independence

Issue	Status	Commentary
1. Prohibit audit firms from providing non-audit services, with the exception of preparation of tax forms and registration statements.	Addressed in Sarbanes-Oxley. Indirectly addressed in proposed NYSE listing standards.	The Sarbanes-Oxley Act makes it unlawful for a registered accounting firm to perform any of eight non-audit services at the same time that such firm is engaged as the independent auditor. The Oversight Board may add other services to this list and may also grant exemptions to specific companies, registered accounting firms or to specific transactions on a case-by-case basis. The proposed NYSE listing standards do not directly address this issue, however, the NYSE does recommend that the SEC prohibit relationships between independent auditors and audit clients that may impair the effectiveness of audits.
2. Require a mandatory rotation (five to seven years) of external auditor.	Not addressed in Sarbanes-Oxley. Not addressed in proposed NYSE listing standards.	The Sarbanes-Oxley Act addresses only audit partner rotation, requiring rotation of the lead or coordinating partner every five years. The proposed NYSE listing standards suggest that the audit committee 'consider whether, in order to assure continuing auditor independence, there should be regular rotation of the lead audit partner, or even the firm itself'.

TABLE 2.1 *continued*

Issue	Status	Commentary
3. Prohibit audit firms from providing internal and external audit services for the same client.	Addressed in Sarbanes-Oxley.	The Sarbanes-Oxley Act makes it unlawful for a registered accounting firm to perform any of eight non-audit services, including specifically internal audit services while the firm is engaged as its independent auditor.
4. Establish a 'cap' ($ or %) for non-audit services (if bright line test not adopted).	CalPERS' staff gathered data on 1,200 public companies' use of their external auditor during fiscal year 2001. Recommend removal from matrix.	Given the requirements of the Sarbanes-Oxley Act, and the authority of the Oversight Board to adopt additional restrictions, it would not be meaningful to pursue a cap on non-audit services.
5. Require a cooling-off period (of at least one year) before a company can hire any employees from their auditor that worked on their audit.	Addressed in Sarbanes-Oxley. Indirectly addressed in the proposed NYSE listing standards.	The Sarbanes-Oxley Act requires a one-year cooling-off period from the date the company may hire one of its auditors in the role of CEO, CFO, controller, chief accounting officer or any equivalent position. The proposed NYSE listing standards require companies to set clear hiring policies for employees or former employees of the firm's independent auditors.
6. Require mandatory liability insurance by all auditors.	Staff continuing to research.	Early drafts of reform legislation did consider mandatory liability, insurance and joint and several liability, however, neither of these issues was included in any of the Bill's later forms or in the final Sarbanes-Oxley Act.
7. Require companies to use two auditors, to double-check each other's work.	Recommend removal from matrix.	

TABLE 2.1 *continued*

Issue	Status	Commentary
8. Support Congressional efforts to amend the Private Securities Litigation Reform Act of 1995 (PSLRA) to restore joint and several liability for auditors, but only for auditors who fail the 'independence' bright line test or who fail to comply with the financial fraud reporting provisions within existing securities laws. Consider other amendments that may be necessary to increase auditor accountability.	Additional issues to be brought to the board as they arise.	Early drafts of reform legislation would have restored joint and several liability for auditors who fail the independence standard (consistent with CalPERS' 'bright line' test), or who knowingly commit a violation of the securities laws, or who fail to comply with financial fraud reporting laws, or where the company audited has become insolvent. However, final legislation does not address this issue.

Accounting standards

Issue	Status	Commentary
1. Join forces with other significant users of financial statements to provide concrete and responsible pro- posals for account- ing standards reform, including:	The board president will designate one or more board members to lead staff in this endeavour. Staff compiling names of potential participants.	Agreement that accounting standards have not kept up with the complexities of the market, and that (minimally) standards need to be revised/added under a more streamlined process than is currently the case.
■ Review the role of accounting standards in the financial markets, and their ability to keep pace with the complexity of the market.	Consider with respect to other workload.	General agreement that financial statements should move towards a 'plain English' approach, with end users' needs being paramount. Part of SEC proposals. General debate centres around whether the USA should move more towards a 'principles-based' model, or remain with what is described as a 'rules-based' approach.

TABLE 2.1 *continued*

Issue	Status	Commentary
2. Coordinate efforts with the California State Board of Accountancy (CSBA), with regard to state-level regulation of the accounting industry.		Note: CalPERS staff testified at a CSBA hearing in February 2002; staff have also met members of the CSBA's legislative oversight committee.
3. Specifically promote the adoption of more rigorous accounting standards for the consolidation of special purpose entities (SPEs).	Financial Accounting Standards Board (FASB) is considering the treatment of SPEs.	
4. Demand broader public exposure (with an annual separate mailing to shareholders) of a company's entrance into forward equity contracts.	This issue will be raised with the Accounting Standards group to be formed (see item 1, above).	
5. Consider possible criminal sanctions that will help ensure fair, accurate and complete financial reporting.	Addressed in Sarbanes-Oxley.	The Sarbanes-Oxley Act requires CEOs and CFOs to certify the accuracy of their corporation's financial statements, and creates new criminal penalties for securities fraud as well as other activities. The Act also contains substantial increases penalties for several existing crimes.
6. Urge FASB to require that stock options used to attract, retain or compensate employees should be reported as expense in income statements.	Staff presented a workshop on the issue in June 2002. No action was taken by the Investment Committee.	Consistent with views of many other institutional investors (particularly those with global portfolios), including TIAA-CREF (see under heading XI of this chapter for further discussion). Consistent with the expected approach from the IASB.

TABLE 2.1 *continued*

Issue	Status	Commentary
Accounting industry oversight		
1. Provide for more effective and independent oversight of the auditing industry. Any oversight entity should have an independent funding source and be comprised of a majority of investors.	Addressed in Sarbanes-Oxley. Not directly addressed in the proposed NYSE listing standards.	The Sarbanes-Oxley Act created a five-member Public Company Accounting Oversight Board. This board will establish rules to regulate the auditing process, conduct periodic inspections of accounting firms, investigate possible violations of auditing rules and, if applicable, impose sanctions. The board will be financed by registration fees charged to accounting firms and annual accounting support fees from public companies. The proposed NYSE listing standards do not directly address this issue: however, the NYSE did support the creation of a new oversight body.
2. Provide that the oversight entity would have subpoena and disciplinary power.	Addressed in Sarbanes-Oxley.	The Sarbanes-Oxley Act grants the Oversight Board power to investigate possible violations of rules regarding the performance of public audits. The Oversight Board may impose sanctions against registered accounting firms, which may include censure, monetary fines and temporary or permanent revocation of registration under the Act. The Oversight Board also has the authority to suspend or bar a registered accounting firm or associated person from being associated with any public company.
3. Impose criminal sanctions for those who lie to an auditor.	Addressed in Sarbanes-Oxley.	The Sarbanes-Oxley Act provides that the SEC may bring civil lawsuits against officers or directors of a public company, or any persons acting at their direction, who attempt to influence any accountant performing an audit for the purpose of rendering the company's financial statements materially misleading. The SEC is granted exclusive civil authority to enforce these provisions, and must adopt rules to implement them within 90 days from the date of enactment.

TABLE 2.1 *continued*

Issue	Status	Commentary
Director independence		
1. Provide for additional disclosure of each director's financial ties to the board and the company, including personal, family, business, political and philanthropic connections.	Recommended and approved.	Consistent with petition for rulemaking submitted to the SEC by the AFL-CIO.
2. Require tougher minimum standards for independence (consistent with CalPERS' standard of independence).	Addressed in Sarbanes-Oxley, specifically in regards to Audit Committee members. Partially addressed in proposed NYSE listing standards.	The Sarbanes-Oxley Act requires each member of the Audit Committee to be 'independent', which is clarified to mean that such members are prohibited from accepting any fees from the company other than for service as a member of the board of directors or committee thereof. The proposed NYSE listing standards require that independent directors must comprise at least a majority of the board. Further, the standards tighten the definition of independent generally, and require that audit committee members receive only director's fees from the listed company (similar provisions to Sarbanes-Oxley). While the independence requirements of the new standards are stronger than in the past, they are weakened by some ambiguity in the definition and provisions that each company will be permitted to determine parameters constituting a material relationship.

TABLE 2.1 *continued*

Issue	Status	Commentary
Governance model		
1. Form a commission made up of regulators, legislative representatives and investors to examine the diverse components of the governance system (including ways in which conflicts of interest may influence corporate decision making), considering the role of investment banks, equity analysts, rating agencies, lending institutions, outside attorneys and other consultants.	Board president to designate one or more board member(s) to lead staff in this endeavour. Partially addressed in Sarbanes-Oxley.	The Sarbanes-Oxley Act requires the SEC to adopt rules no later than one year from the date of enactment to address conflicts of interest facing securities analysts and specific conflict of interest disclosures. CalPERS' Investment Committee has adopted the Investor Protection Principles (IPP) – see under heading IX of this chapter. The IPP are consistent with the provisions of Sarbanes-Oxley.
Other governance issues		
1. Executive compensation disclosure: ■ **improve readability;** ■ **include all sources and forms of compensation (including all perquisites);** ■ **require current disclosure of stock option exercises by executives;**	Investment Committee approved a programme aimed at increased involvement in executive compensation issues at its June 2002 meeting. Partially addressed in Sarbanes-Oxley.	CalPERS staff in the process of developing this programme. The Sarbanes-Oxley Act requires accelerated disclosure of transactions involving directors, executive officers and principle stockholders. Beginning not later than one year from the date of enactment, directors, executive officers and 10% equity owners will be required to report any change in their ownership before the end of the second business day following the day the transaction is executed.

TABLE 2.1 *continued*

Issue	Status	Commentary
■ require compensation of top executives to be compared to the company's philanthropic expenditures.		
2. Invite CalSTRS to participate on both of CalPERS' task forces (i.e. regarding accounting standards and the governance model).	Recommended and approved.	Many public hearings have been held throughout the country, including legislative and CSBA hearings in California.
3. Investigate potential amendments to the PSLRA and related laws to strengthen shareholder rights.	Staff continuing to research.	
4. Establish minimum corporate governance standards for investing (e.g. for active managers, private equity transactions).	Staff continuing to research.	
5. Create a 'report card for corporate governance' that is easily understood by the marketplace.	Staff continuing to research.	Staff research includes the corporate governance rating services already available in the market.
6. Elevate CalPERS' presence and profile in the financial press.	Staff continuing to research.	

TABLE 2.1 *continued*

Issue	Status	Commentary
401(k) reform		
1. Support Con- **gressional efforts to** **provide greater** **retirement security** **to 401(k) plan** **participants.**	Addressed in Sarbanes-Oxley.	The Sarbanes-Oxley Act requires the SEC, in consultation with the Secretary of Labor, to issue rules pertaining to trading during blackout periods. Directors and officers will be barred from trading equity securities in the company during blackout periods if the security is acquired in connection with service or employment as an officer or director.

*On the Oversight Board, see in this table, under 'Accounting industry oversight', item 1.

XI

One item in Table 2.1 requires further comment: the question of the treatment of stock options (see items 3 and 6 under Accounting standards). A huge controversy has been raised in the USA in the past decade over whether stock options should be expensed in the income statement or just shown as a footnote.

> A huge controversy has been raised in the USA in the past decade over whether stock options should be expensed in the income statement or just shown as a footnote.

The most commonly mentioned arguments for expensing options are the following:

1. Expensing options would eliminate the current misinformation on reported earnings, which leads to a misallocation of resources.

2. Some 75% of executive pay now comes in the form of options. Since all other forms of compensation must be deducted from earnings, options should be treated the same.

3. Deducting the cost of options will yield more accurate earnings numbers, which should help restore investor confidence.

4. Since options are now all but free to companies, excessive grants to top executives have been encouraged. But options do have costs: They dilute shareholders' stakes and deprive companies of the funds they would otherwise get by selling those shares in the open market. Such costs should be reflected in earnings.

5. Bringing more discipline to option grants will also reduce the incentives top executives now have to pump their stocks through short-term earnings manoeuvres, in the hope of cashing in big option gains.

Against expensing options, the commonest arguments are that

1. Unlike salaries or other perquisites, granting options requires no cash outlays from companies. Since there is no real cost to the company to deduct, doing so will unjustly penalize earnings.
2. There are no universal standards for expensing options; all valuation methods require big assumptions and estimates. So expensing them will reduce the accuracy of income statements, and leave them open to manipulation.
3. Deducting the cost of options will reduce earnings, which will likely drive down share prices.
4. Rather than take the hit to earnings, companies will issue far fewer options. That would hurt morale, limit a key tool used to lure talent, and inhibit companies from aligning employee and shareholder interests.
5. Technological firms argue that generous option grants have spurred the risk-taking and entrepreneurship so crucial to innovation. Expensing options risks damaging that benefit.
6. Expensing options would have a draconian effect on the market, damaging stock prices.
7. Current disclosure of the cost of options is adequate.
8. Since there is disagreement as to the right valuation method, expensing options would harm the comparability of financial statements.

CalPERS has spent considerable time and resources studying this issue. Although its attitude towards expensing could change in the future, at this moment CalPERS has decided that it cannot entirely subscribe to the idea of expensing. It believes that expensing stock options could be very damaging to the growth of start-up technological companies in general and to the Californian economy in particular. CalPERS also believes the issue is not whether to expense or not to expense but to curb stock compensation abuses. To that end, CalPERS proposes to support regulatory efforts to establish shareholder control of the issuance of options, to encourage the use of performance-based options, and to establish penalties for those companies that abuse the stock option mechanism to the detriment of shareholders.

Looking at the future, I believe CalPERS will continue its efforts to improve transparency and disclosure in all corporate activities. This basic principle applies to financial statements, executive compensation, analysts' conflicts of interest and general protection of the investor. I also believe CalPERS will strive to work with other institutions in the USA and abroad to gain support for its belief in the need for strong, independent boards that are truly concerned about shareholder rights.

Notes

1   This chapter reflects the author's individual insights and opinions and not those of the California Public Employees' Retirement System.

2   Head, Jamie and Sherm, Howard (1987) *Conflicts of Interest in the Proxy Voting System* (IRRC booklet).

3   Stephen L. Nesbitt, 'The CalPERS Effect: A Corporate Governance Update' (Wilshire Associates, 1995)

4   They can be found in the website: www.calpers-governance.org.

5   The CalPERS definition states that '"Independent director" means a director who has not been employed by the company in an executive capacity within the last five years; is not, and is not affiliated with a company that is, an adviser or consultant to the company or a member of the company's senior management; is not affiliated with a significant customer or supplier of the company; has no personal services contract(s) with the company, or a member of the company's senior management; is not affiliated with a not-for-profit entity that receives significant contributions from the company; within the last five years, has not had any business relationship with the company (other than service as a director) for which the company has been required to make disclosure under Regulation S-K of the Securities and Exchange Commission; is not employed by a public company at which an executive officer of the company serves as a director; has not had any of the relationships described above with any affiliate of the company; and is not a member of the immediate family of any person described above.'

6   Complete details can be found in the CalPERS' website: www.calpers-governance.org.

7   The full text of Sarbanes-Oxley can be found at http://news.findlaw.com/hdoes/does/gwbush/sarbanesoxley072302.pdf. In addition, the NYSE's board on 1 August 2002 approved a package of changes to the exchange's corporate governance listing standards. A similar package was approved in July 2002 by the Nasdaq's board of directors. Among other provisions, the

improved standards require a majority of independent directors on the board, full independence on the audit, nominating and compensation committees, and shareholder vote on new equity-compensation plans.

3

EUROPEAN PENSIONS:

PROGRESS, PROBLEMS AND POTENTIAL

ELIZABETH LEGGE
Weavering Capital

Introduction

More and more in the future, share prices are going to reflect pension issues. The investment decisions of pension fund managers already have a huge impact on stock markets, and this impact will grow – but only if confidence in the industry can be built and sustained.

Pension systems are in crisis. If nothing is done, state pension systems in Europe could well collapse. The economic damage of pension systems breaking down is impossible to imagine, but could be comparable to the damage done by the Great Depression or the collapse of the Soviet system in Russia.

> **Pension systems are in crisis. If nothing is done, state pension systems in Europe could well collapse.**

Already, European mainland governments are aware how bitter their citizens feel over the way that this crisis has been allowed to build up. Ordinary people fear that huge increases in personal financial obligations will suddenly be imposed, many believing that one generation at least will have to pay for its parents' retirement needs while saving up for its own – in other words, will have to pay twice over. Because of this there is strong resistance to any reduction in state pension systems.

While the British crisis is that of an industry failing to provide the service needed, on the Continent the crisis lies in too much reliance on pay-as-you-go state systems. In most countries progress towards a private pension system has been small or non-existent: only some 25% of European employees have any kind of private pension provision at all.

Public and private pension systems are so inextricably interlinked that any analysis must include state systems, but this chapter is first and foremost about the prospects and opportunities opening up for the private pension industry. In particular, it is about the difficulties that lie in the way of those opportunities, and the initiatives by the European Commission to bring about Europe-wide pension arrangements that have got the private pension industry metaphorically pricking up its antennae.

1. Where does the future pensioner stand?

Whose interests should be paramount in the pension system? The answer would seem to be obvious: future pensioners. But in today's world it often seems that their interests came long after those of companies, pension providers or even governments. The difficulties experienced by these three groups get too much attention, while the future pensioner is losing out.

> The failures of the present systems hinge upon changing demographics, changing work patterns and, most importantly, changes in the financial arena which have given rise to questions of security and risk.

The failures of the present systems hinge upon changing demographics, changing work patterns and, most importantly, changes in the financial arena which have given rise to questions of security and risk. These include: who should bear the financial risk? how much security should be guaranteed? and how can conflicts of interest be resolved? Scandals such as Equitable Life (see below) draw in reluctant governments to pick up the pieces – so can governments ever distance themselves from a role as provider of last resort? These issues and others need to be addressed.

> In Europe the varying sources of pension provision are often compared to pillars. There are three pillars: government pensions, company pensions and private pensions. Pensions provided by the government are known as pillar 1 pensions (see below for the other two pillars).

What is needed is a system that serves the pensioners' needs first and foremost, and the best people to ensure that are future pensioners themselves. But can governments trust people to look after their future needs? All present systems assume that people cannot be trusted, yet ordinary people have in turn grown to distrust the intentions of their rulers. They also have reason to distrust the private pensions industry. Over recent years the financial services industry in Britain has often been guilty of misselling its products, and of widespread incompetence. As a result people have often been defrauded of the savings they had dutifully put aside for their old age.

2. Is the full extent of the problem being ignored?

As is now becoming all too clear, government pensions[1] are hugely vulnerable to demographic change. Governments have favoured pay-as-you-go systems in which no attempt is made to accumulate savings into a fund that will finance the needs of a retired person; instead the contributions being made by today's workers are immediately paid over to those who have retired. For such a system to work each retired person needs to be supported by several workers.

Pay-as-you-go systems offer governments considerable scope to court political favour by promising better pensions. Pay-as-you-go systems are defined-benefit pensions (see box below), that is, the pension received is only partially related to how much has been paid in contributions. They offer governments the opportunity to manipulate pensions for political purposes, and few governments have been able to resist this temptation.

So long as the proportion of retired people to working people remains favourable and stable, pay-as-you-go systems can work well: they are easy to administer and relatively low-cost. But in Europe this relationship is breaking down; the length of retirement is growing and the number of workers to each pensioner is falling. This is partly because people are retiring earlier and living longer, but largely because birth rates have fallen below replacement levels in most European countries. The ratio of workers to pensioners has fallen from around ten workers supporting each retired person to four or five and is set to fall even further. If current trends continue, then in Italy the day will come when retired people will outnumber working people. A pay-as-you-go system could hardly work in such a situation.

Increasing numbers of over-65s

Today the percentage of the population aged over 65 is around 15%–16% in most European countries, but over the next 35 years that number is set to rise to half as much again or more. By 2030 a quarter of the populations of the five largest EU countries, France, Germany, Italy, Spain and the UK, will be over the age of 65.

A pension is either 'defined benefit' or 'defined contribution'. 'Defined-benefit' pension schemes are company schemes which offer employees a pension that is a percentage of their final salary in accordance with a formula based upon how many years the pensioner contributed towards his or her pension – that is, what is defined is what the future pensioner will receive. (It is possible to buy a 'defined-benefit' pension scheme from a private pension provider but very few indeed offer them.)

'Defined contribution' and money purchase schemes are one and the same thing; any particular level of pension is not guaranteed but instead the person's pension is determined by how much saving has gone into his or her pension fund and by how well those savings have grown as a result of their being invested.

As a result, spending from the public purse on pensions is also set to rise from around 10%–11% to between 11% and 17%. Such a rise in public spending is of dangerous proportions. Possible ways of tackling the situation are:

1. raising taxes generally or contributions paid by employers and employees in order to cover the rise in pension spending;

2. compelling working people to save and provide for their own old age, i.e. the state opting out of its current responsibilities;

3. extending the working lifetime and obliging people to postpone retirement by five or ten years;

4. increasing the workforce supporting pensioners by encouraging immigrants to settle in the country;

5. increasing the workforce by persuading women to have more children (it is too late for this to prevent a crisis within some 30 or 40 years).

6. The impoverishment of retired people.

If option 3 were adopted (so that benefits and tax rates could remain constant), then the age at which people would stop working in Japan would have to be 78 by 2030 and 81 by 2050, and the situation is little better in other countries.

Option 4 has already been partly adopted by Europe, which has begun to draw in immigrants in order to maintain growth and living standards. (No government, however, wants to come clean about this for fear of protests and worsening race relations.) But immigrants are no long-term solution, for sooner or later – usually within a generation – immigrant populations adopt the social patterns of the host country, including birth rates and attitudes to marriage and family.

What governments are increasingly considering is option 2. Not being able to sustain the pay-as-you-go system, and not themselves designed for managing the savings of future pensioners, governments turn to the private sector – either company schemes or private pension providers. Governments prefer company schemes because employers will impose a degree of compulsion, forcing employees to save for their old age. But there are aspects of company pension schemes that work against the interests of the future pensioner.

> The second pillar: pension schemes run by firms on behalf of their employees. These may be fully funded or the company may operate a form of 'book reserve' system.

3. Why companies want to withdraw from pension provision

From the employee's point of view a company final-salary, defined-benefit pension is a very attractive form of deferred wage. But a company also gains certain important benefits from offering a pension scheme: it provides low-cost funds to the company for its own use (so-called 'book reserve' pensions), and the terms of company pension schemes, in particular, long vesting periods[2] have been intended to discourage senior employees from leaving the company. Vesting periods work savagely against those employees who do not stay long with one company: early leavers may forfeit the money they have paid in.

A company providing 'book reserve' pensions retains the accumulated employee contributions as capital available for financing business activities and pension assets are hidden away within the company's corporate assets. Effectively they become a cheap source of funds for the company. In fact, most company schemes are set up in a way that maximizes these *company* benefits. Final-salary, defined-benefit pension schemes penalize employees who change jobs while rewarding those who make a lifetime career with the company.

In the late 1980s in the UK, Robert Maxwell plundered the Mirror Group's pension funds to the tune of £460 million in order to shore up his company when it hit financial difficulties. In the group's collapse, many pensioners found they had been defrauded out of their contractual rights. In April 1992, payments to its 240 pensioners were abruptly stopped. The British government stepped in with £2.5 million to ease their plight, and a month later the trustees of the Mirror Group pension scheme started legal proceedings against five banks and financial institutions in an attempt to recoup £88 million that Maxwell had diverted from the Mirror pension fund as unauthorized loans to Maxwell's private companies.

But fundamentally, *Maxwell had done nothing illegal at the time* and, shocked though the authorities were, there was little they could do. The government was forced to review Britain's 400,000 occupational pension schemes. Ultimately, the Maxwell scandal resulted in legislation intended to ring-fence and protect the rights of employees. This move made it a lot less attractive for companies to offer pensions.

A major problem with 'book reserve' pensions lies with so-called 'phantom profits'. A good example of this is provided by Verizon Communications Inc, the largest US local phone company. In March 2002

A major problem with 'book reserve' pensions lies with so-called 'phantom profits'.

Verizon's annual report announced an annual profit of $389 million. Hidden away at the back of the report was the information that Verizon was claiming $2.7 billion in gains from its pension fund investments. But these were estimated gains, whereas in truth the company pension fund actually lost $3.1 billion in 2001.

Verizon was following legitimate accounting practice as set out by the US Financial Accounting Standards Board: FASB rules say that in preparing income statements, companies should include estimated gains from their pension fund investments. *Estimating* pension fund investment gains allows companies to report phantom profits. In a strong bull market companies have no need to do this, but when stock markets plunge the temptation is great and the danger far worse. It is difficult to know how many company valuations are seriously out of line with the underlying reality. There are signs that a number of US companies have reported phantom profits.

Could it be that the time has come to phase out the second pillar of pension provision, the company pension scheme? Its disadvantages include:

- *Growing burden upon companies.* Most company schemes were set up on the implicit premise that the company could only grow. Final-salary pension schemes were, in fact, never as good as people imagined. They depended on steady growth in the number of people in the system coming up behind and supporting those who had retired ahead of them – exactly what a pay-as-you-go state pension system depends on. They would not be viable if the number of company employees declined substantially over time.

- Not just in Britain, but in Europe too, many companies – while not wanting to deprive their employees of an important benefit – would like to ease themselves away from the responsibilities that go with running a company scheme. Providing a company pension is an extra cost for probably diminishing returns.

- *Pension rights lost when companies merge.* Company schemes become vulnerable when companies are taken over. At present there is often no guarantee that the new owner will continue the pension scheme of the acquired company. More often than not, a new owner prefers to absorb the pension scheme into its own pension scheme, and often the members of the pension scheme taken over are treated as though they were newly recruited employees, losing rights and benefits. This is a matter of some concern to the European Commission, which is working on directives for EU pensions and for EU mergers and acquisitions policies where this issue is to be addressed.

■ *Company pension schemes are rarely portable.* When an employee changes jobs and seeks to close out his participation in his old company scheme in order to take the accumulated pension fund and consolidate it in his new company scheme, he often faces penalties for doing so. Most people leave their savings with the old company scheme, where it is frozen until they have access to it upon retirement.

If an individual entered into his or her own contract with a dedicated pension provider, there would be no need to transfer assets when he or she changed jobs. A consolidated fund potentially should grow more substantially than a fragmented patchwork of pension rights in a number of different company schemes.

The third pillar: private personal pension funds, opened by the individual worker, which are defined contribution pensions.

They have the advantage of being portable: there is no distortion in either the paying of contributions or the accruing pension capital if the employee changes jobs.

The disadvantage is usually that employers do not recognize personal pension funds and do not make contributions into them on behalf of their employees.

---

4. Investing in private pensions: the risk/return balance

For the financial services industry, managing pension funds (as opposed to many traded financial products) has been so much more heavily restricted that, were it not for the huge amounts of capital involved, they would not appear to be particularly attractive business. Other savings products enable the industry to earn greater returns.

In Britain there is far greater freedom than is allowed in the rest of Europe to go after greater returns and to allow greater risk-taking. But that there is a down side to this is shown by the Equitable Life debacle. Not only has it turned out to be impossible to honour promises and guarantees that were made only to win more business, but these risks ought to have been recognized at the time of the policies inception.

Equitable Life, a mutual society, offered its policyholders both a savings plan to build up a private pension fund and an annuity when they retired. It also promised its customers a guaranteed annuity at the time policyholders started saving. Initially, the investment climate and the average returns on annuities were so good that Equitable promised guaranteed annuity rates. A typical guaranteed annuity rate (GAR) customer might have been promised a 12% annuity. For a pensioner with £100,000 in their pension pot that meant an income of £12,000 a year for life. Two things hit Equitable Life: first, the stock market turned down so that the size of the pension fund invested on the stock market began to shrink; second, annuity rates, which are geared to government bond yields, fell.

In a court hearing in July 2000, the House of Lords decided the insurer would have to meet its GAR commitments. But Equitable Life had not got the funds to do this. The 'non-GARs' – those who took out pension plans after Equitable Life had stopped offering guaranteed annuity rates but before the full extent of the company's financial crisis was revealed – have become the ones who have to pay for Equitable's GAR promises (this is because Equitable is a mutual society, owned by and run for its members). Somewhat short sightedly Equitable tended to pay out profits to policyholders rather than add to reserves.

The cost of honouring the guaranteed annuities was first put at £1.5 billion, later revised upwards. The result was that Equitable cut bonuses, the investment growth credited to each savings plan each month. And it has gone on cutting bonuses as the stock market continues to fall and the company struggles to remain afloat.

If private pension providers were obliged to offer a guaranteed return they could do so, but they would then offer what could be guaranteed within a climate of poor stock market returns for example, something like the returns offered on cash or bonds. But what would then happen to 'excess' returns achieved in bull markets? Would this be offered to the pensioners as bonuses, or be retained by the pension providers?

Who should bear the stock market risk?

The risk of a fund falling short of what is required to provide a satisfactory living standard in retirement falls upon the pension provider in the case of a 'defined benefit' pension and on the future pensioner in the case of a 'defined contribution' pension.

But pension funds *must* go after investment growth because without it the amount that future pensioners would have to save out of their working incomes would be punitive.

At the age of 65, life expectancy in western Europe ranges from 17 to 20 years. Most people, then, will need their pensions to provide a comfortable income for that period. If it were not possible to earn a positive return on savings, this would mean that, to put aside enough during the course of a working life of little more than 40 years to support 20 years of retirement, people would have to put aside around a third of their gross earnings each year of work. Since putting aside a third of earnings would be regarded as punitive, it is clear that future pensioners depend upon *the accumulation of the return on their savings along with capital growth* to provide for their old age. They also depend upon favourable tax treatment – which is no longer the case in Britain.

> At the age of 65, life expectancy in western Europe ranges from 17 to 20 years.

Investments on the stock market can go down as well as up, so it is possible a final pension fund could be less than the savings a future pensioner has paid in. People who retire after periods of stock market decline could end up with a much smaller pension than those who retire after a period of strong growth. Most people would expect their final pension fund to hold at least as much as they have paid into it. But investing carries a risk, and this dependence upon capital growth raises an important issue of the risk/return balance.

The risk/return balance, together with the question of who bears the risk (the pension provider or the future pensioner – or even the government in its role of provider of last resort) is possibly the most important issue in the pension debate. Since the total avoidance of risk deprives savers to an unreasonable degree of potential earnings, the risk/return balance needs to be made completely clear to future pensioners.

5. Should people be able to retire later?

Since nobody can guarantee that stock markets will never again turn down, should people perhaps gain more control over when they retire? There is more to this than simply a solution to the problems of growing longevity and how to fund ever-longer retirements.

Firstly, studies have shown that people who are in work tend to remain in good health longer. Retired people make greater claims on health services and social services than do working people. Studies also show that people in work remain more optimistic and outgoing than those without work. Working people undertake more and spend more in doing so while continuing to pay taxes, both on their incomes and on their spending – thus the government's outgoings are lower and its revenues greater.

TABLE 3.1
European working populations

	Active population	Percentage of total workforce in employment	Percentage of 55–64 age range in employment
UK	29.4 million	71.6	52.2
Germany	36.6 million	65.7	37.7
France	26.0 million	62.7	30.7
Italy	23.7 million	54.5	26.9
Spain	17.7 million	57.5	39.1

Secondly, the ratio of working life to retirement today is such that only by working the full expected working life (and saving throughout) can a person ensure an acceptable income for his retirement years. A different ratio – a longer working life and shorter retirement – would mean that an acceptable pension could be ensured in only a part of the working life. Then the gaps that can occur in a person's working life would not be so damaging to his or her well-being in retirement

There is at present a real danger of governments sending out a message that those who reach retirement with not a coin in their pockets will be bailed out and provided for by the taxpayer, and that those who forgo current spending in order to save for their old age will lose out. They would lose out twice over, in fact – not just because they have saved but also because they are likely to be taxed on the pensions they have saved for, and their taxes will support those who did not save. With a better working life-to-retirement ratio, it would be easier for governments to resist the need to bail out those who fail to save.

Working people would be left with the choice of saving more and retiring earlier or failing to save and having to continue working. Because savers could exercise consumer choice, competition among financial service providers would do much to obviate the dangers of moral hazard. The government's role here would be a regulatory one.

The British government is considering removing some of the impediments to people continuing to work after the age of 65, but does not wish to change the statutory retirement age of 65 for the state pension. It is also considering changing the rules on annuity purchases, introducing more consumer choice. Other countries, such as Spain, offer pensioners a choice when they retire: either to transform the capital into a life annuity with a life insurance company, or to leave the capital with the company that has administered the account for years and make scheduled monthly withdrawals (based on a formula incorporating the worker's life expectancy). In the latter case, if the pensioner dies, the balance of capital in his account becomes part of his estate.

6. Britain's pensions problems

Britain has problems aplenty – a crisis even – but their nature is very different from the impending crises on the Continent. In the United Kingdom, one of the first to begin the process of systematically reducing unfunded state provision in favour of funded private provision (beginning in 1980), retirement obligations have been steadily eroded for more than 20 years. Successive governments have reduced the state pension to a level at which those with only a state pension must beg for means-tested help from the state. Today Britain has a state pension system that fails to provide enough for anyone to live comfortably upon its handouts alone.

The private pension sector has grown as the government has increasingly shifted the burden of providing for pensions onto it. Nevertheless, Britain does have its own pensions crisis. A figure of £27 billion has been put on the financial shortfall between what people are saving for their retirements – combined with their statutory pension rights and employers' contributions towards their pensions – and the amount needed to enable working people to retire and live comfortably in their old age.

There are 4.6 million people in private sector defined-benefit schemes and some 1 million people in occupational money-purchase schemes; another 4.5 million are members of public-sector defined-benefit schemes. Thus about 10 million working people have some kind of private pension provision over and above their state pension.

But they are the minority. The British workforce totals around 28 million people, so nearly twice as many people as those with some kind of top-up pension provision will depend entirely on the unashamedly inadequate state system on retirement. And this does not include those who are not part of the workforce, who will also grow old.

Wicked British companies?

The majority of people with private pensions are paying into company schemes. In the beginning employers did not see themselves as under an obligation to provide for the old age of *all* their employees, but rather for professional and higher-paid employees. Nor did companies ever see the pension benefits that they offered as being an alternative to the state system, rather as a top-up to the state pension.

Various governments have tinkered with the legislative framework of company pension schemes, resulting in a hideously complex private pension taxation system. There were no fewer than eight different tax regimes, creating a largely incomprehensible mish-mash of state-imposed tax thresholds and benefit withdrawals.

The tax system itself has compounded the problems companies have had to face in running their pension schemes. The British government introduced legislation in 1986 restricting the tax relief that a company could claim on its pension funds. If the value of assets in the pension fund was greater than 105% of expected liabilities, then tax relief was withdrawn. Pension funds were given five years to reduce the ratio back to below 105% and could do so by cutting contributions, improving benefits or by taking money out of the fund. Taking money out of the fund attracted a 40% tax charge. Improving benefits risked creating a precedent that a company would find difficult to go back on. Not surprisingly, most companies cut their own contributions, but this generated much bitterness.

Inevitably, all that was needed to swing pension funds from surplus into deficit was a fall in stock market values. The decline in the stock market in the three years from 2000 put many company pension funds so far into the red that companies are having to wriggle out of their commitments to their employees in order to keep their liabilities under control.

The excuse that companies needed for ending their final-salary pension schemes has come in the form of a new accounting standard, FRS 17. This requires that companies report the market value of their pension fund's assets and liabilities in their annual reports; they have to present all of their future pension liabilities and compare them against a current snapshot of their assets, which are mainly shares.

Companies hate FRS 17, which may require them to present a very damaging picture of their financial situation even if the obligations inherent in their pension scheme lie far in the future and the whole picture could change considerably before those obligations have to be realized. Before the introduction of FRS 17, the liabilities of companies' pension schemes could be averaged out over time, allowing companies to manipulate the presentation of those liabilities in their company accounts.

A study by the investment bank Credit Suisse First Boston found that FRS 17 revealed that companies currently have a £77 billion aggregate pension deficit, almost equalling their combined profits. CSFB found the situation was even worse for small companies, where the deficit stood at £13.1 billion or 132% of operation profits.

However, FRS 17 was only the last straw that broke the camel's back – there were a number of other reasons why companies wanted to get out of providing a defined-benefit pension to their employees. When the stock market grows at a pace in double-figure percentages, even if it is largely the result of inflation, it is relatively easy to keep a defined-benefit scheme on track. But with tax increases, poor investment returns, weak stock markets, people living longer and a larger proportion of employees expecting to come into the company pension scheme, companies would have been feeling the pinch even without FRS 17.

Removal of pension tax credit

A huge further blow to those trying to manage private pension funds came when Gordon Brown, the Chancellor of the Exchequer, removed the pension tax credit in 1997. Before then, the capital growth of a pension fund was not liable to capital gains tax and the dividends earned from investments were ploughed back into the fund without being taxed. This changed, and neither dividends earned from investments nor capital gains achieved by investments made by the fund were any longer exempt from tax. Tax relief would be allowed only on contributions paid into a pension fund.

> The Chancellor's removal of the tax credit on dividends has harmed and continues to harm the private pensions industry to the tune of £5 billion a year.

The Chancellor's removal of the tax credit on dividends has harmed and continues to harm the private pensions industry to the tune of £5 billion a year. In 1997 the Chancellor seemed to consider this a 'small' adjustment, one that was 'just correcting an anomaly'. It was an idea that apparently came from none other than Arthur Andersen, the accounting consultancy that advised Enron.

It is turning out to be a disaster. The insurers, the financial companies providing pension products and the employers offering final-salary pensions, all relied upon a given framework of regulations and investment opportunities. The massive shake-up of that framework put all their calculations out of joint. Institutions will be very chary of offering long-term investment commitments if the framework within which they have to operate can be changed at a Chancellor's whim. This was one more incentive for companies to pull out of offering defined-benefit pensions.

It did not, in fact, need FRS 17, the dividend tax credit abolition or even the huge decline in stock market values to kill off final-salary pension schemes. Such schemes would have failed anyway for any company whose pensioners outnumbered current employees. Final-salary pension schemes depend upon steady growth in the number of people in the system coming up behind and supporting those who have retired ahead of them – exactly what a pay-as-you-go state pension system depends upon. Companies could protect the benefits they offered to those who stayed with the company throughout their working lives (and, of course, their directors) by placing those who changed jobs a number of times during their careers at a huge financial disadvantage. They could also control the situation by offering pensions only to some of their employees.

In 2002 the number of British private-sector employees covered by final-salary defined-benefit pension schemes was (according to a *Guardian* newspaper survey) only 3.8 million compared with 5.6 million in 1991; only 44% of FTSE 100 companies had final-salary pension schemes for all their employees. According to industry figures, around 4.6 million people – 15.9% of the total workforce – are in private-sector defined-benefit schemes such as company pension schemes where benefits worth up to two-thirds of final salary at retirement are offered.

More and more companies are now saying that their role is to run their businesses, not to run a pension fund. An employee's pay will be what he gets and it will be up to that employee to make what arrangements he chooses or is obliged to make by law. If this is indeed where things are heading, then the government should be considering whether employers should be required to make contributions into whatever pension scheme the employee has.

Where once companies bore the risk of the fluctuating value of capital invested on the stock market, now the individual has to bear that risk. Since there is very little that the individual can do about that risk, he is faced with the insecurity of not knowing how well off or otherwise he will be when he is no longer able to work. This insecurity is compounded by developments in the annuity market. Since annuity rates are related to government bond yields, the annuity a pension fund will buy is much lower when bond yields fall.

Meanwhile, pensions continue for board members

At the same time, it was revealed that 76% of FTSE 100 companies had final-salary schemes for their board members. In a report to the government on executive pay and its regulation in 1995, Richard Greenbury demanded that the financial implications of board members' pay and pension promises should be spelt out in full. The report wanted it made clear to shareholders what capital sum would be required to buy an annuity on the market equivalent to the pension commitments the company had made to its chief executives and directors. In the case of a 60-year-old chief executive receiving a £100,000 pay rise, there would need to be around £1 million to fund the concomitant rise of £66,000 in his pension fund.

In effect, those who work for such a company are being forced to bear risks in order that the company can continue to offer final-salary pension packages to board members. Nor are the company's shareholders likely to be sanguine about what is happening. For example, key shareholders of Unilever, the consumer goods multinational giant, in 2002 demanded that Unilever close down completely its final salary pension scheme in spite of the fact that it was worth £4.2 billion and faced no problems honouring its commitments. Although Unilever's chairman, Niall Fitzgerald, refused to close down the scheme, this demonstrates the growing concern over how companies are running their pension schemes.

British government tries to persuade people to save more

If companies are portrayed as villains for withdrawing from final-salary, defined-benefit pension provision, they are not the only ones. The government's own actions have done much to compound the crisis. Let us look at two of their initiatives.

'Stakeholder pensions'

A key feature of government pensions policy[3] is the 'stakeholder pension' – private pension schemes to be offered by the financial and insurance sector where the charges are held down below 1% of funds under management rather than fees between 0.5% and 2.5% for other pension products.

In fact, the government has shown a remarkable lack of business nous with its scheme. It imposed conditions without considering that, for the insurance companies offering stakeholder pensions, the returns were too low to be regarded as viable business. At the same time the targeted audience for stakeholder pensions – those earning £20,000 p.a. or less – has shown little interest.

The administration and regulatory costs are such that only savings of £80 a month or more could be deemed viable business. For anyone with an annual income of £30,000 a year (well over the average income) this £80 a month would represent just over 3% of salary, a relatively high imposition. In the light of that, selling a stakeholder pension to anyone earning less than £30,000 is a dubious proposition.

> **The targeted audience for stakeholder pensions has shown little interest.**

Further, if the insurers were to make any profit on the products at all, given the low charge structure and the obligation to provide pension guarantees, they needed to avoid policy surrenders in the early years of pension saving. Since higher-income policyholders are less likely to surrender the policy early, the insurers had every incentive for targeting their sales efforts towards higher income households – which was not what the government intended.

Thus, in the first year of their existence only 320,000 stakeholder pensions were taken up by those earning between £10,000 and £20,000 a year. This 320,000 – only 2% of those without any kind of private pension top-up to the state pension – represented 42% of stakeholder pensions sold.

Many insurers did not bother to offer stakeholder pensions at all: of those that did, few bothered to put themselves out to market the products. At the launch 48 providers signed up to offer stakeholder pensions; a year later this number had fallen to five.

It has been compulsory for employers to offer a 'stakeholder pension' for employees but not for the employer to make any contributions or for employees to take up this pension and pay into it themselves. All but a few companies have done the bare minimum, which is to inform their employees of a firm offering 'stakeholder pensions' on behalf of the employer. Some 90% of employer-designated schemes have no members at all.

The State Pension Credit

As the government is forced back to supporting those without savings and means-testing benefits, those who have any savings are losing out. Why save and do without today when you will never get the benefit of your savings because your entitlement to state help is correspondingly reduced by the amount of your savings?

The government has chosen to limit the degree of disincentive by introducing its State Pension Credit, which came into force in October 2003. The aim of the new credit is to reward people who have built up small savings and pensions and who could otherwise lose out on state benefits. With the credit, instead of losing

> The aim of the new credit is to reward people who have built up small savings and pensions and who could otherwise lose out on state benefits.

£1 of benefits for every £1 saved, a saver will only lose 40p. But it still remains questionable whether it makes sense to save £1 in order to have 60p's worth of value in the end (and that 60p itself will be subject to income tax), especially when all other pension saving is tax-free. Experts in the industry have estimated that anyone who ends up with savings or a pension fund of less than £40,000 (in 2003 prices) is likely to fall into the pension credit regime.

The fundamental problem with means-testing is that – State Pension Credit or no State Pension Credit – it deters people from saving. Means-testing itself is deeply hated as people have to provide evidence of all their financial affairs. If the state system provides such major disincentives to extra saving, people will only save enough if forced to. Compulsion hits the poorest, lowering their living standards which are often already low. Since the state pension system is compulsory anyway, this would amount to a sudden and probably large increase in compulsory pension saving. The alternative to compulsion is to remove the disincentives.

Before making saving for a pension compulsory, the government ought to ask why the original system of compulsory saving for a state pension is not working as it should. The government's answer would probably be that people are living

> The problems arising from people living longer are relatively small compared to those that arise from people being forced into retirement at ever-earlier ages.

longer and therefore requiring much more in their old age, but it is probably true that, had the state seen fit to set aside in full the share of National Insurance contributions intended for pensions and ensured that their real value was maintained, the problem today would have been minimal. The problems arising from people living longer are relatively small compared to those that arise from people being forced into retirement at ever-earlier ages. To tackle this problem the government would need to fight ageism in the labour market.

What about reform?

Basically, the government makes fine pronouncements about reform but has chickened out when it comes to doing anything constructive. Frank Field was given the task of 'thinking the unthinkable' with regard to the impending pensions crisis but when he did so he was sacked. Derek Scott, economic adviser to the prime minister, was pushing for some radical and bold solution, including raising the pension age for all to 70; he, too, has stepped down. A government-appointed commission, chaired by Adair Turner, the former director-general of the Confederation of British Industry (CBI), then considered whether to continue with a voluntary system or to introduce compulsion. The resulting December 2002 Green Paper, a consultative document, was weak on solutions, having quietly dropped any ideas that had provoked outrage before publication. One such was the ending of the 25% lump sum that people are entitled to take from their pension fund tax-free upon retirement – the Treasury was itching to close this tax incentive and get its hands on the tax income from those lump sums.

Even so, the damage had already been done. People are not going to save unless they feel confident that they will receive the package they have been promised. Any government that forces huge swathes of the population into much-hated means-testing is not going to be thanked. So today *much saving that might have gone into proper pension products is being diverted into housing*.[4]

This is not just because most Britons trust housing as an investment that will evade the depredations of inflation; they trust housing, too, as a way of providing a far greater return than any other investment. A person's main residence escapes capital gains tax when sold and, by and large,

> Housing is sometimes described as the fourth pillar of pensions.

people feel that they have control over their housing investments. Theirs is the decision to buy and sell, to trade up or down, to realize some of the value invested in their house and so on.

As people grow more cynical about the professionals who manage their pensions, the more they are likely to turn to housing. In the UK in 2001, owner-occupier households were sitting on property valued at £1.5 trillion – and its value has risen since then. Of course, it could fall, but over the long term it is unlikely to do so. Tax advantages on a main residence are compounded because on a small overcrowded island the growth in housing stock will continue to be less than the demand for it.

So while British people turn to their homes to protect them financially, what did the Green Paper come up with? The answer is very little – although it does start to look at simplifying the tax regime for pensions. The eight different tax regimes that apply to company and private pensions would go and be replaced by one, with an individual lifetime savings limit of £1.4 million (under review). In other words, anybody who puts aside up to £1.4 million in a recognized pension product during the course of his or her working life will be able to do so without paying tax on those savings. The pension when he or she draws it down will be taxable, just as it always has been.

Already financial pundits are arguing against the £1.4 million limit. This limit is imposed not just on contributions – it includes any growth in the fund as a result of investment. Given the way stock markets can go up and down, a saver might find it impossible to ensure that the fund remains below the £1.4 million limit. But if it does go above that limit quite stringent penalties are proposed.

For the rest, the government wants to ensure that people are better informed throughout their working lives about their likely income in retirement so that, if their pension looks like being less than expected, they may be spurred into saving more. The government also wants to make it easier for the financial industry to offer cheaper products and more attractive forms of annuities; wants to persuade people to work longer; and plans to prevent employers from setting mandatory retirement ages. The tax rule that prevents people from continuing to work (usually part-time) for their old employer after the age of 65 and when they have started to draw their pensions is to go. But the state retirement age will remain unchanged.

7. The EU's drive for a single pension framework

By and large, the feeling in continental Europe is that working people should be able to look forward in retirement to a guaranteed income that is a percentage of either final salary or average salary over a number of years – in effect a defined-benefit system.

Britain's much publicized difficulties have been seized on by many on the Continent who are opposed to private pension arrangements and wary of a too loosely regulated industry answering to shareholders rather than to pension-savers. The main elements of the British pension system they find disquieting are:

- the degree to which the investments of British private pensions have become like driftwood on the tide of stock market movements. The Equitable Life scandal is presented as an example of what can go wrong;

- the ease with which companies can go back on their commitments to their workforces and the growing number of companies turning away from final-salary, defined-benefit-type pensions;

- legislation reducing the freedom of companies to use pension funds themselves as a form of cheap capital – in Europe this is a common practice.

But there is the issue of EU workers moving from country to country, who need to ensure a fair pension when they retire. Pension provision in Europe is a variegated patchwork that penalizes those who seek work in another EU country. Many who work outside their own country find that they lose pension benefits or rights because they worked elsewhere, or they find that their pension funds are not fully consolidated. The number of EU citizens who work outside their home country is currently over five million (out of a total EU population of 375 million) but it is rising – and rising at an increasing pace.

Every study made of the current situation in Europe stresses the impossibility of continuing along current paths: horror statistics are produced on the social dangers inherent in not making appropriate provision for ever larger retired populations. Facing this Gordian knot, governments are increasingly focusing on the need for working people to rely *less* on state systems. Even those governments whose electorates bitterly oppose change need to find a way of shifting towards private pension arrangements. Most of them also sincerely believe that private pensions arrangements can deliver better living standards for people in their old age. Some of the arguments for this are:

- *Increased pensions.* The rate of increase in wages represents the ceiling for any possible increase in pensions in a mature pay-as-you-go system, but over the long term the yield of an investment portfolio would almost certainly be higher than the rate of increase in wages (except when stock markets plunge).

- *Savings.* The net result of private pension arrangements is expected to be an increase in national savings, especially if the state encourages working people to save more than a specified minimum and offers tax incentives.

- *Capital productivity.* Because those savings are channelled through competitive and transparent capital markets, and the government cannot use them to finance public expenditure, the capital generated is used with greater efficiency than is likely to be the case if used by government (but some countries' capital markets are not very competitive, transparent or efficient).

- *The pension system is depoliticized.* Since the level of benefits of the pension system no longer depends upon government decisions, which may be coloured by political needs, pensions should cease to be a political football – thus eliminating the uncertainties of present and future pensioners (but not necessarily eliminating uncertainties generated by stock market swings).

Most of these arguments were put forward in Chile when its government decided on a major reform of the pension system in the early 1980s (see box). Since then other countries have looked at the Chilean experience and found its outcome encouraging.

The key point of the Chilean pension reform introduced in the early 1980s was that all working people were to make compulsory contributions into *individual savings accounts*; in short the system switched to being a fully funded defined-contribution system. Neither the state nor employers could henceforth be relied upon to provide for people's retirements. This was a radical move at the time and it has provoked considerable interest elsewhere where state pension systems are failing.

The EU Commission in Brussels is working towards an EU-wide pension system that breaks down the barriers between individual nations' different systems. Frits Bolkestein, the European tax commissioner responsible for the drive to create a single market in private pension provision, wants to break down the impediments to cross-border pensions. *Ultimately* (but not yet) he wants to enable both companies and individuals to manage their pension affairs anywhere within the EU as though the whole European Union were one single country. Just as a firm with branches in Munich and Hamburg is able to set up one single pension scheme for all its employees, so the aim is for a firm with branches in Munich and Madrid to be able to do the same. Similarly, the individual whose career takes him from one country to another should not have to suffer as a result of his pension savings being fragmented in many different schemes.

However, the Commission is well aware that national governments are not yet ready to accept so drastic a move. As a starting point it has set out four objectives:

- to ensure the security of pension beneficiaries;
- greater affordability and efficiency;
- cross-border membership;
- a level playing-field between providers.

The legislation that underpins the single market is supposed to guarantee the freedom of movement of people, goods and services. Any impediments to free movement (and much in current national pension arrangements does impede that freedom) can be challenged in the courts. Getting agreement will nevertheless be difficult – as the experience of introducing a common system of taxation for cross-border savings shows.

Investment constraints

The constraints on the private pension industry in terms of its investment possibilities vary enormously from country to country. British and Dutch funds are free to invest in a 'prudent' manner, so long as they do not invest more than 5% of the fund in any sponsoring company. German funds have to meet no fewer than five separate limits – not more than 30% in EU equities, or not more than 25% in EU property, or not more than 6% in non-EU equity, or not more than 6% in non-EU bonds, or not more than 20% in overall foreign assets. In Denmark and Austria pension funds may invest up to 40% of the funds they manage in equities; in France the limit on equities is 25%.

The percentage of pension funds that may be invested in equities in particular has long been a very thorny issue, since most national governments impose strict restrictions on equity investment, forcing pension funds to invest a high proportion of funds in government bonds, and in particular in the government bonds of the nation concerned. This is a contentious issue: some countries favour strict and rigid limits on how much may be invested where, while others prefer the greater flexibility of so-called 'prudent person' judgements. Countries that favour strict limits fear this more fluid approach and see in it the potential for fraud. Other countries see strict and rigid limits as unnecessarily restrictive, preventing the industry from obtaining the best results. Rather than impose quantitative rules and limits on national governments and private pension providers, the Commission has decided that a 'prudent person' framework would be more appropriate.

Studies carried out by the Commission between 1984 and 1996 found that where there were fewest restrictions the annual real return on pension fund investments was on average 9.5%. Where there were strict limits on pension fund investments and allocations, the average annual real return was 5.2%. But a gung-ho desire to eliminate all restrictions has to be tempered by the need for products to deliver what is required and expected of them.

The EU is proposing that up to 70% of any pension fund may be invested in equities. Another proposed change is that pension funds will be allowed to hold up to 30% of their investments in currencies other than the one in which they have commitments. This will give the large international firms an advantage because they have global research and management capabilities, particularly with equities.

Progress so far

The Brussels directive on pensions first came out in October 2000; it then had to get the approval of EU national governments. A number of states held out bitterly for concessions. In June 2002 France was the last country to agree in principle to the Brussels proposals, having held out for much stricter quantitative limits on funds' investments than Bolkestein wanted. Spain, too, could not accept that the rules gave enough protection for savers, but eventually came up with a compromise plan that would allow member states to set their own rules for domestic pension schemes. For the time being, then, funds that operate in only one country will continue to be regulated by the national authorities.

The directive, on the other hand, will set out the rules for cross-border schemes, which will be subject to more stringent rules on solvency and allowable investments than domestic schemes. This has given rise to criticism that the tighter regulations that will apply to pan-European pension provision will deter multinational companies from setting up pan-European pensions for their workforces.

8. The thorny issue of taxation?

A major impediment to Europe-wide private pension provision lies in the very important question of how saving for a pension should be taxed. No sizeable pan-European private pensions industry is likely to develop until this question has been addressed.

Denmark, for instance, was faced with serious financial difficulties because a good few Danes were choosing to retire to warmer countries, paying taxes there while drawing their pensions from the Danish government. Its attempts to inhibit such behaviour were clearly against the EU ideal of the free movement of people and their right to live wherever they wish within the EU. In Belgium, employees whose pension fund is located in another EU country are not eligible to claim tax relief on their contributions, although such relief is available to them if their fund is managed in Belgium. The Commission wants to stop such anomalies.

> A good few Danes were choosing to retire to warmer countries, paying taxes there while drawing their pensions from the Danish government.

Given the intensity of feeling among EU citizens over pension provision, governments need to provide tax breaks and incentives for younger people taking out private pension plans. The incentives need to be potent and effective.

Yet governments seem to be more concerned that such incentives do not become loopholes for tax evasion and damage their fiscal budgets; they are struggling to find the fewest tax incentives, backed up by as much compulsion as their electorates will bear, in order to minimize the potential damage to their fiscal budgets. They are likely to fail. With inadequate tax incentives, many people are likely to trust to luck rather than comply, and compulsion brings a political backlash.

> With inadequate tax incentives, many people are likely to trust to luck rather than comply, and compulsion brings a political backlash.

A 2002 OECD survey found a wide variation in the tax treatment of pension funds in different EU countries, which acted as a barrier to the single market in financial services. Tax incentives for pension saving could be interpreted as a form of government aid to its own financial services industry, at the same time inhibiting participation in other EU countries' pension schemes, since non-resident citizens and companies do not usually get the same tax privileges as nationals. This could generate a competitive advantage for some EU countries' pension funds and insurance provision compared with others.

Should contributions be taxed on pension payments?

Some European countries allow saving for a pension to go untaxed and then tax the pension when it is drawn down. Britain is an example. In other countries, such as Germany, contributions have to be paid out of after-tax income but the payments in retirement are tax-free (except for civil servants. Their contributions are paid directly by the state, and their pensions are taxed).

Clearly, there is a disincentive for British workers to go to Germany unless they are envisaging living out their retirements in Germany as well because they will be taxed twice over. For Germans working in Britain the opposite is true and they potentially enjoy making untaxed contributions and later untaxed pension payouts.

The German government in its recent moves to reform the German pension system and to introduce private pension top-ups to the state system disappointingly dropped plans for changing over to a system of 'deferred taxation', that is, pensions are taxed but not contributions.

Countries that offer greater tax privileges tend to be those that have gone furthest in pushing their citizens towards making private provision for retirement. Tax privileges for retirement savings amount to 2.4% of GDP for the UK and Ireland compared with 1.0% of GDP in The Netherlands and only 0.1%

of GDP in Germany. These tax privileges were largely introduced in order to reduce the pressures on the state pension system.

The EU Commission's tax and customs department, DG TAXUD, has a new director, Robert Verrue, a Frenchman, who has indicated that his department intends to step up measures to get rid of tax distortion and obstacles between member states. His concern is pensions and company tax, particularly pensions. A massive study by DG TAXUD found huge and widespread distortions in the taxing of pensions.

Back in 2000 the Commission said it would launch court cases against member states with tax rules that penalize those who want to work in a different EU country or who want to retire to a different country from where they worked. The Commission already has cases under way against Denmark and Finland. But it raises a fundamental issue: each EU member state retains full authority over national taxation policy – a jealously guarded right. To change anything to do with taxation requires unanimous support from all member states.

So while the Commission presses for a single market in pension services, it knows that differing tax regimes will make it impossible to bring about unless the necessary changes can get unanimous support. The Commission is pressing for a lifting of the unanimity requirement where taxation has an important EU dimension. Its current drive is to make the EU's tax system easier and more efficient for industry; it is no secret that the Commission wants to see a common corporate tax base for companies operating across Europe, even if the tax rate imposed by different governments varies from country to country. It is a measure of how important and how difficult this issue is that it has generated so much talk of court cases. (See Chapter 5 for further details.)

> While the Commission presses for a single market in pension services, it knows that differing tax regimes will make it impossible to bring about unless the necessary changes can get unanimous support.

Meanwhile the Commission's strategy is to try to get member states to offer the same tax relief on payments wherever the fund into which the payments are made operates. This should allow financial service providers to compete across Europe.

At the same time, to reassure national governments that pension payments will not be used to evade tax, the Commission wants a system for making all details on contributions, employee status, fund status and so on openly available. Member states would maintain their own tax arrangements but anomalies would be sorted out by the European Institution for Occupational Retirement Provision.

The Commission is also talking about possible new European legislation that would remove the obstacles that workers face when switching occupational pension schemes. As we have noted already, entitlements in company pension schemes are all too often contingent on discriminatory conditions such as minimum ages and waiting periods before entering a scheme, and vesting periods.[5] The Commission is calling for a basic level of harmonization, together with rules to make vesting periods shorter.

Top industrialists in Europe have also pressed for radical reform of national pension systems. Firms are very conscious they would benefit if they could set up a single pension fund for all their employees wherever they were employed. Ford, for example, has calculated that it could save around 40 million euros a year if all its European employees were in one pension scheme. Individuals who choose to work in different EU countries would also gain. While the Spanish compromise (see under heading 7 above) may be something of a setback, firms are likely to move increasingly towards setting up pan-European pension schemes.

The issue of speeding up progress towards a single system returned to prominence in summer 2002 when a group of 20 multinational companies said it would launch a legal campaign to end the tax discrimination that stands in the way of pan-European pensions. A test case is being brought by the Pan-European Pension Group, which includes Swiss Life, Kvaerner and Mercer Human Resource Consulting. The case is expected to end in the European Court of Justice in Luxembourg.

Tax harmonization is likely to become the biggest impediment to a pan-European system. So far it has been hard enough to get agreement to the idea of Europe-wide pensions; harmonizing the taxation of pensions and saving for pensions is too prickly a bunch of thorns to grasp.

9. European private pension difficulties

Germany

Out of a population of around 80 million people in Germany, some 23.5 million are retired. State pension transfers, which rose to 56.8 billion euros in 2002, are the government's second biggest outlay. The balance is paid jointly by employers and employees.

The German government has made the first moves towards making private pensions compulsory for workers alongside the state scheme. The idea provoked a very hostile reaction but the government is committed: the state pension is to fall by 2030 to 64% of final salary instead of the current 70%. This reform started giving private pension schemes tax concessions from 2002, with individuals initially saving up to 1% of their income. By 2008 individuals can pay up to 4% of income into a top-up private pension scheme. The government will set aside around 7 billion euros a year for tax breaks and subsidies in order to persuade Germans to save up to 4% of their income in private pension schemes. Berlin officials were confident these incentives would encourage around 90% of the 35 million people who pay into the state system to set up additional private pension provision. So far it is not working like that: initially, only 2 million signed up for private pension plans.

The pension industry is unhappy, too. The new schemes must satisfy 11 criteria to qualify for government help. Only bank deposits, investment plans and pension insurance policies guaranteeing a regular retirement income would be entitled to the proposed incentives. The pension industry did not like the fact that to be eligible for tax concessions schemes must pay a life-long pension and must guarantee to pay out at least as much as is paid in.

This last requirement means that pension plans must not lose money regardless of market performance – raising the issue of risk/return balance and who should bear the risks of investment volatility. If a fund must pay out at least as much as is paid in, the German pension industry is likely to adopt the most cautious and restrictive investment strategy.

Future pensioners also found much to criticize. They cannot touch their money until they reach 60, and even then face strictly limited choices: no more than 20% of the fund may be taken as a lump sum and the rest must be used to buy an annuity.

There was disappointment, too, that on the issue of taxation the government decided to leave the system as it was, with contributions being paid out of after-tax income and the pension being tax-free. Furthermore, the subsidies the German government will pay out to encourage workers to top up their state pension are lost if they move abroad.

However, even if German workers do embrace these private pension schemes, recent studies show that they will still not be saving enough. Few people in Germany are aware of how big the shortfall is, but the BfA, Germany's state institute for employee insurance, has been writing to employees to put them in the picture as to what they can expect in their retirement. In all of this there are similarities to the British situation.

> Few people in Germany are aware of how big the shortfall is.

For most workers, occupational schemes provided by employers look more attractive. Until now, company pension schemes have usually only been offered by big companies, and have accounted for only 10% of pensions. But under the new rules workers will be able to insist that part of their pay goes into a pension scheme. As a result, new industry-wide schemes are coming into existence, drawing in smaller companies: already some 16.3 million employees have won the right to such pension payments. These may well squeeze the government's private pensions out of the picture completely.

Unfortunately, German companies favour 'book reserve' pensions (see under heading 3 above). In the immediate post-war years an understanding was reached whereby companies accepted that a major part of their profits should be reinvested in the company rather than paid out in high dividends to shareholders. This high level of investment led to high productivity growth which benefited the whole economy. It was once seen as 'taming' investment capital, but increasingly it is seen as 'trapping' it, because it can mean that new industries find it hard to obtain seed capital.

It has been estimated that 'book reserve' pension provision accounts for around 60% of German pension liabilities out of a total of 331 billion euros. Could any company defraud its employees and former employees out of their rights on the lines of the Robert Maxwell fraud in Britain? No one expects this, and it should be noted that companies are required by law to insure themselves against the risk of defaulting on their pension liabilities.

All the same, a number of DAX 30 companies, including DaimlerChrysler and Siemens, have begun to take steps to create greater transparency. For at least part of their pension commitments they have set up a form of trust, a legally separate entity which takes a share of their pension funding off balance sheet. This is because there is growing pressure from investors, particularly international investors, for transparency so that companies can be compared with their peers in other countries where the 'book reserve' system does not operate. In effect, they were faced with the possibility of investors penalizing them and pushing up their financing costs.

Among the alternatives to 'book reserve' pensions comes the system next most favoured by companies, the *Pensionkasse* – an association, usually an insurance association, which manages pension assets on behalf of one or more companies. The German government's legislation to promote individual private pension funds to enable individuals to save more for their retirements is seen as boosting the *Pensionkassen*.

France

Different French Prime Ministers have tried to win French people round to the idea of topping up the state pension with private savings, but France is more hostile to private pensions than anywhere else. Like most EU countries, its pension system is pay-as-you-go, but the number of workers paying contributions is shrinking. Today, every ten workers pay for four retired people; by 2040 they will have to pay for seven. The average EU 'real retirement age' is 64, but in France it is below 58. Back in 1960, when the population was growing, the cost of pensions was 4.4% of GDP and a pay-as-you-go system made sense. Official estimates today see the cost of pensions rising from around 12% of GDP to anything up to 16.7% of GDP by 2040.

> The average EU 'real retirement age' is 64, but in France it is below 58.

TABLE 3.2

French pension arrangements*

	Private-sector workers	Public-sector workers
Minimum number of years of service to qualify for a full pension:	40 years	37.5 years
Pension is based on the average gross wage for a number of best-paid years of work:	25 years	10 years
Age of retirement:	65	60
Pension increases indexed to:	Retail prices	Average salaries

*Prior to legislation introduced in 2003

In 1993 Edouard Balladur introduced some reforms for private-sector pensions, the key feature of which was the setting up of the FSV (*Fonds de Solidarité Vieillesse*, the old-age solidarity fund). The FSV weakened the link between contributions and pension. Two years later Alain Juppé tried again. The pension arrangements of public-sector workers had remained much more generous than those in the private sector (see Table 3.2). The earlier changes had not applied to civil servants, so Juppé set about harmonizing public-sector pension regimes with those of the private sector, particularly with regard to the length of time contributions had to be paid in order to qualify for a full pension. But irate public-service workers took to the streets in protest and public opinion forced the government to backtrack. In France public sympathy is with the public sector.

Those demonstrations ensured the failure of the *loi Thomas*, the law authorizing private pension funds to top up the public pay-as-you-go system.

These private pension funds were to be offered by employers, and funded by contributions from both employer and employees. Upon retirement the individual had to buy an annuity. The contributions would be exempt from taxes but the annuity would be liable to normal taxation. However, the *loi Thomas* was never implemented and was repealed in 1999.

The demonstrations also played a part in bringing down Juppé's right-wing government in the May 1998 general election, so French governments not surprisingly feel beleaguered on the pensions issue, unable to face the electorate with unpopular reforms. When Lionel Jospin came to power in 1998, he promised 'diagnosis, discussion and decision', and first indications suggest that this will be concentrated upon whether and, if so, how the imbalance between private-sector workers and public-sector workers, who count for a fifth of the labour force, should be eliminated.

Tiptoeing round the issue, Jospin's first moves with regard to pensions were to strengthen the pay-as-you-go system. A reserve fund financed by the surpluses of the FSVs was set up to provide minimum pensions for older retired people. Then in October 2001 a voluntary long-term savings scheme known as PPESV was introduced. Under PPESV workers were offered tax breaks for entering a scheme where contributions are deducted from wages and then topped up by employers. To many this is a pension fund in disguise; the president, Jacques Chirac, has dared to talk of 'pension funds *à la française*'.

Insurers, mutual banks, credit agencies, commercial banks and employers have for a long time all wanted to develop pension funds. There is increasing acceptance that some form of mixed system combining pay-as-you-go and funded pensions must come. And the French population has already begun contributing more to life insurance and pension savings. In 1986, only 31% of French households owned such a product, but by 2000 46.6% did.

Finally, in 2003, the French government returned to the issue and, despite protests and demonstrations, pushed through new legislation. The most controversial part was the raising of the number of years that public-sector employees must work in order to qualify for a pension – from 37.5 to 40 and later, along with the private sector, to 42.

Italy

In many ways, the Italian welfare state is less well developed than most other European countries, but the exception to this lies in the area of pensions. For more than ten years the percentage of GDP spent on pensions has been much higher in Italy than in any other EU country, and today it is almost double the

For more than ten years the percentage of GDP spent on pensions has been much higher in Italy than in any other EU country.

EU average. In 1999 public spending in Italy on pensions stood at 15% of GDP and constituted 66% of overall welfare spending.

Every year pension payments far exceed the contributions paid by workers and employers. The problem is getting worse and at a faster pace than in many other countries. Italy not only has one of the lowest birth rates in Europe but also a faster increase in life expectancy. Italy's low birth rate of 120 babies per 100 women means a likely fall in the population from some 57 million today to 41 million in 2050, a much quicker collapse than the decline in the Roman Empire.

The government had wanted to see private pension schemes launched before tackling the huge problem of the state pension system. But the latest move has been retrogressive. In the early 1990s the government had started phasing out so-called 'seniority' pensions which allow early retirement at 57 if the worker has been in work for 35 years. This was to have happened by 2004, but Silvio Berlusconi is now proposing to allow the present system to continue until 2008. This is because there is fierce opposition from workers and trade unions. Even employers are lukewarm; they fear labour unrest and dislike the proposed ending of 'book reserve' pensions. Employers currently deduct 7% of a worker's pay, and the employee receives a lump sum when he/she retires or changes employer. Although, since 1993, new employees can choose to have this deduction paid into a pension fund, most in fact leave the money with their employers. As in Germany, these funds provide firms with cost-free working capital.

The government wants all this money to be paid into private pension funds, and to sweeten the pill has offered employers a cut of three to five percentage points in their contributions to the state pensions system for new workers, even while assuring these workers that their benefits will not be cut.

In December 2002 Roberto Maroni, the Minister for Welfare, insisted that the pension reform would be pushed through 'regardless of the hiccoughs'. For a country where 15% of GDP already goes on pension benefits and where a fifth of the population will be pensioners by 2015, pension reform is indeed urgent.

Other EU countries

Not all EU countries are facing impending crisis. The Netherlands has a fully-funded pension system and its pension funds are major investors throughout the euro zone. The Netherlands also does not face the same degree of ageing as many other EU countries.

In 1970 the Swedish government introduced a tax break on mutual funds that was simply too good to be ignored. This started a process of rising savings. More recently Sweden brought in a major pension reform with a switch from defined benefits to defined contributions, and contributions into a private pension fund became compulsory. Swedes must pay 18.5% of their earnings into a pension scheme. Furthermore, the state pay-as-you-go system is now linked to life expectancy, so that the size of the pension received is determined by the likely period over which it will be paid.

A number of governments (particularly in Scandinavia) have begun to set up information systems to enable people to ascertain much more precisely than before just how much they will have to live on when they retire and what kind of living standard they can expect to enjoy. This may well have the effect of bolstering the private pensions industry. The Norwegian government now has a state-administered website that Norwegians can log on to, input key data about themselves and find out in considerable detail what they will have in their old age. Under this scheme Norwegians can consolidate their state pension entitlement with any private pension savings schemes they may have. They can input varying estimates of inflation and growth of the return on their savings so see how different outcomes alter their likely pension income, and they can simulate the different outcomes they would experience if they increased or decreased their rate of saving. All of this is intended to give them a sense of ownership of their pension savings and a measure of control over them.

10. The future of the private pension industry

How big might the private pension industry one day be? At this stage the answer to this question can only be speculative. But it is clear that the sums involved will one day be huge, for if Europe's workers can be nudged into putting more into pension schemes, then that money has to find a home.

Currently only about 25% of the EU workforce is covered by private pension provision, but this is far from being evenly spread. That 25% is almost entirely to be found in The Netherlands and Britain, with private provision growing somewhat reluctantly in Germany and Spain. Other EU countries have a lot of catching up to do. So the proportion of the EU workforce saving for a private pension alongside public-sector pension arrangements is certain to grow and could well rise over time to around 75% or more of the EU workforce.

> Currently only about 25% of the EU workforce is covered by private pension provision, but this is far from being evenly spread.

TABLE 3.3
Pension fund assets
Total assets of private pension funds – preliminary 2001 OECD data

	Total assets $ billion	Percentage of GDP
United States	5115.9	75
United Kingdom*	1226.3	85
Japan	811.6	21
Canada	418.8	48
Australia	417.9	62
Netherlands	383.2	113
Switzerland	268.6	102
Germany*	63.0	3
Ireland	48.5	52
Italy	48.1	4
Denmark	39.0	22
Austria*	22.8	1
Belgium*	13.4	6
Norway	12.9	8
Spain	12.8	2
Portugal*	12.4	12
Finland	10.9	9
Sweden*	6.8	3
Poland	4.9	3
France	0	0

*2000 data

It was officially estimated in 2000 that overall in Europe funds worth around 2.3 trillion euros were under the management of the pension industry. Experts have forecast that this could rise to over 3 trillion euros by 2005, a 30% increase within a few years. The 2.3 trillion euros under pension fund management may be compared to the 4.5 trillion euros managed by the insurance industry. The private pension industry clearly has the potential to equal the insurance industry in size.

When the first legislation for German pension reform was passed, in the summer of 2001, banks and insurance companies envisaged a whole new business sector sprouting up with significant growth and earnings perspectives. Deutsche Bank estimated that an additional 300 billion euros would flow into private pension funds over the coming decade; Commerzbank estimated that by 2008 90 billion euros that would have been going into company retirement funds will wind up instead in the new pension funds. However, because of the way the German government shaped the reform, with strong emphasis upon a capital guarantee on contributions, private pension provision in Germany is likely to be in insurance-type pension schemes; fund managers outside Germany are unlikely to gain much business. This is because regulation of insurance business varies from country to country within the EU.

More recently a study by Deloitte Research and Goldman Sachs estimated that there would be funds worth around 4 trillion euros in private pensions accounts by 2010. This would rise to 11 trillion euros by 2030. Long-term savings in Europe would reach 26 trillion euros by 2010 and much of that would be savings for pensions. The potential that lies behind these numbers is enormous. It is not surprising that the financial industry is watching developments very keenly.

Some British investment banks are considering taking over company pension funds and are looking for ways of presenting a financial product that would fit the need. If they get it right, it will be another example of the City's innovativeness. If they get it wrong, the blame is likely to be considerable. The financial world is growing more complex year by year, and requires an ability and readiness to find new ways of fitting new needs. But to prevent such initiatives from going wrong, the regulators must be much more on the ball than they sometimes seem to be at present. Is this a strength or weakness of the British financial scene?

There are still many tripwires to be negotiated. Ordinary people fear and distrust the changes proposed in pension provision. Faced with strong opposition, governments tend to put the problem aside, and confidence in the financial services industry is weak. Progress will be much slower than is usually forecast. Opening up private pension provision to providers in other countries will be particularly slow.

The fear remains that progress just might be so slow in some countries that a crisis hits. This would result either in a government being forced into huge borrowing to support the elderly or in groups of people being deprived of their rights, or some combination of the two. The easiest way of limiting the damage if something like this threatened would be to make people work longer.

All of this is based upon the assumption that people when they have given up work have only a pension to live on. Fifty years of peace and economic growth in Europe have made Europeans relatively rich; many possess assets that may well be able to help support them in their old age.

Are people saving too little? On the face of it the answer has to be yes. But if assets are added to the picture and people are given greater freedom to

> If assets are added to the picture and people are given greater freedom to continue working after the age of 65, then the crisis could well be averted.

continue working after the age of 65, then the crisis could well be averted. In the meantime, the savings industry should be developing the products that serve people's needs. Governments could do a great deal more to offer incentives for more pension saving while still accepting the role of provider of last resort. However, this is a role that governments do not want: they may be tempted to impose a needlessly stringent risk/return balance in order to protect their own interests, which might be self-defeating.

Notes

1   A distinction can be made between Bismarck and Beveridge principles. The former grants earnings-related benefits where entitlement is conditional upon a contributions record. By contrast, a Beveridge system is one in which benefits are directed at the whole population, are typically flat-rate and financed through taxation – the principles of Beveridge are unity, universality and uniformity. The Continent has embraced the Bismarck system while Britain went for Beveridge.

2   The vesting period is the length of time (often a number of years) the employee must pay into the scheme before he/she has a right to claim a pension from the scheme when the employee retires. Clearly there will always be a number of employees who will not have paid contributions for long enough to have a right to a pension when they retire, or because they left the company too early; thus the company is able to bolster the pension fund at the expense of those who change jobs.

3   The British government is still tussling with the pensions system and new proposals are coming out constantly.

4   Housing is sometimes described as the fourth pillar of pensions. In Britain increasing numbers of people are deliberately seeking to buy a second property that can be rented out and generate an income. Others place their trust in being able to sell their family home and move somewhere smaller and cheaper upon retirement. In both cases people feel greater confidence in the ability of property to appreciate in value than in the ability of pension fund managers to ensure the growth of investments.

5   On vesting periods, see note 2, above.

section II:

QUESTIONS OF FINANCIAL REPORTING

4

GRASPING THE INTANGIBLE

ALISON THOMAS
*Global Director of Research, PricewaterhouseCoopers
Research Fellow, St Catherine's College, Oxford[1]*

Overview

Reports of the death of the traditional financial reporting model are greatly exaggerated. Although fashionable to disparage its relevance, it remains, without doubt, the most widely used method of communicating the *historic* performance of company managers. But, unfortunately, as the small print on every mutual fund advertisement says, one cannot use past performance as any guarantee of future returns. And it is typically the future returns that are of interest to the users of financial reports.

> The market's short-term memory span tends to assume that Enron was the start of the end for the current reporting framework.

Examples of the inadequacy of the current reporting model as a predictor of future success abound. The market's short-term memory span tends to assume that Enron was the start of the end for the current reporting framework. Although admittedly the most spectacular collapse to date, it is in fact merely one in a long line of high-profile market failures.

The magazine *Management Today*, for example, publishes annually a list of the UK's 'top' companies. Ranked by ROI, an analysis of the subsequent fate of the award winners makes for interesting reading – see Table 4.1. These formerly world-class companies feature frequently today in every business school's case studies. Although the details of each company's fall from grace differ, one fundamental recurring theme emerges. The current financial reporting model fails in its most basic task; it does not allow the user to evaluate the quality and sustainability of a company's financial performance with any degree of certainty. Or, more simply stated, to differentiate good management from bad, luck from skill.

If it were just a matter of a few investors burning their fingers, the weaknesses of traditional accounting measures might perhaps not be a cause for public concern. However, it is becoming increasingly apparent that the cost of this inability to evaluate the sustainability of corporate performance is far greater than the financial and social consequences of a single corporate failure. This issue affects us all.

On its own, the fear that a sell-side analyst might downgrade a company's stock is enough to make managers avoid investments that the stock market cannot readily assess. The likelihood that such an investment could be misinterpreted as an unexpected cost is too great – and the cost in terms of stock price performance too damaging – for managers to ignore. The consequence of this is an under-investment in 'invisible' long-term projects such as training or customer retention programmes.[2]

TABLE 4.1
Management Today: UK's top companies

Year	Company[a]	Market value	ROI[b]	Subsequent performance
1979	MFI	57	50	Collapsed
1980	Lasmo	134	97	Still profitable
1981	Bejam	79	34	Acquired
1982	Racal	940	36	Still profitable
1983	Polly Peck	128	79	Collapsed
1984	Atlantic Computers	151	36	Collapsed
1985	BSR	197	32	Still profitable
1986	Jaguar	819	69	Acquired
1987	Amstrad	987	89	Still profitable
1988	Body Shop	225	89	Still profitable
1989	Blue Arrow	653	135	Collapsed

[a] Where a company has been top ranked for more than one year, the next best performer has been included. For example, Polly Peck topped the charts in 1983, 1984 and 1985.

[b] Pre-tax profit as a percentage of investment capital.

Furthermore, at a macro economic level, as these intangible assets are being systematically mispriced by the market, a company's cost of capital does not reflect the appropriate risk-adjusted rate that the future cash flow streams should command.[3] Projects that would add to the wealth of the nation are thus not financed, while projects that should not get the go-ahead are embraced.

The potential consequences of this inadequate communication mechanism are clear. As the UK government's own research shows, the long-term competitiveness of this nation is falling behind its major international peers.[4] Economic growth is constrained.

In this chapter, I look briefly at why the traditional reporting model appears to be failing in its most fundamental roles and then consider some of the practical attempts that have been made to plug the holes identified. I will examine some of the new frameworks for reporting that have appeared over recent years and question why such frameworks, though eminently sensible, have been adopted by so few companies. Through an analysis of the obstacles to change, I will offer a practical solution that should encourage more to move towards the transparency that our corporate sector – and indeed our wider economy – needs.

The model needs new clothes ...

So what are the fundamental objectives of a financial reporting model and why are the current standards failing to meet the needs of the user?

The financial reporting model as we know it today started to evolve in earnest at the turn of the last century. At this time, the capital demands of a growing base of mass manufacturers necessitated a shift away from the previously common organizational model of the 'owner-manager' to the inclusion of external sources of capital. As ownership became more dispersed, it became common for the owners of a company to have no direct knowledge as to whether the capital that they had entrusted to the manager was being efficiently utilized or whether it was being squandered.

> The financial reporting model as we know it today started to evolve in earnest at the turn of the last century.

This informational asymmetry led to the creation of a standard set of externally verifiable financial measures that were designed to provide investors with a way of assessing:

- the quality of corporate performance;
- the sustainability of corporate performance; and
- whether the governance structures of the firm were sufficient to prevent the misappropriation of corporate funds.

The structure of the reporting model that evolved basically met these needs. Return on capital employed, cost per unit of production, value of inventory held are all critical elements of a reporting model for a company in the heavy industry environment. The standards that emerged were thus sufficient to allow the user to evaluate, however crudely, both the quality and the sustainability of corporate performance for the bulk of the industrial base of the land.

But, of course, the world did not stand still. Today, service industries dominate the industrial landscape. Typically, success in these enterprises is not dependent upon a large, fixed asset base. Indeed, for many such companies the value of plant and equipment is trivial. Instead the business model today is critically dependent upon other factors of production – in particular, the management of intangible assets such as brand, employees and the organizational capability of the firm to innovate. And yet, despite their fundamental importance to any business today, these assets are left completely invisible by current standard reporting mechanisms.

Of course, such observations are far from new. Indeed it has been estimated that over 1,000 books and articles have been written on the subject of goodwill alone since 1880.[5] However, the importance of this debate has increased to a critical point as the economy's intangible base has grown. In the ten years from 1977 to 1987, goodwill increased as a percentage of the net worth of bidding companies from 1% to 44%.[6]

So the issues are well known. Recent experience has highlighted to investors the dire consequences that can accompany an inadequate reporting model. Given this, why have reporting standards not changed?

Grasping the intangible: great idea – why the delay?

When a mass-manufacturer wished to signal its long-term strength, it had to demonstrate that it generated an adequate return on its huge base of fixed assets and that its costs were low. But how can a technology company signal its future prospects on the basis of its intellectual capital base? In contrast to physical assets, intellectual capital derives much of its value from the fact that it can be deployed simultaneously in multiple tasks, that it can have increasing returns to scale (as knowledge is cumulative) and that knowledge assets can learn from feedback loops.

Despite these highly differentiated attributes, intangibles could still be evaluated if there were an organized exchange where they trade. However, this is not typically the case. Furthermore, even if there were some pricing mechanism, one would have to address the issue of property rights. Except in the case of intellectual property that is protected by a watertight patent, the ownership of intellectual assets is often in question – which makes them inherently more risky than plant.

The fact that reporting standards have failed to keep pace with the new economy does not necessarily signal a lack of willingness – it merely reflects the complexity of the task. Indeed, it is to the credit of a number of academics and standards setters that, despite these challenges, they have tried to grasp the reporting nettle through a variety of interesting initiatives.

Old models: new assets

The first wave of research in the field of intangible asset evaluation tried to apply old reporting model concepts to new kinds of asset. Comfortable with the concept of a balance sheet that reveals all assets and liabilities, people have tried – and continue to try – to describe a routinized method for placing a value on the intangible assets of the firm.

One of the more noteworthy academics in this school is Baruch Lev. He argues that it is possible to value intangibles through the use of a production function:

$$EP = \alpha(\text{physical assets}) + \beta(\text{financial assets}) + \delta(\text{intangible assets})$$

where EP is economic performance and α, β and δ represent the contributions of a unit of asset to the enterprise performance.[7]

Given that physical and financial assets are routinely evaluated by existing reporting techniques, and given that one can 'estimate normal rates of return', the contribution of the intangible can be evaluated.

The contribution of the intangible can be evaluated.

Although an interesting conceptual framework, Lev's methodology remains insufficiently tested in 'real world' settings for users to have confidence in the reliability of the estimates of the coefficients employed and the underlying model used to define 'normal rates of return'.

In practice, therefore, regulators have tried to take the first few steps towards addressing the intangibles dilemma through more conventional means. Thus, for example, the US's Financial Accounting Standards Board has recently revised the standards for accounting for intangibles. Known as FAS 142 'Goodwill and Other Intangible Assets', the new rules try to encapsulate some of the attributes that differentiate intangibles from conventional fixed assets. Most notably, it has removed the requirement to amortize intangibles over a finite life. Instead, it allows some intangibles to have indefinite lives with no amortization. Such assets will only have to be written off when they are deemed to be 'impaired'.

For the ever-prudent US authorities, this standard represents a significant shift in their recognition of the economic imperative to make visible the intangible assets of a firm. However, it still leaves those charged with implementing the new standard with a tricky question. In the absence of any routinized market, how can one assess whether an intangible asset has become impaired?

Fortunately, this 'balance sheet' approach to the intangibles problem is not the only solution on the table. Others have tried to re-evaluate the very concept of corporate reporting, pushing the boundaries of the traditional financial-based framework towards a broad basis of measures that can combine to present an overall picture of corporate health.

Fortunately, this 'balance sheet' approach to the intangibles problem is not the only solution on the table.

Venturing beyond the balance sheet

One of the earliest attempts to develop a holistic framework for reporting arose from the work of the Brundtland Commission, whose 1987 report, *Our Common Future*, introduced the now ubiquitous phrase 'sustainable development' and emphasized the idea that issues of balance and equity were essential to the concept of long-term development. This fundamental tenet has been developed by SustainAbility into what is now known as the 'triple bottom line'.[8]

Triple bottom line refers to the expansion of the traditional economic bottom line to incorporate wider notions of accountability and responsibility and to recognize the importance of non-financial drivers in the development of a sustainable business. The three areas of the triple bottom line are: economic prosperity, environmental quality and social justice. These ideas should, it is argued, permeate all levels of governance and strategy in order to achieve long-term success.

> Triple bottom line refers to the expansion of the traditional economic bottom line to incorporate wider notions of accountability and responsibility and to recognize the importance of non-financial drivers in the development of a sustainable business.

These notions have made a significant impact on the reporting world, with Shell's high-profile adoption of the framework sealing its credibility. However, the SustainAbility model was insufficiently prescriptive to allow stakeholders to compare performance over time and among peer groups. Overcoming this limitation was one of the original motivations for the formation of the Global Reporting Initiative (GRI).

Originally convened by the Coalition for Environmentally Responsible Economies (CERES) and the United Nations Environment Programme (UNEP), the GRI is one of the most ambitious efforts to develop a set of non-financial standards. It is a long-term, multi-stakeholder initiative, which aims to develop and disseminate globally applicable 'Sustainability Reporting Guidelines'. Companies can then use the guidelines voluntarily to make visible their management of the triple bottom line.

Implementing the GRI is not without its conceptual and practical difficulties. Most notable of these is that it presents its list of measures and metrics in a generic reporting format. This is despite the fact that one of the most obvious conclusions to draw from the reporting debacle of the past 100 years is that a 'cookie-cutter' approach to disclosure doesn't work: the factors critical to a bank's future success, for instance, are very different from those that drive a mining company. Although the GRI is currently trying to address this concern, achieving consensus industry by industry remains a challenge.

However, despite this obvious limitation, some standards setters are already incorporating the spirit of the GRI initiative into their reporting requirements. In Germany, for example, the Institut der Wirtschaftsprüfer (IDW) has introduced new guidelines for the preparation of management reports. Statements must now encompass 'all disclosures required for an overall assessment of the economic position of the enterprise, business activities and risks of future developments'. All factors that are seen to have a 'cause and effect relationship with the position of the enterprise' have to be reported, including 'political events in the community', working hours, conditions of employment, the compensation system, company kindergartens, expenditure on training, environmental protection measures taken, recultivation measures, the use and removal of waste, the risk of liability for environmental damage – the list is exhaustive. Moreover the guidelines are explicit in demanding 'clarity and intelligibility' in all disclosures. Thus they expect all 'disclosures in the management report should be made in a clear, unambiguous and understandable manner', with comparability in terms of measures used over time. If measures used to report on these items change in any year, then all previous years must be restated.

These reporting requirements are onerous indeed. They are all the more surprising given that they have been imposed in a country that is renowned for its tight corporate governance structure. Given the concentration of ownership within the market, one might argue that the level of informational asymmetry between owner and manager – and thus the need for additional disclosure – is far less than that present in the Anglo-Saxon markets.

However, even this admirable effort is a mere drop in the ocean when placed alongside one of the world's most ambitious attempts by a regulator to tackle the intangibles dilemma.

The Danish Trade and Industry Development Council and the Copenhagen Business School have formed a task force to examine how a company may make visible its intellectual capital (IC) base.[9] Their approach, like the German initiative, tries to expand the number of measures available to stakeholders, but at the same time recognizes the need to tie these expanded measures to financial returns.

To investigate the reporting of a subset of intangible assets, intellectual capital, the task force aims to analyse the experiences of companies that have experimented with IC reports, and to develop an understanding of best practice in order to establish standards.

The ten IC accounts studied by the Danish task force differ in their detail but share common features, which can be broadly split into three categories: 'what there is', 'what is done' and 'what happens'. In the first, the company's resources, customers and technology are visualized. Under the second heading, there is an attempt to describe the processes that drive value creation by this asset class. Finally, the company's ability to utilize the opportunities offered by intellectual capital development and management is assessed.

The objective of this type of initiative is thus to try to make visible the financial consequences of human resource development, readjustment, reshuffling, acquisition and turnover. However, its focus on factors that can be immediately valued limits its scope. By looking at other measures such as staff demographics, training statistics, loyalty numbers and so on, one can, over time, monitor whether the stock of intellectual capital is growing and then determine how changes in, say, training are correlated with financial returns.

> By looking at other measures such as staff demographics, training statistics, loyalty numbers and so on, one can, over time, monitor whether the stock of intellectual capital is growing and then determine how changes in, say, training are correlated with financial returns.

This more holistic, longer-term, model of corporate reporting underpins *Building Public Trust*,[10] in which PricewaterhouseCoopers sets out its vision of the future reporting model. Advocating three 'tiers' of information, it recognizes not only the need for non-financial information, but also the necessity of moving beyond the 'one-size-fits-all' view of corporate reporting through the provision of information that makes visible the different dynamics that are at play in various industries:

- tier one: global GAAP (generally accepted accounting practices);
- tier two: industry-based standards;
- tier three: company-specific standards.

Though conceptually quite straightforward, this represents quite a bold step forward for a firm traditionally associated with the regulatory-driven, financial-based reporting framework. In this vision of the future of reporting, PwC is not calling for a wholesale departure from the traditional financial model. Indeed, it sees financial outcomes as the common denominator for the effective evaluation of all companies, regardless of territory or industry. But to understand the quality and sustainability of corporate performance, measures that extend beyond the financial are clearly required. The second tier of the reporting model starts to address this need with a call for standard metrics that may be specific

FIGURE 4.1
ValueReporting framework

Market overview →	Strategy →	Value creating activities →	Financial performance
■ Competitive environment ■ Regulatory environment ■ Macro-economic environment	■ Goals and objectives ■ Organizational design ■ Governance	■ Customers ■ People ■ Innovation ■ Brands ■ Supply chain ■ Environmental, social and ethical	■ Financial position ■ Risk profile ■ Economic performance ■ Segmental analysis

Source: PricewaterhouseCoopers

to a given industry but which are comparable across all players within that industry. In the oil and gas industry, 'proven and probable reserves' would be an example of such a measure.

However, a complete understanding of corporate returns needs more than even these additional, industry-based standards. Every company approaches the opportunities and risks within their industry in a unique way. Those differences need to be clearly articulated for the user to understand the sustainability of corporate performance.

Although a sensible conceptual framework, the model as presented raises the obvious first question: what type of information is needed, industry by industry, to populate each of the tiers? PricewaterhouseCoopers has spent the past six years trying to build an understanding of just that. Through a series of global industry surveys, it has asked CFOs, sell-side analysts and the investment community to identify the success factors they consider critical for a given industry. The results of these empirical analyses have been codified into the ValueReporting framework,[11] a generic version of which is given in Figure 4.1.

From this codification of the survey findings, it can be seen that users of the corporate reporting model are looking for four basic building blocks of information. The first category of information that investors demand, and that managers deem essential for good business practice, the *Market overview*, revolves around an analysis of the economic and competitive landscape of the firm. Given this analysis of competitive positioning, a company then needs to be able to articulate clearly its *Strategy*. Under *Value creating activities* the firm is then encouraged to

> Users of the corporate reporting model are looking for four basic building blocks of information.

make visible the competencies and resources at its disposal that will enable it to implement its articulated strategy. And then, last but not least, are the *Financial outcomes* from corporate activity. Note the emphasis that is put on the importance of communicating the company's economic performance.

This framework, though presented here in its generic form, is tailored to reflect the findings of each global industry survey. Thus, for a retailer, the research highlights various customer and store-based metrics; for a bank, customer penetration and retention, among other things, are emphasized, and so on. The result is a framework that provides the user with a robust starting point for understanding the quality and sustainability of a company's performance and making sense of all the disparate pieces of information that may be offered. This is probably best illustrated with a simple example.

Take the case of a hypothetical retailer, Tell All Disclosures Inc. It announces that its revenues for the year are up by 10%. How am I to evaluate this performance? Traditionally, I would try to gain comfort regarding the quality and sustainability of this number by poring through financial statements – but how far can that get me in understanding the company's returns? What can I draw on, within the financial report, that would allow me to differentiate good management from bad, luck from skill?

The ValueReporting framework would approach this challenge by considering the market conditions in which the firm operates. An obvious question might be 'How has the peer group performed?' Let us assume that it is discovered that Tell All's competitors saw an average increase in revenues of just 2%. How does that alter my sense of comfort with the 10% reported by the company? I am now more curious, but little the wiser. How has that higher growth rate been achieved?

The ValueReporting framework suggests moving on to the company's stated strategy. Has Tell All been making acquisitions, or been growing the store base aggressively? Is that the reason for its superior growth rate? Let us assume that no such structural decisions have been made. Faced with this additional piece of information, I am perhaps a little less comfortable with the 10% revenue growth number.

But perhaps the company has managed its internal resources with great skill? To investigate this hypothesis, the tailored ValueReporting framework would suggest I examine such measures as customer satisfaction. If it turns out that this has actually fallen over the period, a very uncertain picture emerges. Has the company grown by pushing product aggressively to a reluctant customer base? Will the returns rate increase as unwanted product flows back into the firm? Might it have even used an unconsolidated vehicle to park inventory? Even if today's numbers are a true reflection of a momentum built in years gone by, the sustainability of the performance must surely be questioned.

Although this may be a trivial example, I think it illustrates the type of structure we need if the information provided by management is to make sense of corporate performance. It is not necessarily an increase in volume of data that is required. Indeed, in some cases, I would argue there is already an excess of data obscuring the information that would allow underlying performance to be understood. What is required, however, is for management to pay greater attention to articulating in a credible and consistent fashion the kind of 'dashboard' information used to control the firm's assets.

> What is required is for management to pay greater attention to articulating in a credible and consistent fashion the kind of 'dashboard' information used to control the firm's assets.

Many companies today produce a social report, for example, that talks of employee metrics. However, very few companies help the reader to 'join the dots' through an effective structuring of the information provided. Strategic intent and the competencies and resources available to the firm to deliver on strategy are rarely linked. Critical blocks of information are ignored. For that reason, the propensity of the investor is to judge corporate performance using a single or mere handful of indicators, such as earnings per share or profit. This cannot be in the interest of management.

If managements wish their firms to be fully valued by the capital market, they need to provide a sufficiently robust understanding of their performance so that readers can evaluate whether today's performance has been achieved through skill or as a result of a management acting for the short term at the expense of future growth. Has management been investing to maintain or grow market position, or has it been acting in a fashion likely to detract from future prosperity, cutting back on staff training, environmental safety procedures, investment in new technology and so on? Equally, if, because of a substantial investment in, say, a customer relationship management system, financial numbers disappoint today, a firm can only expect investors to 'look across the valley' to the positive outcome of this investment if it has previously articulated customer satisfaction as a critical long-term success factor. In short, if management leaves us in the dark, it can be no surprise if the scarce resources of the land continue to be misallocated.

But could the provision of such information give competitors too great an insight into the 'game plan' of their peer? I would contend that in most industries competitor analysis is part of the fabric of life – people move between employers; customer surveys are commissioned; relative brand analyses are conducted. The number of secrets is small indeed! Furthermore, in most cases, the ability to copy a peer is constrained by the competencies and resources of the firm. Coca-Cola could provide a detailed analysis of customer satisfaction, market share, organizational structure and so on in the full knowledge that no other company could take such data and become, over-night, the new Coke.

We know the 'what', but 'why'?

A picture is emerging of the future of corporate reporting that makes sense conceptually and has sufficient detail, industry by industry, for practitioners to move forward. The actual measures required to populate the three-tiered reporting model are well understood. But for wholesale change to occur across all sectors, another key piece of the jigsaw needs to be put in place, namely the economic rationale for adopting a more holistic reporting model.

Having a clear understanding of the economic benefits of improved corporate reporting is essential for a management team faced with the challenge of structuring its reporting strategy. Any information worth its salt is costly to produce and disseminate. Furthermore, in a few cases the enhanced disclosure might also reveal something of strategic interest to competitors. For these reasons, faced with these costs, managements need to have a framework to help them to identify where their greatest economic benefits may lie.

Why report? The economics of improved disclosure practice

The original motivation for the drive for companies to offer voluntary non-financial disclosure to improve stakeholder communications may have come as a reaction to short-term problems. In a 1999 article in the *Guardian*,[12] Roger Cowe cited a list of disasters that had forced companies to rethink their reporting strategies. Brent Spar, Nike and child labour, Microsoft and allegations of social irresponsibility, even Mr Ratner and his ill-advised comment that his company sold 'crap' – all have stimulated a plethora of companies to start taking non-financial measures of success seriously.

There is growing evidence, however, that the motivation for incremental disclosure is now changing. Many companies now report non-financial measures that provide the external stakeholder with information on how they are managing those relationships that define their long-term licence to operate. And rather than those disclosures being a defence mechanism – a knee-jerk response to disaster – these companies are finding that such supplemental reports create competitive advantage in the marketplace.

The exact nature of this advantage seems to vary company by company. Talking to the financial controller of a FTSE 100 company about the benefits of its substantial investment in greater corporate transparency, I was told that the group's 'employment brand' had increased substantially. It had quantified its ability to retain and attract the best and brightest; through surveys, it had attributed much of the observed improvement to an enhanced corporate image and had thus concluded that its communication strategy was not just 'the right thing to do' but had also yielded substantial economic and competitive gains.

In a similar vein, empirical analysis suggests that customers prefer to deal with a known supplier. Uncertainty about the sustainability of a firm, about its ethical standards and about the continued employment of critical employees may lead a customer to find an alternative source for the product, or to demand more favourable terms.

Case studies from the extractive industry frequently cite the importance of a credible and holistic reporting framework when trying to win new government licences or to attract new partners. In this case, a corporate culture of transparency provides the government or potential partner with an added incentive to welcome a potential bid.

For many companies, however, it is the relationship between greater transparency and the cost of capital that is of greatest interest. By communicating in a credible and consistent fashion the value of the opportunity set they are creating, will managements be rewarded for their efforts through a lower cost of capital? Will they gain a competitive advantage in the capital market?

This question was addressed in a paper by Gietzmann, Shilo and Thomas,[13] who demonstrated a relationship between the quality of reporting critical elements of information in the pharmaceutical industry (as defined by the PwC Pharmaceutical industry survey) and the volatility of stock prices surrounding corporate releases. Companies that fail to communicate their research and development pipeline well, or fail to talk about their competitive environment, experience a large degree of stock price volatility surrounding corporate disclosures in those areas. The uncertainty that their reticence creates is clearly costing them in the capital market.

It is equally interesting to note in this work that a pharmaceutical company that does not clearly articulate, say, its brand strategy, or customer satisfaction metrics, appears to add little to the uncertainty surrounding its share price. It is not the volume of data that matters, but the quality and relevance of the information provided. If a pharmaceutical company is thinking of prioritizing its communication stream, therefore, it is better served by ensuring an accurate understanding of the drugs in its pipeline than talking about its brand strategy, customer satisfaction and so on.

This analysis is currently being extended into the debt market. Early evidence here suggests that corporate transparency may explain a significant portion of the variation in the cost of debt for companies that have the same debt rating. This conclusion could have significant and immediate cash implications for corporations today.

A slightly different angle to understanding the value of improved communication to the capital market has been taken by Holliday and Pepper,[14] who have demonstrated the economic benefits of incorporating a broad set of stakeholders into corporate decision-making. If a management 'dashboard' that extends beyond financial measures enhances underlying corporate performance, then, by implication, by integrating stakeholder measures into an analysis of management's performance, the financial community can allocate its resources more efficiently. In order to exploit this economic opportunity, however, enhanced and credible communication of corporate activity is required.

Similarly, my own study[15] examined the relationship between consumer opinion and financial returns in the banking industry and found that consumer satisfaction metrics were a leading indicator of changes in both stock price and cash flow returns. It thus makes sense for a bank to communicate the success with which the customer base is being managed, rather than leave investors to assume the worst.

Two other studies[16] have found that an investment in human capital drives above-average productivity and financial performance. If this is made visible, the users of reported information can understand the foundation that is being laid for future success.

Indeed, the body of empirical research that helps the manager and analyst to understand the *economic* significance of a broader set of financial indicators is now vast and growing rapidly as the understanding of the drivers of long-term value creation expands.

So now what's the hold-up?

We have a framework for reporting that seems to be perfectly sensible. We have a plethora of studies that show the economic benefits that accrue to the transparent. So why aren't companies stampeding to embrace change?

FIGURE 4.2
The reporting grid

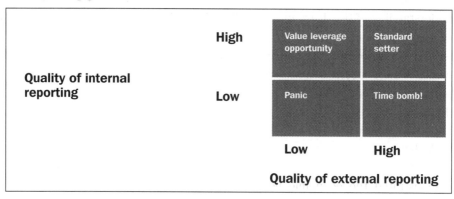

Source: PricewaterhouseCoopers

To understand this, we need to delve a little deeper into the practical issues that constrain change. Consider the assessment matrix in Figure 4.2, designed to understand the state of a company's reporting today and to help to frame the ambition of a company's reporting strategy. This matrix clearly sets out the relationship between the quality of internal reporting and the quality of external reporting. It stresses the necessity of excellent internal control systems before 'going public'. So a company that has poor internal information, that is perceived by the outsider to be reporting holistically, is categorized as a 'time bomb'. In short, its inadequate control structures will eventually be recognized by the marketplace and corporate trust will evaporate. Equally, a company that has great internal information could easily gain credit for its good management by becoming more open in its reporting – a value leverage opportunity exists. But this matrix is also can be used to illustrate one of the critical reasons why changes in reporting practice have been held up.

Consider how the investor perceives the company. At present he is in a position to make an assessment – subjective or quantified – on the quality of a company's external reporting. But how useful is that assessment when evaluating a potential investment? If the investor thinks the company somewhat reticent in its communications, what conclusions can he draw? Is the lack of information simply because the management is uncertain about the appropriate means of communicating non-financial information? Or is management's reluctance to talk about its customers, employees and so on related to a dearth of such information within the firm – a situation that an investor may rightly categorize as 'panic'?

Such ambiguity of signal can exist equally when a company apparently offers the investment community a plethora of data. Is this company truly in control? Or is it being a little creative in the numbers reported? Given the information available today in most industries, it is impossible to distinguish between the two. And human nature dictates that, in the absence of any further reassurance, all companies will be tarred with the same cynical brush by the investor. All companies will thus face a high cost of capital – which reflects the degree to which the inability to distinguish good management from bad is endemic within the market.

Credibility of data is thus critical. There is little point in spending large sums on gathering and disseminating additional information if your efforts will be met with a shrug. Fortunately this difficulty is not insurmountable. Indeed, we have some well understood examples that can guide us as to the best way forward.

Take the oil and gas industry. In the spirit of the three-tiered reporting model, the key players have for many years reported a set of measures that are both industry-specific and reasonably standardized in terms of the definitions used. Proven and probable reserves are an obvious example of such metrics. The relative uniformity of the methodology employed in producing the data, though by no means perfect, does allow both cross-industry comparisons and a degree of assurance that the numbers produced are an accurate reflection of a firm's activity. A similar model for reporting has evolved in the pharmaceutical industry, where the research and development pipeline data are reported using a format that is reasonably consistent across all participants.

So why has the reporting model progressed so notably in these particular industries? Why have other industries not followed suit? One can only speculate. However, some obvious considerations might include the homogeneity of the value creation process within these two industries. An upstream oil and gas company is critically dependent upon its ability to find and extract fuel in a cost-effective manner. A pharmaceutical company needs a drug pipeline to survive. Contrast this with the business model underlying technology companies, for example. The variety in the underlying drivers of value within the industry makes it difficult to identify the measures that encapsulate the value of the opportunity set that is being created by management.

Similarly, the measures that make visible the broader set of competencies and resources required in other less 'clear cut' industries are more ambiguous. Oil, whether in the ground or in a refinery, has a known market value at any time. A drug that is in the research and development pipeline has a known target therapeutic area and can be assigned a probability of success. Customer satisfaction data for a retailer, however, are far trickier to interpret. Rising satisfaction trends relative to peers may generally be a 'good thing', however, there will come a point where investing even more money in making a customer happy will not be rewarded. There is a limit to the number of socks that one is likely to buy.

It might also be speculated that the oil and gas and pharmaceutical industries are relatively concentrated in a number of major participants. This may have facilitated the speed with which they have converged to a reporting norm.

Finally, and perhaps most importantly, the economic necessity for the two industries to find a way to communicate the value of long-term investments was critical for their survival. Both the pharmaceutical industry and the oil and gas industry invest today in the hope of yielding a cash flow from that investment in ten years' time. Without a routinized method of demonstrating the value of the opportunities created by management through this investment, the ability to finance economically attractive long-term propositions would be constrained.

Do these distinctive characteristics mean, however, that the extractive industries and the pharmaceutical industry will remain exceptions to the reporting rule? Do the additional complexities in other industries' business models render any attempt to improve the reporting framework futile? Far from it. It will simply require a little bit more coordination among the various stakeholders involved in the reporting supply chain (see Figure 4.3).

> **Do these distinctive characteristics mean that the extractive industries and the pharmaceutical industry will remain exceptions to the reporting rule?**

Everybody in this supply chain has a part to play. But for now, let us focus upon the difference that just one key constituent, the auditor, can play.

FIGURE 4.3
The reporting supply chain

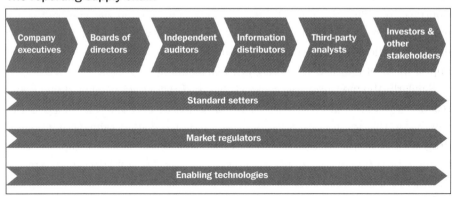

Source: PricewaterhouseCoopers

The role of the auditor is to provide an opinion on the accuracy of the financial data reported by the company. As, historically, financial data offered an adequate proxy for the quality and sustainability of performance in a mass-manufacturing environment, the auditors' role was highly valuable. Their assessment provided assurance of the information needed by the investor to evaluate his holding.

But how things have changed! In a recent survey conducted for the Australian CPA,[17] nearly 60% of passive shareholders and 40% of auditors believed that financial reports are just another piece of advertising – a shocking indictment of the profession.

However, the situation is not beyond redemption. We have seen that a major stumbling block preventing companies from adopting the kind of industry-specific reporting model that users demand – and from realizing the economic benefits that ensue – is the inability of the investor to differentiate a 'panic' situation from a company that is merely reticent in its communication, or a 'standard setter' from a 'time bomb'. If we know the shape of information that constitutes good quality external reporting, surely a sensible starting point is to ask auditors to provide assurance that such information exists in a credible form on the inside?

In order to do this, do we first need pre-defined standards for the measure-ment of customers, brands, employees, environmental protocols and so on? Although this may be a long-term ambition, substantial progress can still be made even without such standards. An indication of how this may work in practice may be taken from the few companies around the world who are leading the charge.

Take Shell, for example. Long recognized as a leader in reporting, it has recently acknowledged the difficulty for users in factoring additional information into assessments of the firm if they are not told whether the data is reliable or not. So, alongside the measures that it produces, it uses symbols that indicate the level of comfort that one may have in the relevant data.

How can one have degrees of comfort? To an auditor this is a well-worn question. At the simplest level, an auditor can provide assurance that the measures provided have been properly calculated – basically, that the sums underlying the numbers are correct. The next level will question whether the method employed for collecting the data is sound. Here, the auditor will differentiate between a client who produces his customer satisfaction measures, for example, on sheets of paper on an *ad hoc* basis collected from each division and a client who has a routinized system for collecting and analysing data – a system embedded into the process controls of the firm. The highest level of assurance would be for the auditor to state not only that the processes are in place but that they are 'appropriate'.

So do these distinctions in the level of assurance help, in practice? Consider the case of a retailer. Customer and store metrics are critical for evaluating whether this year's financial performance has been achieved at the expense of future growth opportunities. Currently, if the store tries to communicate its progress in these areas, an investor has to trust the management that the statistics reported have been consistently and accurately measured over time. If management's compensation is in any way tied into financial or stock price performance, the investor may be sceptical.

By presenting this information, however, with even just the first level of assurance, the user would immediately gain a genuine sense of the trend in corporate performance over time in these critical areas. Although a current lack of industry-based standards may prevent direct comparisons of measures, the trend data for each company will afford an interesting start.

What if a company does not wish to reveal data in commercially sensitive areas? Even here, if data are not disclosed for competitive reasons, investors could be assured that the metrics relevant to that industry do exist within the firm in a reliable form, and thus be able to differentiate between 'those who could but don't' and 'those who would but can't'.

As the quality of control structures in the intangibles area will vary widely by firm, so might the level of assurance provided by auditors. This might be usefully achieved through a move away from the effectively binary audit opinion ('qualified' or not). Perhaps the audit profession might learn from the bond-rating agencies and adopt a system that allows them to signal on a scale from 'AAA' to 'junk' the quality of a firm's overall control structures.

Is this vision of the future reporting model a mere fantasy? Here, I recommend that readers investigate the reporting of a company such as Coloplast, a Danish medical products group that is truly a global leader in reporting. The depth, breadth and clarity of its disclosure is exceptional. All critical value drivers are identified and the strategy employed to manage the related resources and competencies is clearly articulated. Milestones are defined, monitored and associated with quantified long-term objectives. That the firm is able to produce such information is impressive.

The signal that Coloplast provides through reporting is clear. Management is not merely offering platitudes about its 'number one asset' or its customer focus, it is living by this model. Moreover, the information provided is sufficient to provide the user with an insight as to the success with which strategy has been implemented and the likelihood that the performance achieved to date is sustainable in the future. The added confidence that gives investors when assessing the company today will undoubtedly be reflected in the value they place on the stock.

In conclusion: what gets measured gets done

If you reward a manager for producing higher earnings, then higher earnings is what they will produce. Forget investment in new products, employees, customers, environmental protocols or new plant to help aid efficiency. If they result in a negative surprise in that all-important earnings number, then they can wait.

The economic consequences of this Pavlovian response can be harmful at the company level, and disastrous if compounded to the macro level.

I have argued in this chapter that a root cause of this inefficiency is the paucity of information available to those charged with allocating the scarce resources of our nation. The good news is that this is not an irreversible issue; the bad news is that substantial reform will only occur if a number of players in the reporting supply chain rise to the challenge.

> A root cause of this inefficiency is the paucity of information available to those charged with allocating the scarce resources of our nation.

Companies need to be prepared to take a hard look at the quality of the information available within the firm and to question whether they have taken the dominance of the financial model too much to heart. Does the 'dashboard' of the management team make sense, given the industrial context?

Auditors too need to take a hard look at the value that they are adding to the reporting supply chain. In the UK, accountants state that the numbers reported present a 'true and fair' view. Although that may be the case within the narrow confines of accounting conventions, surely it is time to consider whether corporate reporting presents a 'true and fair' view of the underlying business.

Over time, standards setters will need to work with industry groups to codify emerging standards so that comparability of data may be achieved. I would argue, however, that in most cases we are not at that stage yet. The accounting conventions of today arose from the codification of the best practice that emerged after a prolonged period of experimentation by companies that wished to assure investors that their money was being wisely managed. In a similar fashion, I would contest that we are now in need of another period of experimentation where companies are encouraged to explain more fully the dynamics of their business and the success with which they have implemented

> Over time, standards setters will need to work with industry groups to codify emerging standards so that comparability of data may be achieved.

their articulated strategy. From this, some industry standards may emerge, some conventions may arise.

Finally, investors will need to learn a new vocabulary. They will need to understand how to evaluate a company's overall performance instead of merely the latest reported earnings. Although this clearly happens implicitly with the investment community today, the establishment of models of corporate outcome based on the fundamental drivers of the business will require an overhaul of the short-term valuation techniques that dominate the industry today.

None of this is trivial. None of this will occur overnight. But, 'what gets measured gets done'. If we don't reward managers for investing for the long term, if we confront our companies with a pool of capital whose price reflects the inability of investors to differentiate good management from bad, the cost to the economy is clear. If we want society to prosper, can we afford to fail?

Notes

1 Note that the opinions expressed in this chapter are those of the author and do not necessarily reflect those of PricewaterhouseCoopers.

2 See, for example, Bebchuk, L.A. and Stole, L.A. (1993) 'Do Short-term Objectives Lead to Under or Over Investment in Long-term Projects?', *Journal of Finance*, Vol. 48, pp. 719–29; Stein, J. (1988) 'Takeover Threats and Managerial Myopia', *Journal of Political Economy*, Vol. 96, pp. 61–80.

3 See, for example, Gietzmann, M., Shilo, A. and Thomas, A. (2002) 'Winning the Competition for Capital', *European Business Forum*, Spring.

4 UK Department of Trade and Industry R&D Scoreboard, 2002, accessible online at www.dti.gov.uk.

5 Hughes, H.P. (1980) *Goodwill in Accounting: A History of the Issues and Problems*. Georgia State University.

6 Higson, C. (1990) *The Choice of Accounting Method in UK Mergers and Acquisitions*. Institute of Chartered Accountants of England and Wales.

7 Lev, B.L., and Sougiannis, T. (1996) 'The Capitalization, Amortization and Value of R&D', *Journal of Accounting and Economics*, Vol. 21, pp. 107–38.

8 See www.sustainAbility.com

9 Danish Department of Trade and Industry (1997) *Intellectual Capital Accounts*.

10 De Piazza, S. and Eccles, R. (2002) *Building Public Trust*. Wiley Press.

11 See Eccles, R., Herz, R., Keegan, M. and Phillips, D. (2001) *The Value-Reporting Revolution: Moving Beyond the Earnings Game*. Wiley Press.

12 Cowe, R. (1999) 'Winning with Integrity Called to Account: Multinationals are waking up to the fact that social irresponsibility can hit the share price', *Guardian*, 27 November.

13 Gietzmann *et al., op. cit.*

14 Holliday, C. and Pepper, J. (2001) 'Sustainability through the Market – Seven Keys to Success', *World Business Council for Sustainable Development*, April.

15 Thomas, A. (2000) *Banking on Favourable Terms*. University of Bristol Discussion Paper No. 00490.

16 Black, S. and Lynch, L. (2000) 'Human Capital Investment and Productivity', *American Economic Review*, Vol. 90, pp. 685–701; Bassi, L., Ludwig, J., McMurrer, D. and Van Buren, M. (2000) *Profit from Learning: Do Firms' Investment in Training and Education Pay Off?* American Society for Training and Development White Paper, September.

17 CPA Australia (2002) *Confidence in Corporate Reporting*, November.

5

WHITHER THE BEAN COUNTERS?

THE CURRENT AND FUTURE SHAPE OF ACCOUNTING[1]

ANDREW BLACK
with ETIENNE PICIOCCHI
Building Value Associates

How has the present system of accounting evolved, and could it be improved? Can there be an agreed international accounting standard? When an accountant carries out an audit, who is the main client? This chapter aims to explore these and other questions that currently beset accounting currently – all of which, it seems to us, have an important bearing on the quest for value in today's economies.

In the course of our exploration, we will look in some detail at the IAS (International Accounting Standards) and accounting systems currently in place in the USA, the UK and France, with a glance at Germany. We will then tentatively draw some conclusions as to the direction that accounting might be headed in the future.

'Counting the beans'

'Bean counting', as accounting is sometimes pejoratively called, is one of those taken-for-granted services. Just as we assume that electricity will be available at the flick of a switch, so accounts and the presentation of financial statements are often assumed simply to 'happen' somewhere off stage, preferably without too much fuss.

Of course, there are times when the beans counted somehow don't quite add up. Someone may have had their hand in the till, and this has been revealed by the application of sound accounting practice. This 'attest' function is possibly what the accountants and auditors are most commonly associated with. It is also a role of public trust they, individually, take very seriously, ensuring that the more successful accountants become pillars of the community, members of the rotary club and similar organizations.

But there are other areas where the work of the 'bean counters' has an impact – notably the capital markets. The origins of the UK's accounting system, one of the earliest to be formally organized, go back to the fact that lenders of capital to the equity market needed security and a reassurance that they were not about to be 'ripped off'. Capital markets have become increasingly demanding of information about a company's present and future prospects – information that is both accurate and frequently delivered. These concerns may occasionally be at odds with the more backward-looking attest function, which is primarily designed to ensure the family silver has not been stolen.

In mainland Europe the picture can look rather different. Attestation is certainly there, but here accountants are part of a complex mechanism designed not only to ensure the family silver is still there, but that taxes are correctly apportioned and paid. Thus they take on a pseudo-civil-servant role, acting as intermediaries between their corporate clients and the governments who regulate and control them.

> In mainland Europe accountants take on a pseudo-civil-servant role, acting as intermediaries between their corporate clients and the governments who regulate and control them.

Seen from this angle, accountancy combines prudential considerations (that the goose laying the golden eggs will continue into the future) with becoming an intermediary between the tax authorities and the client company. Creditor interests are also given a high rating, so lenders have a good view on the assets and other features that companies offer as security on loans.

Over the years individual national accounting systems have developed in a number of interesting, and occasionally incompatible, ways, although mostly with similar objectives. As the world's financial markets have grown, so these national variations in accounting standards have increasingly became a problem for anyone analysing companies, especially companies that operate internationally. Conversion from one standard to another became an extensive cottage industry, where accountants and analysts tried to 'square the circle'. One of the better examples of this was the DVFA (*Deutsche Verein der Finanz Analysten*), which would spend long hours converting German-based accounts into a kind of half-way house towards an IAS system. The results would be anything but timely.

Nevertheless, the labours of these and other analysts were not entirely in vain: the accounting profession began to see the system-wide implications if there were no further steps towards integrating accounting systems. The EU also clearly has an interest in ensuring that the internal market for commercial and financial services is measured more or less accurately along the same lines. An internal market cannot work effectively without harmonized accounting systems

As we note throughout this book, a blizzard of events and difficulties has gripped the world of accounting and financial reporting. A lot of this has taken place in the USA, where some of the biggest corporate names have imploded. Enron, the seventh largest company by market capitalization at one stage, and Andersen Consulting, one of the privileged members of the 'Big Five' accounting firms, are no more – swept away by bankruptcy and charges of criminal dishonesty and fraud. Such problems are not limited to US companies alone. There is a long list of corporate failures associated with weaknesses in the audit and accounting practices.[2]

Our aim here is not simply to lump all failed companies together and conclude that they all suffered from some kind of faulty accounting. Rather we are trying to establish whether there is some kind of pattern in the companies that have become embroiled in accounting scandals. More particularly, we want to look at the nature of accounting itself: do accounting systems themselves contain weaknesses that throw the entire system of financial reporting into question?

We are not alone in the view that some very real issues require resolution, and that the system does indeed have inherent weaknesses. Taking this further, we think that further reforms are urgently needed in order to restore confidence in the quality of financial reports. The problems go beyond the limits of any one national authority to resolve: they are, if you like, endemic.

One of the most pressing is the recognition of revenue. Several recently failed companies were 'confused' about whether to enter the sum of a transaction or more properly the commission or fee earned on it. Succumbing to temptation, companies sometimes opted for including the entire sum, and not just the commission, thus inflating their income many times. The auditing agencies may have cooperated on these matters, grappling with the ambiguities in the underlying accounting conventions themselves.[3]

The recognition of revenue, the subject of an IAS working party, is an ongoing issue within accountancy. It is not just the question of what revenue should be recognized, but also when it should be recognized. Under the system of accrual accounting, efforts are made to match costs and revenues over time – which can mean spreading out revenues into the future in order to match the cost stream associated with it. But this is seldom certain; there are occasions when it may be both expedient and perhaps also prudent to take the income up front – to borrow from the future, as it were, or record the income when it is booked, on another view.

People can quite legitimately have different opinions on this question. Decisions can be taken on the treatment of these revenue and cost flows that are entirely legal; nevertheless they can lead to the true nature of an undertaking being seriously distorted. And more dangerously, collusion can occur between the company (the client) and the auditor.

Other issues that have arisen are associated with special purpose entities or vehicles (henceforth called SPVs in this chapter). These are designed, along with other 'off balance sheet' transactions, to obscure a company's true debt position. Again, these vehicles are entirely legal, and yet can lead to distortions of the accounts and ultimately to that company's bankruptcy. On this topic, too, an IAS working party is in action: this is an effort to address a problem that has been around for several years. There may not be an immediate 'fix', given that

SPVs were established for perfectly legitimate reasons (these include, *inter alia*, the funding of buildings and helping to provide capital for banks with troubled loans) and entirely within current rules applying to financial reporting.

It may be worth casting our minds back to the late 1980s and early 1990s and re-examining some of the issues thrown up by the savings and loans crisis – the 'thrifts' – when the US taxpayer had to pay out huge sums to salvage a large part of the domestic savings and loans industry. Here too, a number of allegations and court cases highlighted the sometimes dubious role played by auditors.[4]

A hypothesis may be beginning to form, then: that accountants and auditors have been heavily involved in recent business collapses. They are involved in several senses:

- as auditors, they have cooperated with management to create solutions to 'problems', and in their status as auditors they have been able to sign off and hence approve of these actions;

- as accountants, in that accounting systems are struggling to keep up with changes in commercial and financial practices, leading to increasingly arbitrary, and possibly uneven, application of ambiguously worded rules and guidelines;

- as individuals, who may on occasion 'jump ship' to work for their client directly as accountants in charge of internal audit processes – knowing very well what will be possible to 'get past' the auditors.

None of these involvements are exactly new. What is new is the consequence of getting it wrong for the public interest. As a number of observers, including Arthur Levitt, the former head of the USA's Securities and Exchange Commission (SEC), have said, accountants rarely speak of the 'public' interest.

If the accountancy and audit professions have a case to answer, to date their answers have been muted, muffled and not very enlightening. Recently public concern, especially in the USA, has risen to such a height that the profession has effectively been 'decapitated', and its new masters are for the main made up of people who are not even allowed to be accountants. This is a remarkable development. In the pursuit of its own interests, and especially in maintaining its privileged position backed by self-regulation, has the accountancy profession neglected broader financial and shareholder interests, to the detriment of society?

Who do the accountants and auditors work for?

This seemingly innocuous question is surprisingly difficult to answer. In the case of most professions the answer is the person who pays the bills, i.e. the client. So who are the accountants' clients? In the main they work for the company managements. The boards of these companies appoint auditors to provide them with the official signature that the financial reports are 'true and fair', or have an *image fidèle* in French. Frequently, the CEO is responsible for the auditor's appointment, although recent practice is starting to change this.

In theory, auditors also work for the shareholders. After all, financial reports are prepared for the annual general meeting of the shareholders, who are expected to attend and find out how their money has been spent. In legal terms, everything is done in the name of the shareholders, although they have surprisingly little to do with the audit process in large modern corporations.

Since the actual audit process involves a sharing of information between company management and auditors, these two groups clearly enjoy much closer relations than the shareholders and auditors. Over time, it is likely that auditors, beholden to the management in terms of fees, will be cooperative in finding 'constructive' solutions to financial reporting issues. Having found the skeletons, you could say, auditors are also well placed to ensure they remain well and truly buried.

> Over time, it is likely that auditors, beholden to the management in terms of fees, will be cooperative in finding 'constructive' solutions to financial reporting issues.

Auditors often point out that they report on what is put in front of them, which is relatively well defined under the attest function, and are not obliged to look either to the right or to the left of them. If what they see makes sense, then that is what is reported. One is reminded of the ditty much quoted after the 1929 stock market crash:

> We have audited this balance sheet and say in our report
> That the cash is overstated, the cashier being short;
> That the customer receivables are very much past due;
> That of these are some good ones, they are very, very few;
> That the inventories are out of date and principally junk;
> That the method of their pricing is very largely bunk;
> That according to our figures the undertaking's wrecked,
> But subject to these comments, the balance sheet's correct.[5]

Audits are now legal obligations, and for publicly quoted companies are quite demanding. For their part, publicly quoted companies have got larger, more complex and hence more difficult to put into neat boxes. The dilemma is that auditors are dependent on the company for information: they can request more information, but won't necessarily be given it. The auditors can always resign the audit, if the factual basis for their enquiry is too limited. The trouble is, this doesn't happen very often. Indeed, in a now substantial number of cases auditors have been only too willing to not look properly, accept management excuses and generally cooperate with management in order to find an 'acceptable' solution. After all, qualifying the accounts is messy and time-consuming: rather than reach an impasse, better try to smooth out the wrinkles behind closed doors.

> Auditors are dependent on the company for information: they can request more information, but won't necessarily be given it.

This is not to suggest that the profession does not mostly consist of hard-working decent people trying to do as good a job as they can under sometimes trying circumstances. But on too many occasions auditors have taken a rather too partisan view of a situation in favour of management. Genuine public and investor disquiet has led to important changes affecting the accounting profession.

It is important to point out, given the recent spate of legislation and scandals, that other interest groups and stakeholders also have an interest in the outcome of an audit. As a US Supreme Court ruling against Arthur Young & Co. (now part of Ernst & Young) put it several years ago:

> by certifying the public reports that collectively depict a corporation's financial status, *the independent auditor* assumes a public responsibility transcending *any employment relationship with the client.* The independent public accountant performing this special function owes its ultimate allegiance to the corporation's creditors and stockholders, as well as to the investing public. *This 'public watchdog' function demands at all times that the accountants maintain total independence from the client at all times* and requires complete fidelity to the public trust.[6]

The Supreme Court highlighted a number of key issues in this passage, written, it should be noted, in 1984 (*plus ça change*). It lay great emphasis on the independent nature of the auditor: it is this that has been such a bone of contention in recent Enron-style scandals. There are many instances where auditors have earned substantially greater fees from non-audit work with their audit clients. This has raised eyebrows before, but now, in the USA, action has been taken. Under the auspices of the SEC and the Public Company Accounting Oversight Board (PCAOB), a number of activities have now been declared off limits for auditors – until, that is, the same Ernst & Young pressured the PCAOB for approval of existing non-audit activities already in place, arguing that no special dispensation was required for those.

(And while we are on the subject, perhaps a subtle redefinition of what properly belongs to the audit is also desirable. Thus the list of non-audit work can be minimized, largely because it is now being conducted as part of the official audit! Such is the lobbying power of the larger accounting firms in the USA.)

There is an even more substantial issue. Most of the larger accounting firms make a lot of money selling tax work to their clients. Doesn't this compromise the auditor's independence, in the sense outlined by the Supreme Court? In the case of Enron, one of the most significant problems in its recent demise was the role played by the SPVs that were established for both loan and for tax reasons. It was the auditor's tax department that sold the SPV schemes to the client to lower its tax payments; the schemes were then approved by the same firm's audit function, and ultimately led to bankruptcy. Nowhere in this process was there an 'independent' auditor. Current lobbying by the larger accounting companies to keep their lucrative tax work sits ill with other protestations about improving the quality of the audit.[7]

> Most of the larger accounting firms make a lot of money selling tax work to their clients. Doesn't this compromise the auditor's independence, in the sense outlined by the Supreme Court?

Returning then to the question of who accountants and auditors work *for*, several answers seem possible. Technically, the auditors work for the audit committee of the board of the company whose accounts they are auditing. Audit committees are often appointed by a company's chairman and CEO, so in a narrow sense auditors work to the senior management of their client.

However, there is clearly public interest in their work. Investors, in whose names the audits are performed, come away much the poorer when things go wrong. The suppliers, customers and employees of the company also have a very material interest in knowing whether or not their company is sound. And the government itself, with its need for tax revenue, and also as a lender and problem-solver of last resort, should have an unbiased a view as possible about a company. After all, it will probably have to help clear up the social consequences caused by misleading financial reporting.

Under the current system these interest groups are often, in our view, treated cavalierly. The only way they can influence the selection of auditors is through voting at the AGM. You have no say if you have no votes; and those with votes, the large institutional shareholders, will in many cases go along with the management choice – even if this turns out to be detrimental to shareholder interests.

As for the question of reporting fraud, considerable ambiguity is to be found. On paper, no reputable accountants would willingly acquiesce in fraud. But the rules on whether they have a duty to report it, and if so to whom, are not at all clear. Their first responsibility will be to their client. But if that client is doing something deceitful, a conflict of interest arises and regrettably professional standards have slipped on occasion. Should there be clearer guidance as to how auditors should react in these situations? As we will see below, measures are already being implemented in the USA that should result in a tougher line on suspected fraud.

Despite current unease, many practitioners think that present arrangements are for the best, even though they are far from perfect. Let us look at this in more detail – in particular, consider whether in the likely move towards a more global accounting standard we might learn some important lessons from the 'non-Anglo-Saxon' world.

The incidence of scandal

Most of the companies in note 2's list (p. 142) of those that have experienced financial difficulties are to be found in the United States. Yet no less a person than Sir David Tweedie, the current head of the International Accounting Standards Board (IASB), is on record as saying that the US GAAP (generally accepted accounting principles) represent the best corpus of accounting practice anywhere in the world, and is used extensively as a model for the IAS system.[8]

Until fairly recently, many seriously suggested that US GAAP would be the basis for an emerging global accounting standard, and that any other system should take a back seat and let the US accounting profession 'do the driving'. Fewer voices argue for this solution today.

Experts, Tweedie among them, have observed that the US system has been largely standards-led. This very specificity has also been a defence against the litigious nature of US society, which has led to a more rigid rules-driven system. The extra detail this involves in turn can obscure rather than reveal the underlying accounting position. The result is compliance with the letter rather than the spirit of the law. In contrast, the IASB argues that the 'auditor should take a step back and consider whether the accounting suggested is consistent with the underlying principle. This is not a soft option.'[9]

This discussion is taking place, of course, in the context of the broader US picture: a large increase in stock-market prices, fuelled by public interest in the dot-com and information technology sectors, followed by a huge 'correction' and a three-year bear market. Many new companies had stock quotations that were based on wildly irrational and optimistic views of the future. They did not even have an operating income to speak of and were sustained by the piles of equity they had accumulated when investors had more money than sense.

As often happens, it soon became evident that there are no free lunches. So in order to stave off disaster, some companies have been tempted to try adapting the numbers, embarking on unfamiliar new financing schemes. Again, Enron is a good example: a relatively conventional pipeline company expanded into trading energy futures and options, and had to shoehorn this into an existing set of financial reports. But this was not exclusive to Enron, as the revenue-swapping arrangements among telecoms companies show.

So it was the great corporate excess followed by the great corporate 'hangover' that contributed to the stresses experienced by the US system. Not that the USA was unique: there was similar exuberant optimism in Germany with the *Neuer Markt*, and to a lesser extent in the UK and France. Dot-com fever was highly contagious, and most of the major financial markets caught a good dose.

> Dot-com fever was highly contagious, and most of the major financial markets caught a good dose.

Interestingly, auditing systems outside the USA appear to have coped rather better with the sudden changes in market fortunes. There have been scandals and failures, but on nothing like the scale experienced across the Atlantic. Are there important lessons to be learnt here?

There is a view, frequently expressed in 'Anglo-Saxon' circles, that the US system is so much more transparent that it is possible to see problems that are not even visible in Europe and elsewhere. Collusive attitudes between the various boards, management and auditors in mainland Europe mean, it is said, that potential problems can be covered up.

On balance, we think there is more evidence for the 'learning the lessons' point of view. Significant changes have taken place over the past few years as part of the EU integration process. Some countries, notably France, have enacted important measures – the Vienot Reports[10] for instance – that go a long way towards creating an institutional infrastructure similar to that of the USA and the UK, with some useful additional features that we will discuss below.

We think that the incidence of scandal in the USA is leading to a major reappraisal of institutional models. It now looks increasingly as if the model to be adopted will not be US GAAP with minor additions. Instead it could be a Europe-based set of propositions, hopefully combining the better aspects of both local and IAS systems.

The world is growing smaller

The loss of confidence in the US accounting system comes at a timely moment in the deliberations of the global accounting profession. As we have seen, there are advantages in having a global system:

■ maintaining different national standards pushes up the cost of raising capital, since it tends to perpetuate local 'pools' of capital and hold back the emergence of a truly global system;

■ no one national system has all the answers, neither is it likely to gain acceptance across the world – a snub to US GAAP;

■ if one national authority tries to raise accounting standards, it risks encouraging companies to relocate to areas where compliance is more lax.

For these and other reasons, the IASB is now taking centre stage in moves to reform and improve the global accounting system. It is a great opportunity, but one that is also fraught with uncertainty.

The political pressure is very much on, since the EU has already said that all member states should be using the IAS system by 2005. Some countries, such as Austria, are already using it. This sounds encouraging, until you realize that the system to be so grandly introduced is still under construction. Also, most national accounting authorities seem to be taking a wait-and-see attitude, leaving it to the IAS to resolve the problems of the world.

> This sounds encouraging, until you realize that the system to be so grandly introduced is still under construction.

Ideally, current moves towards convergence would seem to be a good thing. But the derivation of accounting systems is by no means a 'clean' process. It is by no means value-free, and strong vested interests are involved.

Take for instance the issue of 'expensing' stock options. This is a practice that provided a relatively cheap way of rewarding the executives of small start-up companies such as the dot-coms. Initially, it was also argued that the practice linked share price development with executive remuneration – one of the aims of value-based management.

However, problems immediately arose about how these stock options should be treated for accounting purposes. The accountants at FASB (the Federal Accounting Standards Board, the US accounting authority before the PCAOB) initially proposed that such stock options should be 'expensed', treated as a cost – a view also expressed by Warren Buffet, the 'sage of Omaha'. But the new Silicon Valley entrepreneurs in California, stock market analysts, venture capitalists and others disagreed. Expensing stock options in the USA would, it was calculated, reduce declared corporate earnings by between 8 and 9% – too much, they argued. Their view prevailed: the accountants wobbled and accepted what was the less coherent position. Congress also wobbled and prevented the FASB from making the required changes. (In Chapter 2 of this book, Joe Arau from CalPERS, normally a fearless champion of shareholder interests, also declines to support the expensing of stock options.)

Unfortunately, agreement is unlikely on almost all the main accounting issues (see below). Any compromise may well lack consistency, and an agreed international accounting system could end up being inferior to current national models. Yet all major countries will have to accept the new standard if it is to work.

Some similarities and differences in approaches to accounting

As we have already indicated, for most purposes (but not for all) one can think of an 'Anglo-Saxon' US/UK accounting system on the one hand and a more mainland European system on the other. Most other parts of the world have tended to copy or adapt one of these two basic models.[11]

The US/UK system is essentially about preparing financial statements for investors and is less interested in the creditors and other major stakeholders. In particular, the tax figures struck in the annual accounts will not necessarily form the basis of actual tax payments to the IRS/Inland Revenue.

> The US/UK system is essentially about preparing financial statements for investors and is less interested in the creditors and other major stakeholders.

As for valuing assets, the two systems differ in their emphasis on 'fair value' approaches. French and German accounting systems opt for the historic cost approach, or taking the lower of the historic and the book value of the asset. Elsewhere in this book serious criticisms are levelled at this approach and the resulting distortions with respect to a number of key performance measures.

Recent practice in the UK has been to introduce a closer market valuation of assets. In the case of pension funds this is underlined by the new FRS 17 rule (see Chapter 3), which has introduced much more volatility into pension fund valuations.

From the French/German perspective this rule can be criticized by arguing that it is reasonable to take certain holding periods into consideration before using market valuations. (In passing, we should note that these holding periods are often determined by the tax system, thus maintaining a closer link between tax and accounting reports.) Contrary to the implications of FRS 17, companies don't normally seek to liquidate their pension funds immediately: valuations should reflect the funds' long-term nature. Behind this argument lie detailed questions about how to properly value a range of longer-term liabilities such as leases and various kinds of debt.

A more general criticism is that market-based valuations may not be credible if the markets concerned are not well developed. Worse still, you may have to use 'theoretical' market models whose results could prove highly misleading – e.g. with some options and futures valuations – even if they are closer to the truth than a clearly fictitious number based on depreciating historically determined aggregates.

The Anglo-Saxon and European systems differ in other important ways too. In the latter, national commercial and tax laws play a more prominent role in determining the shape of accounts. In France, the *Code de Commerce*, the *Loi sur les Sociétés* and the *Plan Comptable General* (PCG), which is approved by ministerial rulings, hold sway. Tax law will take precedence over accounting law in some situations – highlighting the fact that the European system is more closely supervised and administered by government. The US/UK system has been predominantly self-regulating – although this too is now starting to change.

> The Anglo-Saxon and European systems differ in other important ways too. In the latter, national commercial and tax laws play a more prominent role in determining the shape of accounts.

Trying to summarize further, we can suggest that the 'European' system reflects:

- a tax-based approach compared to the Anglo-Saxon 'true and fair' basis;

- a rules-driven approach (content over form) on the Continent compared to a principles-based approach;

- a safer, more prudential approach, compared with a more market-relevant (but hence more volatile) approach.

Clearly each of the main systems can learn from the other in some areas, hopefully in order to reach an improved synthesis.

In order to get a better grip on these issues, we will now turn to a more detailed (but still brief) look at recent developments in the USA, the UK and the IAS system, followed by France with a glance at Germany, before considering how the integration project is likely to proceed.

USA: the giant stumbles

The USA has prided itself on having an exemplary set of accounting rules. Yet back in the nineteenth and early twentieth centuries it was not always regarded as a model of financial propriety. The US system evolved over the years as an accretion of rules, rulings and bodies authorized to develop and maintain accounting standards. As the number of accountants grew, along with clients and fees, so did rules, rulings and recommendations. Indeed a veritable forest of rules, many of which are ambiguous, with all kinds of exceptions and dispensations, has been created. One of the unintended results of this has been the demise of Enron and the dawning awareness that all is not well in the land of accountancy. How did this come to pass?

A stylized history of US accounting

The early development of US accounting owes a lot to prior developments in the UK. As UK capital expanded abroad, in particular to the USA during the second half of the nineteenth century, so UK accountants followed and set up local accounting practices.

The first accounting society, the American Association of Public Accountants (AAPA) was established in 1887 and for many years the emphasis on professional individual development continued relatively unaffected by the huge changes taking place in the US economy. These included the formation of large trusts and the gradual emergence of federal government competence and authority in managing inter-state trade. Accounting in the USA tended towards the establishing of corporate liquidity, and so towards creditors and the banking community.

The emphasis on the capital markets in general, and on equities in particular, strengthened in the 1920s as fresh equity became an important source of capital for America's new and dynamic corporations. During this process there was a steady rise in the influence of the income statement (profit and loss account) and also the flow of funds statement. Advances in the use of consolidated accounts largely came from outside the profession. In the early twentieth century there were four main types of financial statement:

- those documenting changes in the cash position;
- those documenting changes in current assets;
- those documenting changes in working capital; and

■ those showing the state of overall financial activity.

Following the 1929 stock market crash and subsequent depression, it became clear that financial controls and reporting requirements were inadequate. The reforms of the New Deal included efforts to achieve more order and consistency in the matter of financial reports.

The biggest innovation was the establishment in 1933 of the Securities and Exchange Commission, which was given statutory authority to set accounting standards and to have oversight over the audit profession. Crucially, though, this authority was delegated back to the accounting profession, by now represented by the American Institute of Certified Public Accountants (AICPA).

The main organizational developments in US accounting are summarized in Figure 5.1 – a highly simplified account. It is useful to distinguish between three separate and yet related developments:

1. The ultimate bearers of responsibility for the accounting system in the USA are the US Congress and to some extent the Treasury and Commerce Departments. These branches of government only rarely get involved with the actual setting of rules. Rather, they tend to intervene by setting up new federal structures that then become agencies whose role is to ensure the development and maintenance of accounting standards.

2. The SEC plays a central role in regulating the capital markets, and has an operational oversight over the accounting profession. It is mainly interested in ensuring that sound financial reports facilitate the operation of the capital markets. Effectively it has struck a deal with the accountants: they have a monopoly over authorizing and legitimizing financial statements needed for IPOs and other financial reporting reasons. But this franchise comes with several strings attached, the most important of which is that accountants must be independent and represent the public interest. It is at this point that the system has most frequently broken down.

3. The accountancy profession regulates its own affairs with respect to setting professional standards. Though clearly these must meet the needs of the marketplace, self-interest can become an issue. It can sometimes be difficult to separate what may be required for internal professional regulatory purposes from broader social requirements.

The first signs that all was not well came in the late 1960s and early 1970s, with a large bankruptcy at Penn Central Railroad and problems with investment tax credits. Other longer standing issues came to the fore: in the eyes of its critics, the Accounting Principles Board (APB) had not really been that good at formulating accounting principles. The APB consisted of 21 part-time members, all of whom were accountants, and required a two-thirds majority to pass any new regulations, so progress was relatively slow. The profession seemed unprepared for any crisis.

The outside world, however, was getting impatient. The SEC intervened, and under the auspices of Francis Wheat, produced a report (the Wheat Report) that abolished the APB and replaced it in 1972/3 with the Financial Accounting Standards Board (FASB).

There were important changes in the way the FASB went to work. Now it was recognized that the job of standard-setting required a more professional approach, a select group of seven members were chosen by an organization called the Financial Accounting Foundation,[12] which was the FASB's paymaster and provider.

An important departure was that a clear non-accountancy interest was represented in the new organization. Originally the FASB's seven members consisted of four from the public accounting firms, one from industry (the 'preparers'), one from academia and one industrial executive. Of course, if the accountants chose to vote together, they would have had a majority over the others. To avoid this, it was decided that new regulations could only be approved by a five–two majority, ensuring that the accountants had to convince at least one other member to vote with them. However, in 1977 the accountants' representation was reduced to three, and two 'preparers' representatives were included, along with one member from the investor community and one from academia. Recall our earlier question about who the accounting profession's clients are: in the FASB there were now two client 'preparers' influencing the determination of accounting rules – numerically outweighing the interest of the investing community.

It has been argued[13] that the new FASB structure ran into difficulties. In its earlier years it promulgated a great many new rules. This may have been facilitated by a relaxation of the voting rules, with only a simple majority now required for a new regulation. But FASB was no longer as representative of accounting interests as its predecessor APB had been. Its efforts to develop a comprehensive conceptual framework were hindered by a reluctance to acknowledge the 'distributional' issues affecting its constituent members. In addition, two rather inadequately formulated rules, FAS 8 on currency translation and FAS 19 on oil and gas exploration, encountered criticism.

As a full-time organization, the FASB had become a bureaucracy in its own right. Funding was always tight, giving leverage to the FAF (see Figure 5.1) if ever a proposal moved in the 'wrong' direction. And, of course, like other bureaucracies, the FASB needed to come up with new rules to justify the expense of the organization and to maintain members' support and interest.

As we have noted earlier, the FASB's 30-year reign also included the crisis of the 'thrifts' (savings and loans associations), which led to the destruction of $10 billion for depositors and tax payers, and to fines on the leading accounting firms of between $500 million and $600 million. Despite this, the US accounting regime seemed relatively calm and ordered before it was overwhelmed by the Enron crisis.

FIGURE 5.1
Organizational changes in US accounting

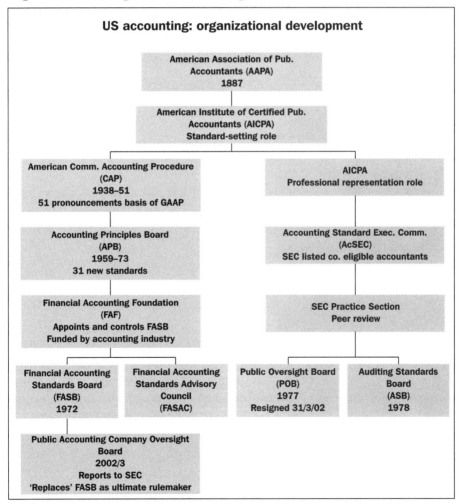

Enron and after

In the hearings that led to the establishment of the SEC in 1933, a senator – after hearing a well argued case for having mandatory audits – asked the then head of Deloittes, Colonel Carter, who was going to audit the auditors. 'Their conscience', came the immortal reply.

Nearly 70 years later, the *Wall Street Journal* observed:

> It's hard to deny that the boom of the 1990s produced some faster and looser behaviour by business … US companies re-stated their earnings 607 times in the past three years [1999–2002], more than in the entire previous decade. Granted a company's income statement isn't everything, but it ought to be more than fiction.[14]

There is no need to dwell at length on the Enron case, since this has been covered at great length elsewhere.[15] But a few observations should suffice. This was the seventh largest corporation (by market capitalization) in the USA, worth around $100 billion: it was, as Senator Lieberman put it, 'not just a tempest in a teapot. It is an unprecedented corporate storm.' In 1999 *CFO* magazine had awarded Enron's CFO, Andrew Fastow, a prize for developing 'remarkably innovative financing techniques'. The company improperly recorded $1.2 billion in equity. Income fell by $51 million in 1997 after the readjustment of 48.6% of the original total. The company conspicuously failed to consolidate the debt on its SPVs. The catalogue of misdeeds goes on.

This was not all. Andersen's audit opinions were simply lies. 'They [Andersen] were both Enron's accountant and its strategic business consultant. The fox was truly guarding the chicken coop.'[16] Andersen's charged Enron $52 million for non-audit services. In the words of Lynn Turner, former chief accountant of the SEC, 'while Enron has correctly been described as a business failure … it was also a failure that the audited numbers did not report the true economic condition of the company in an accurate or timely manner to the investors'. Yet a lot of what was done at Enron was not, technically speaking, against the law or the rules of US GAAP.

The collapse of Enron, followed by serious financial problems at companies such as Worldcom, galvanized the US Congress into action. Note it was Congress that acted, not the accounting profession: and the muddled and timid response from the FASB and the AICP was echoed elsewhere. Almost all the dogs that should have barked on Enron didn't: two-thirds of analysts still had Enron as a 'buy' right up to the date of its bankruptcy, and the credit agencies failed utterly to see what was coming.

Unusually concerned at the spectacle of large well-established corporations simply imploding overnight, two congressmen, Senator Sarbanes and

Representative Oxley, collected sufficient political support to pass an Act that, in our view, has fundamentally changed the accounting landscape. The ramifications are likely to be felt for years to come.

The head of the SEC, Harvey Pitt, resigned, and was replaced by William McDonaugh. The Public Oversight Board (see Figure 5.1) announced its own extinction,[17] and in a radical departure from earlier organizational arrangements Congress swiftly set up the entirely new Public Company Accounting Oversight Board. This board has full delegated rights to oversee the SEC Act with respect to setting accounting standards and regulating accountants, and auditors have to register with it. Under section 103,

> The Board ... determines ... through adoption of standards proposed by one or more professional groups of accountants ... or advisory groups convened ... and amend or otherwise modify or alter, such auditing and related attestation standards, such quality control standards, and such ethics standards to be used by registered public accounting firms in the preparation and issuance of audit reports.[18]

The board consists of five members 'from among prominent individuals of integrity and reputation, who have a demonstrated commitment to the interests of investors and the public, and an understanding of the financial disclosures required of issuers under the securities law and the obligations of accountants with respect to preparation ... of audit reports'. The head of the PCAOB is not allowed to have been an accountant for the last five years, and only two of the board's members can be accountants.

Section 201 lists the many services that are outside the scope of the audit practice. Auditors may not offer their audit clients the following services:

1 book-keeping or financial service statements;
2 financial information systems, design and implementation;
3 appraisal or valuation services, fairness opinions or contributions in kind reports;
4 actuarial services;
5 internal audit services;
6 management functions or human resource advice;
7 broker, dealer, investment advisor or investments;
8 banking services;
9 legal services and expert services unrelated to the audit;
10 any other services deemed to be impermissible.

True, there is some amelioration of these conditions. If the services on offer are less than 5% of the audit fees, or if they are not recognized as non-audit services by the management at the time of the engagement, or if the audit committee approves, some of these services can be performed. But in the current climate, audit committees may prefer to be safe rather than sorry, trying to keep everything as clean as possible.[19] Still allowed, however, is the provision of tax services by auditors to their audit clients. Clearly there are unresolved issues.

This list of prohibited activities came as a bolt from the blue for many in the accountancy profession. It has certainly hastened the break-up of the 'big four' companies, which have hastily sloughed off their management-consultancy and other 'unrelated' divisions.

It seems to this writer that Congress's intervention has finally made accountants realize that the authorities now really mean it when they say they want independent auditors. The idea that the audit has to be seen to serve the public and investor interest has received a huge boost. (Furthermore, CEOs have to sign declarations that their accounts are indeed true and fair, and face criminal prosecution if they get it wrong.)

The whole process of regulation is now funded by a levy of publicly quoted companies, and is entirely independent of the accounting profession. Accounting firms have to report to the PCAOB annually to renew their licence to operate.

Tightening up the rules

As the dust settles, there are signs that it is 'business as usual' for many auditors. Perhaps they can live with the 'worst' excesses of government intervention or slowly reverse them. Audit fees can rise, and things can go back to where they were, minus a significant proportion of fees that are now either inaccessible or have to be traded with the competition.

Such an assessment is, we think, mistaken. We foresee a period in which the power of the PCAOB (the Roundheads, to use a historical analogy) is gradually consolidated, and the FASB and the AICPA's power is gradually diminished. The 'decapitation' of the profession has now effectively occurred.

An indication of the way things are going is the fact that other actors are starting to move into the standards-setting arena now that the FASB has been largely displaced. It was recently reported[20] that changes in the consolidation rules are now being proposed by the PCAOB, not by the FASB. There is a proposal to tighten up on the interpretation of FASB No. 46 to include not just SPVs but other entities such as corporations, partnerships, trusts and other legal structures, even if they don't have equity investment with voting rights. Even non-voting equity holders in these special vehicles may have to be consolidated if they provide sufficient funds to support the vehicle's activities.

It is thought that this measure, if implemented, could affect up to 234 of current S&P 500 companies, including groups as large as GE and Citibank. This would represent a very significant tightening of the rules on consolidation, and would go a lot further than anything the FASB has suggested.

Even more radical is the suggestion that the PCAOB will establish one or more advisory groups to set public audit standards. The FASB may be able to attend, but it will no longer be in the driving seat. These groups will include corporate finance and corporate governance people and investors' representatives as well as accountants.

The standard-setting cat is now well and truly out of the bag, and it seems unlikely that the accountancy profession will be able to reassert control over standard-setting. The jury is still out on whether the new system will be an improvement on the previous status quo. But, as critics would argue, it could hardly be any worse.

The UK: 'It could never happen here'

With one bastion of the global financial system damaged by serious accounting problems, there are serious worries about contagion elsewhere. What then of the UK? In looking at the situation in Britain, we will consider not only developments here but also the progress of the IASB and an emerging global accounting standard.

The UK lays claim to one of the oldest, and hence most developed, accountancy systems in the world. Yet there has been a tendency towards conservatism and institutional lethargy here. As with the USA, interested parties only act in response to financial scandals, reacting with a flurry of changes followed by lengthy periods of tranquillity before the next storm.

One of the UK system's more frequently cited strengths is that it really tries to uphold the principle of 'true and fair'. This means the profession aims to follow a principles-led approach, where content takes precedence over form. As Sir David Tweedie puts it, this is not a 'soft option'.

Strenuous efforts have been made in the recent past to assure law-makers that the self-regulatory system is still the best model. In the process some interesting innovations have emerged, and in some respects the UK has moved ahead of the US regulatory model. The clear difference between the two countries is that the UK

> The clear difference between the two countries is that the UK authorities are much more wedded to an internationally compatible solution that will involve both the EU and the IASB.

authorities are much more wedded to an internationally compatible solution that will involve both the EU and the IASB.

Before looking at the current situation, let us summarize the main milestones in the development of accounting in the UK. There are several strands to this, one important one being the question of corporate governance. While to some extent this is a separate issue, it is often closely intertwined with the nature of financial reporting, and so will be included here.

Table 5.1 summarizes some of the main differences between the UK and the continental European approaches to accounting systems and regulation. With the co-location of the IASB in London, the UK accounting authorities and their international counterparts have a close working relationship. There is also a considerable personal continuity in that the former head of the British Accounting Standards Board (ASB), Sir David Tweedie, is now the head of the IASB.

TABLE 5.1

Similarities and differences between UK and 'continental European' accounting systems

UK system	European ('continental') systems
Limited statute law. Mostly driven by case law, e.g. rulings on dividend payments (note some convergence with European systems through 1981 Company Act).	Roman law and well-developed commercial codes anchored in the legal system.
Equity from institutional shareholders and private individuals.	Equity from large shareholders, banks and the government.
Separation of ownership and control.	Closer alignment of owner/shareholder interests.
Accounting rules precede taxation rules. First profits tax in 1937.	Public accounting rules laid down by taxation authorities.
Auditors 'needed' to fill legislative 'gaps'. Experts outside of government.	Fuller legislation and more government experts. Less need for audit.

The British accounting system has evolved slowly. It started with the 1844 Joint Stock Company Act which required that financial books of accounts should be kept. There should be a 'full and fair' presentation of a balance sheet for shareholders, but there was no agreement as to what should be in the balance sheet; and there was no requirement for a profit and loss account at all. The 1856 Joint Stock Company Act reversed the requirement for mandatory accounts, but it did strongly suggest that accounts should be voluntarily kept. A model of accounts and clauses on audits laid down an unofficial template of how these things could be done.

Interestingly, in the light of subsequent developments, the reason for abandoning mandatory accounts was that this was felt to be a private matter between a company's shareholders and its directors. The crucial link here was between the shareholder and the director: in those days, the 'auditor' was actually a shareholder who either volunteered or was delegated to look into this aspect. This shareholder auditor would often seek outside advice, in other words a real auditor. (Some aspects of this process remain attractive to this day!)

Accounting and auditing rules began to be seriously implemented with just three specific types of organization: banks (once they became limited companies), railways (prone to bankruptcies) and public utilities (attractive to private investors). It was only in 1907 that filing balance sheets became compulsory under the new Companies Act. Unfortunately the legislators forgot to specify what sort of balance sheet, and it was not unknown for the same balance sheet to be trotted out for several years – a loophole only closed in 1929.[21]

One of the first crises to hit the world of accounting occurred in 1929 with the bankruptcy of the Royal Mail Steam Packet Company. Despite having had good audited figures, and having declared a £439,000 profit in 1926, the company failed to repay a £10 million loan that was guaranteed by the Treasury. The chairman, Lord Kylsant, and the company secretary, Mr Moreland – a partner at a leading firm of accountants – were charged with publishing a false and fraudulent balance sheet.

In what is a perhaps interesting model for the future, both executives were ultimately acquitted. The reason given was that the profit declaration came about as a result of a transfer from reserves, which in those days did not have to be declared (similar to the reserves identifiable in the German accounting system). These 'secret' reserves could then be fed back into the P & L account to produce profits. The accountancy profession assured the judges that such transfers were common practice, and that the normal investor would understand that 'profits after adjustment for taxation reserves' might not be the same as a more conventional description of profit.[22.]

There was no rush to bridge this gap between 'truth' and the accounting view of the world. The rules did not change and little happened of note until in 1948 group accounts became compulsory, there was an increase in the level of disclosure and the profit and loss account now had to be audited. Accountants were authorized to operate under delegated powers under the Companies Act, but the determination of rules and practices was left entirely in their hands.

Little changed until a spate of bankruptcies in the late 1960s, including such companies as Fire, Auto and Marine Insurance, the IOS and Rolls Razor, a manufacturer of washing machines. Takeovers of AEI by GEC and the attempted sale by Robert Maxwell of Pergamon Press also revealed discrepancies in stated profits numbers.

With public disquiet suggesting that the government should take a closer interest in regulating the accounting and audit profession, the ICAEW (Institute of Chartered Accountants for England and Wales) published a 'Statement of Intent on Accounting Standards' in 1969. This led to the establishment of the Accounting Standards Steering Committee (ASSC) in 1970 to systematize current accounting practice and begin to codify it.

The bulk of ASSC members were accountants, either practising auditors or accountants working for industry and commerce. There were also representatives from users, or 'preparers', and from the public sector; and one academic.

While this was a welcome first step in bringing the unruly growth of accounting practices under one roof, there was still no enforcement of rules. 'No member was ever disciplined for breaching accounting standards *per se* during the ASSC's 20-year existence.'[23] The ASSC was also criticized for lacking a clear conceptual framework within which accounting should work. More particularly, there was little effort to iron out differences in the varying industrial and sector standards that were being applied. Further, the committee was funded entirely by the accounting industry itself, which gave rise to the perception of bias.

It took another series of scandals associated with the names of companies such as Polly Peck, the International Leisure Group and the Sock Shop to prompt another look at the state of auditing. Sir Ron Dearing set up a committee in 1988/9, and his report was to have a far-reaching effect on the accounting industry. The scandals shared a number of features:

- the companies had received a clean bill of health from their auditors;
- the companies were led by powerful, charismatic leaders;
- there had been little action from the non-executive directors;
- there had been little involvement from institutional investors.

These features all suggested that there were weaknesses in the system, and it was decided to set up a structure similar to that used in the USA, but with one or two important differences. The details can be seen in Figure 5.2.

The present system, basically established in 1988/9, is anchored in the delegated authority from the Companies Act, via the Department of Trade and

FIGURE 5.2
UK accounting institutions' current structure

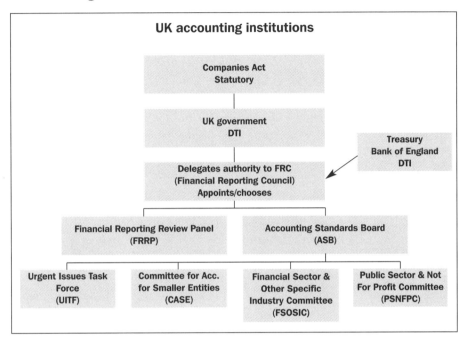

Industry. The self-regulating nature of the system is ensured by a further delegation of authority to the Financial Reporting Council. However, for the first time government interests are explicit, even if exercised with a light touch. Government ministers and the Bank of England help select the members of the FRC, which is funded with a levy on companies quoted on the London Stock Exchange, as well as with contributions from government, industry and the profession – helping to avoid any charge of bias.

The UK system, prior to the Enron disaster, had already accepted the principle that the system required buy-in from more stakeholders than accountants alone, whose role is explicit and important. Yet a large degree of self-regulation remains.

Corporate governance and regulating the auditors

There are two strands to recent developments in UK accounting. Following the Dearing Report, the accounting profession made timely moves towards opening up the discussion about regulation with a wider range of stakeholders. The scandals revealed weaknesses in the UK system of corporate governance, and efforts were made to deal with them by strengthening the oversight roles of non-executive and independent directors.

The 1992 Cadbury Committee Report laid out the following principles which should govern board behaviour:

- Separation of the role of chairman and chief executive.
- There should be a majority of independent non-executive directors (NEDs) on the board.
- There should be an audit committee with the majority of members being NEDs.
- There should be a remuneration committee with a majority of NEDs.
- There should be a nominations committee also largely made up of NEDs.

When these recommendations were made, only five out of the FTSE 100 companies had met all of them. Both the Cadbury Committee itself and its successor, the Greenbury Committee, tried to encourage further compliance with these recommendations. By 1993 some 54 companies in the FTSE 100 were reported to be complying – a significant improvement. The Greenbury Committee also recommended that the head of the remuneration committee should report to the shareholders – a theme later picked up in the 2003 Higgs Report regarding the role of the senior independent director, or SID. The SID is supposed to open direct channels of communication to the shareholders.[24]

While efforts were being made to improve the corporate governance system, one important area had been rather neglected: the question of who should regulate and discipline the accountants and auditors. It might be argued that this is being taken care of by the FRRP (see Figure 5.2), which is designed to investigate 'defective' audits. There are some doubts about just how effective the FRRP is. Most of its deliberations are behind closed doors and rarely reach the outside world. This makes sense from the point of view of the company being investigated, but less so when it concerns members of the profession who may be implicated in faulty audits or more serious misdemeanours. At the moment sanctions on companies with defective audits seem not to be balanced by sanctions on the auditors who performed them.

In the Table 5.2, the state of auditor investigations being held by the FRRP between 1992 and 1996 is shown. At that time there had been three fines levied on accountants ranging from £500 to £1,500 – which, as one writer put it, hardly had the accounting firms 'trembling in their boots'.[25] The table highlights the fact that no inquiry really resulted in any significant public admonishment of auditors.

TABLE 5.2

Consideration by ICAEW of cases referred by the Financial Reporting Review Panel, 1992–96

Item	Date	Company	Auditors	Outcome
1	28 Jan 92	Williams Hlds	Pannell Kerr Forster	IC 1 Sep 92: – PRCNFA
2	15 Oct 92	Trafalgar House	Touche Ross	IC 3 Aug 93: – NPFC
3	26 Oct 92	British Gas	Price Waterhouse	IC 20 Apr 93: – NPFC
4	22 Feb 93	Eurotherm	Arthur Anderson	IC 1 Nov 94: – NPFC
5	17 Mar 93	Foregn & Colonial	Price Waterhouse	IC 3 May 94: – NPFC
6	5 Apr 93	Penrith Farmers	N T O'Reilly & Ptrs	IC 28 Mar 94: – NPFC
7	27 Jul 93	Breverleigh	Copeland & Co	IC 15 Nov 94: – PFCNFA
8	10 Aug 93	Royal Bank of Scotland	Coopers & Lybrand	IC 24 Feb 94: – NPFC
9	24 Sep 93	Control Techniques	Coopers & Lybrand	IC 1 Mar 94: – NPFC
10	19 Oct 93	BM Group	Kingston Smith	IC 29 Nov 94: – NPFC
11	25 Oct 93	Ptarmigan	Ernst & Young	IC 1 Mar 94: – NPFC
12	26 Nov 93	Chrysalis	KPMG/Stoy Hayward	AC 20 Feb 95: NPFC
13	28 Jan 94	Intercare	Price Waterhouse	IC 5 Jul 94: – NPFC
14	11 Feb 94	Pentos	Coopers & Lybrand	IC 4 Oct 95: – NPFC
15	24 May 94	BET	Coopers & Lybrand	AC 4 Apr 95: – NPFC
16	2 Nov 94	Butte 1993	Cooper Lancaster Brewer	Still under enquiry
17	29 Mar 95	Alliance Trust	KPMG	IC 6 Feb 96: – NPFC
18	21 Jun 95	Courts	Coopers & Lybrand	IC 6 Feb 96: – NPFC
19	15 Feb 96	Securicor	Baker Tilley	Closed 1 Nov 96: – NA
20	28 Mar 96	Brammer	KPMG	Still under enquiry
21	9 Apr 96	Foreign & Colonial	Price Waterhouse	Closed 12 Jul 96: – NA
22	24 Jul 96	Sutton Harbour	Nevill Hovey & Co	Still under enquiry
23	2 Oct 96	Butte 1995	Cooper Lancaster Brewer	Still under enquiry

Abbreviations

IC	ICAEW Investigations Committee.
PFCNFA	Prima facie case but decided to take no further action.
NPFC	No prima facie case found.
NA	Investigation by officials who found no case for Investigations Committee

Source: Letter from the Minister for Corporate and Consumer Affairs to Austin Mitchell MP, 17 April 1997

These concerns have been echoed elsewhere. Consider the following quote:

> We clearly see a transition in the role and responsibility of the auditor from fostering fraud detection in the infancy of this profession and more distancing itself from it, as auditing became more concentrated and self interests gained a higher weight than public interest.[26]

New reforms

Fear of contagion is a powerful thing, and the US example has sent a wake-up call to the global accounting profession to get its house in order – with increasing assistance from outside parties. Currently the UK government is giving serious thought to introducing a stricter regime for both accountants in general and for auditors in particular. The details are shown in Figure 5.3.

Figure 5.3 highlights the idea of a structure within a structure that typifies much of accounting. The professional bodies, both auditors and more general accountants, maintain a grip on qualifications and exams and on controlling entry into the profession. Whereas this once sufficed as a policing and monitoring function, it increasingly has to run parallel to a more transparent interface between accounting/auditing activity and the other major stakeholders. There is some tension between the demands placed on the accountancy profession by the public regulatory side and what the accountants would ideally like for themselves. Currently, 'outsiders' are intervening in the profession in an unparalleled way – which in our view is likely to accelerate the codification of the profession, and quite possibly move it closer to US and continental European models.

Outstanding accounting issues

Change is happening not only in the infrastructure of accounting. Improvements in the state of accounting practice are also on the agenda. It is important to grasp how far-reaching these discussions are, and how serious the shortfalls in current practice are.

We have commented earlier on the problems raised by SPVs, which go to the heart of a number of accounting issues. A recent statement from the ASB reveals substantial work on revising and improving accounting practices in the areas shown in Table 5.3. The striking thing about this list – which is supplemented by a blizzard of suggested reforms, or FREDs (Financial Reporting Exposure Drafts) – is how deep they go. While some may take comfort from the

FIGURE 5.3
Regulating UK auditors

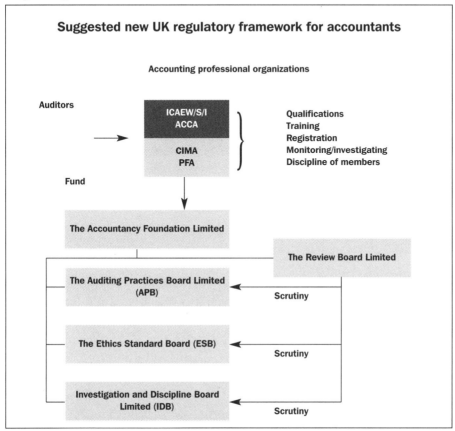

idea that these issues are now being attended to, the idea that the house of accounting is in such disrepair, and requires serious attention, may seem alarming.

On the audit side, the ASB is working hard to develop guidelines for the areas of:

- financial instruments
- revenue recognition
- consolidation policy/practice (related to the SPV issue)
- de-recognition
- leasing
- operational and financial reviews
- insurance accounting.

TABLE 5.3
The ASB contemplates reforms

Financial reporting standard and topic	Subject or abuse reform is intended to prevent
FRS 4: Capital instruments	To make it more difficult for corporate debt to be treated as equity
FRS 5: Substance of transaction	To sort out the treatment of operating assets and finances and their treatment on the balance sheet. To curtail the use of early revenue recognition (something largely resolved in SHV models)
FRS 7: Fair value	To try and prevent the shifting of profits from one period to another
FRS 12: Provisions, contingent liabilities and contingent assets	Ditto
FRS 8: Related party disclosure	

In their desire to improve things, and in particular to bring about some convergence with an international standard, policy-makers are realizing how widespread the shortcomings in existing practice are. Again, a glance across the Atlantic can be salutary. If CEOs are expected to sign off on accounts as being true, fair and accurate, then the codes of practice used should be expected to be relatively homogeneous and consistently applied. When basic building blocks such as revenue, or when an asset is sold, remain difficult to define, one may wonder how successful reform efforts will be – especially if it is the 'principles-led' approach that is supposed to gain the upper hand over something more 'rules-driven'.

In summary, it looks as if the UK accounting industry really has called in the builders, who are swarming all over the edifice at the time of writing. To its credit, the UK has managed to avoid the problems affecting the USA: it is still unclear whether this is due to luck or to good judgement. In any event, the UK experience is being used as one of the foundations for the developing IAS system.

And the IAS ...

We suspect that activity levels at the IASB are much higher than they would have been in the absence of the Enron disaster. As we have pointed out earlier, an international accounting standard, widely recognized and accepted across the world, would be an important element in the creation of a more truly global capital market.

Organizationally, the IASB is funded from a wide range of institutions across the world, running on revenues of around $12 million a year – a modest sum in view of its current huge responsibilities. It has a board of trustees, led currently by ex-Fed chairman Paul Volcker, with members drawn from the USA (five), the EU (seven, including two from the UK), Japan (two), Canada, Brazil, Hong Kong (all one each). The IASB itself explicitly works with the various national accounting organizations, the main ones being from the USA, the UK, France, Germany, Japan, Canada and Australia. Notable absences from this list include China, India and Russia.

As we noted above, in 2005 the EU intends to use the IAS standard as the basis for EU corporate accounts, and already many countries are moving rapidly to transfer to this system – no doubt in order to be seen to be good global corporate and accounting citizens.

The IASB is currently in the vanguard of rule-setting – largely because the other great contender for this role, the USA, has its own extensive internal problems. Indeed, both at the Sarbanes-Oxley hearings, and at subsequent meetings with FASB, the IASB is giving clear support to those in the USA who want to bring standards closer together. Table 5.4 shows the main tasks facing the IAS – which have a reassuring similarity to the agenda being dealt with in the UK.

TABLE 5.4
Main tasks being dealt with by the IASB

Main issues	Country delegated to coordinate efforts to set a new standard
IASB principles for small and medium-sized companies	IASB staff and advisory panel
Lease accounting	UK
Initial measurement and impairment	Canada
Accounting for financial instruments	IASB staff
Management narrative	NZ + Canada + UK
Extractive industries	Australia + Canada + Norway + S. Africa
Accounting for service arrangements and 'concessions'	UK

Source: IASB Annual Report 2002

So is a new and shiny accounting 'gold' standard going to emerge out of all this activity? As indicated earlier, the various national accounting systems have significant differences in their underlying philosophies. These will have to be resolved at the IAS level if there is to be any hope of a Global GAAP being generally accepted. Perhaps any new IAS standards will primarily apply to large internationally active corporations, and will be used to present the consolidated accounts for the purpose of financial reporting to shareholders. Progress has already been made in this area.

This, however, leaves the rest to be considered, and here the picture is not so reassuring. There is still a disjunction between the tax-based accounting systems of continental Europe and those from the 'Anglo-Saxon' parts of the world. Efforts towards a harmonized view on tax payments in the EU will lead to attempts at the harmonization of tax systems,[27] and these will be accelerated by companies seeking tax relief for losses incurred in one part of the EU against profits earned elsewhere. If this is to be allowed – and it would be strange if it wasn't in a single capital market – there will have to be greater standardization in taxes and tax allowances. Many exemptions granted for foreign enterprises will have to be reviewed to ensure that 'foreign' now means non-EU.

Probably a parallel system of accounting will continue. For the larger companies, IAS will prevail, assuming some current standards can be resolved. For the smaller companies, local tax-based accounting systems will probably persist. One unintended consequence of the efforts to reform accounting standards may be an unavoidable increase in the number of reports to various authorities – all of which would create work for the accountants!

Continental Europe: the case of France

This chapter so far has concentrated on developments in the USA, the UK and the IAS. It is time to turn our attention to a different tradition, which has also existed for a long time, and whose existence we have alluded to at various points already.

We will take a brief look the French system, since we think it may hold the key for some future developments. As elsewhere, the French accounting system has been undergoing some important changes, as has the system of corporate governance.

Before 1998, the main sources of regulation came from decisions made by the tribunals or commercial courts. Accounting regulations, as such, emanated from various bodies, including the Conseil National de Comptabilité, or CNC (the

National Accounting Council, under the supervision of the Ministry of Finance); the Commission des Opérations de Bourse, or COB (equivalent to the Securities and Exchange Commission); and the two professional bodies for accounting and auditing, the OEC (l'Ordre des Experts Comptables) and the CNCC (the Compagnie Nationale des Commissaires aux Comptes).

This means that the French system has been used to operating in a broader environment than the UK/US equivalent, and has done so for a longer time. Other features have contributed to the system's stability:

- One of the main principles of French accounting is 'prudence'.

- Companies that consolidate their accounts must have two different auditors. This allows for reciprocal control and consultation on difficult technical matters and is claimed to reinforce auditor independence – but may also encourage some auditor collusion.[28]

- There is a six-year tenure period for auditors. Contracts can be, and often are, renewed after the six years. But at this point the auditor can be replaced honourably (this might be worth looking at in the context of the US/UK situation).

- The audit committee is not obliged to look for the cheapest auditor, but rather the one that is likely to give the best service.

- The auditor is expected to give up all other kinds of ancillary work for the client after taking up the audit mandate. This includes legal, tax, IT and valuation work. Some ancillary work is allowed if it is complementary to the audit.

- Any auditor application to a publicly quoted company must be presented to the COB, which subsequently gives its opinion. It is difficult for a company to ignore a negative opinion.[29]

Given the closer association between the legal and commercial laws and codes and accounting rules and regulations, the misappropriation of corporate assets, fraudulent financial statements and the spreading of false information are all criminal offences. (Compare the new strictures on CEOs in the USA and the penalties they face if their accounts are found wanting.)

What lets the French system down, however, is that any such criminal case takes an inordinately long time to come to court. Owing to the delays, the chances of the accused ultimately being acquitted are relatively high. Proceedings have been brought against the former CEO of Vivendi, but there is little expectation of a speedy end to the investigation.[30]

In April 1998, an additional official accounting body was created, the Comité de la Réglementation Comptable (CRC) which is responsible for approving new accounting standards. This body was created to address the following issues:

- French accounting standards were often general and could be interpreted in several ways. The CRC's standards are designed to be more specific and therefore make the financial statements more transparent.

- French accounting standards had previously been set by several sources.

The CRC seems to be a cross between the UK's FRC and the ASB and/or FASB. Unlike the FRC, it does set and approve rules, but like the FRC it takes its cue from another body, the CNC, which functions like the ASB in this system. The CRC is designed to give the rule-setting process more consistency. So the CNC proposes changes to the rules, which are then reviewed and ultimately issued by the CRC.

Another leaf taken from the Anglo-Saxon world is the use of a Comité d'Urgence (Urgent Issues Task Force), which comprises a smaller number of CNC members. It can issue interpretations and guidance on existing standards. As elsewhere, among the burning issues it has dealt with are consolidation rules, accounting changes, construction contracts and accounting for liabilities and provisions. Meanwhile, a Financial Security Bill presented to the Cabinet in February 2003 puts more emphasis on audit rotation and the separation between auditing and consulting. Also, an independent High Council of Auditors will be created to monitor the profession.

Also as elsewhere, France has seen important changes in corporate governance, introduced by the Vienot Reports. These are similar in intent to the Cadbury Committee, and have argued for clearer separation between the CEO and chairman roles. There are also proposals for a wider set of committees to deal with audit, remuneration and nominations. The roles of non-executive directors are also to be strengthened: they should chair some of the ancillary board committees.[31]

This raises an intriguing point. In both France's single-board structure and in the UK/USA, there is a strong suggestion that the single board should extend its activities through various special committees to improve corporate governance. But it seems to this writer that the dual-board structure as practised in Germany and elsewhere already does this. With its *Aufsichtsrat* (supervisory board) and *Vorstand* (executive board) the German structure also has a more explicit role for employee representatives, who participate at the supervisory board level. As with many other elements in the accounting and corporate governance debates, differences in form can sometimes obscure similarities in function and content.

Conclusions and thoughts for the future

Clearly the world of accounting is undergoing serious challenges and changes, and a lot is riding on the outcome of various deliberations.

A number of themes have been apparent throughout this chapter. The accounting profession has very rarely acted proactively to prevent crises from happening. Horses have bolted, leaving empty stables, while regulators consider ways of closing the door, if not retrieving the horse. Only relatively recently have the authorities started to think about installing a second door made up of a wider non-accounting group of experts and regulators to keep an eye on the stable.

Which once again raises the question of the accountants' and auditors' ultimate customer. There are clear social interests in avoiding Enron-type situations. Central banks have been regulating the banking sector relatively successfully since the Second World War: banking failures are now relatively rare events, and the panics of the nineteenth and twentieth centuries are mostly distant memories.

We think that the shareholder interest needs to be pushed closer to the audit process. We are attracted by the earlier practice of letting the shareholders really organize the audit. At the very least the auditors need to report to a NED, or possibly the SID of a large public corporation who is in charge of the audit committee.

But as the degree of social intervention in the audit process increases, so the demands for greater codification and consistency are also rising. A clearer link to the legal framework expressed through stock exchange rules or through company law also seems to be needed. There are unresolved tax issues running through all this, too. Potentially the process of working towards global standards will break down obstacles erected by national governments and bring forward the date of a more harmonized EU-wide tax system.

There are also signs that accountants are beginning to fulfil a more social function. One day this might be recognized by payments from governments or NGOs. If this prospect appals the accountants, then perhaps they will realize that there might have to be more specialized audits meeting the needs of separate audiences – possibly raising the question of whose views or numbers are ultimately correct. This could be resolved by the advance of technology such as the use of XBRL, making it possible to 'slice and dice' financial reports into different formats for different purposes.

Audit regimes have been rather less successful, we have noted, when it comes to spotting fraud. When it is spotted, it is mostly too late, and the consequences are unevenly felt through the economy. It seems to us that the auditors have often escaped relatively lightly in relation to the turmoil they have helped create.

We have tried to show that in today's complex world, there are some very serious accounting issues that are taking a long time to be resolved. In the spirit of the rest of the book, we think that the innovations and advances reached through the application of SHV methods of valuation may have helped reduce the kind of problems we face today. Some SHV practitioners, for instance, have been adjusting for operating leases for some time, thus trying to get closer to a 'true and fair' picture. We have also taken a much harder view on the consolidation issues, and have tried to include the assets a corporation has 'economically used' rather than watch them be defined out of existence as a result of SPVs. More importantly, some of us have argued for the superiority of a cash-flow-based approach over alternatives. Perhaps the view that the profit and loss account should be scrapped, and financial reports should consist of a balance sheet and a cash flow statement, has its merits.

There remains a lot to do, we suspect, before the financial systems that we know are fully to be trusted.

Notes

1 The author is grateful to Etienne Piciocchi for help with some parts of this chapter.
2 The list of companies that have failed, or are being investigated for their accounting practices is growing longer. The chief names on it are: Freddie Mac, Network Associates, Enron, Dynergy, WorldCom, Global Crossing, Adelphia Communications, BCCI, Maxwell, Levitt, Polly Peck, Dunsdale, Wallace Smith, Garston, Vivendi Universal, Comroad, Condomi, BKN International, Metallgesellschaft, Holzman, Hypovereinsbank, Bremer Vulkan, Balsam, Schneider Affair, Riegebank, Bank Burgenlandfall, Libro, Cybertron, Y Line Computer Associates, Tyco, Xerox, Halliburton, Bristol Myer Squibb, Q West Communications, Imclone System, Harken Energy, K Mart, Lucent Technologies, Health South ... Note, this is not a complete list.
3 The following admission by the IASB is revealing in this respect: 'Revenue

recognition has been one of the most contentious topics in accounting. Surprisingly for an issue that is of such fundamental importance, the approaches to it in standards and conceptual frameworks (both the IASB's and other standard setters') *are inconsistent, and guidance on some crucial issues is non-existent'* (28 IASB Annual Report 2002, p. 11 (author's italics)).

4 It is sometimes now forgotten that many of the leading auditing companies were fined large amounts – $400 million in the case of Ernst & Young – for colluding with the Thrifts in producing misleading financial statements. See Shields, Janice C. (1993) *Bad Audits, Not Deep Pockets*. US Public Interest Research Group, July.

5 Quoted in AICPA (1969) *The Rise of the Accounting Profession, Vol 1. From Technical to Professional 1891–1936*, p. 167.

6 Emphases are the author's. *United States* v *Arthur Young & Co*. 465 US (805) 1984.

7 Senator Charles Grassley and Max Baucus, member of the Committee on Finance in a letter to William Donaldson, current head of the SEC, wrote: 'As a wake up call to all of us, Enron's use of a close web of tax promoters, and advisors ... accountants, lawyers and investment bankers – to construct complex schemes to avoid taxes and manipulate financial statements raises serious questions regarding the role played by these promoters and advisors.' In a similar vein, Sprint fired two senior executives who benefited from tax shelters, rather than firing the auditor, who was behind the schemes. (See the Congressional Committee on Taxation for further details.)

8 Tweedie, Sir David, The Fall of Enron. How Could It Have Happened? Hearing before the Committee on Governmental Affairs, US Senate, 24 January 2002.

9 Ibid.

10 See Daniel Bouton, 'Promoting Better Corporate Governance', Report of the Working Group, press briefing, 23 September 2002, published by MEDEF and AFEP-AFREF.

11 This is not to overlook important differences between UK and US GAAP. Indeed, the waters are getting sufficiently muddied to say that there is a coalescence within Europe around the IAS – significantly influenced by the UK, as compared with another group of countries associated with the US GAAP.

12 It is useful to document the organizations sponsoring the FAF. These were the AICPA (US accounting organization), the American Accounting

Association, the Financial Executive Institute, the Securities Industry Association, the National Association of State Auditors, Comptrollers and Treasurers, the Institute of Management Accountants, the Government Finance Officers Association and four 'at large' members chosen by the FAF. The accountancy profession is well represented here, and these members through their control of the FAF also ensured that the 'right' people were selected for the FASB, presumably also including the non-accounting members.

13 See Sunder, S. (1988) 'Political Economy of Accounting Standards', *Journal of Accounting Literature*, Vol. 7, pp. 31–41.

14 'Andersen Agonistes', *Wall Street Journal*, 5 March 2002.

15 See testimonies and hearings for the 107th and 108th US Congress, US Senate Hearings before the Committee on Governmental Affairs Jan.–Feb. 2002. Also hearings before the US Senate Banking Committee. See also Chapter 7 in this book.

16 Senator Bennett's testimony, 24 Jan. 2002 hearing before the Committee on Governmental Affairs, US Senate: 'The Fall of Enron: How could it have happened?'.

17 Resigned on 31 March 2002 after failing conspicuously to see the Enron events coming.

18 See Sarbanes Oxley, Conference Report Amendments of Senate to Bill F:\p7\ACCTREF\H3763CR.HSE.

19 But see above on Ernst & Young's efforts to change this ruling.

20 Katz, David M. (2003) *CFO Magazine*, 2 July.

21 See Day, R.G. (2000) *UK Accounting Regulation: An Historical Perspective*. Bournemouth University, p. 5 – for this and for other points in this section.

22 Ibid. p. 9.

23 Ibid. p. 16.

24 Derek Higgs, 'Review of the Role and Effectiveness of Non-executive Directors', report to the DTI, January 2003.

25 The auditors in question were those of a company called Butte (1995) fined £1,500; Wenham Major which audited Concentric plc, fined £1,000, and Coopers & Lybrand which audited Strategem; and Harvey's which was fined £500. It is true that C&L were fined £1.2 million for their part in the Maxwell pensions scandal. This pales into insignificance when measured against the £400 million of mis-appropriated pension fund assets. See Sikka, Prem (2002) *Regulation of Accountancy and the Power of Capital*. University of Essex.

26 Hesse, Heiko (2002) *Corporate Frauds, Accounting Scandals and Auditing. Quo Vadis?* EC247.

27 See European Commission consultation document – February 2003 International Accounting Standards (IAS) and a consolidated tax base for companies' EU-wide activities.

28 In many large corporations, audits are split between several accounting firms in several locations. In the USA/UK the final consolidated accounts are normally prepared by just one firm.

29 For more details, see Bouton, David op. cit.

30 Arnold, Martin (2002) 'Investigation Unlikely to Move Fast', *Financial Times*, 31 October.

31 As well as the Vienot Reports, more recently there has been the Bouton Report and a report from the Institut Montaigne.

THE SHAREHOLDER INCOME STATEMENT:
A PROPOSAL FOR REPORTING CORPORATE CAPITAL MARKET PERFORMANCE BASED ON TOTAL SHAREHOLDER RETURNS (TSR)[1]

COLIN CLUBB
The Business School, Imperial College London

1. Introduction

The aim of this chapter is to present a possible approach to reporting corporate capital market performance which focuses on the analysis of total shareholder returns (TSR). My starting point is that reporting corporate capital market performance might be a useful extension of the scope of financial reporting. While this view, I would argue, is broadly consistent with the concern for providing information on corporate performance from an investor perspective that underpins modern financial reporting practice, a convincing case for such an extension of financial reporting depends both on system design issues (concerned with how one might report capital market performance) and broader institutional and societal issues (concerned with the extent to which such a development might serve useful economic and social ends). The focus of this chapter is on system design issues, in particular the development of a simple but nevertheless theoretically grounded approach to reporting actual capital market performance. The potential usefulness of my proposed system is also considered, although I conclude that there is a need for more detailed analysis of the broader possible impact of extending financial reporting to include capital market performance reporting.

> Reporting corporate capital market performance might be a useful extension of the scope of financial reporting.

The remaining sections of the chapter are organized as follows. Heading 2 discusses developments that have stimulated my proposed approach to reporting capital market performance. Heading 3 provides an explanation of the structure of the proposed 'Shareholder Income Statement' (SIS hereafter) emphasizing the relationship between the SIS and the concept of 'economic income' and applies the framework to BT plc over an eight-year period 1994–2001. Heading 4 concludes by briefly discussing issues in relation to the usefulness of capital market performance reporting.

2. Past developments and background

The system for reporting *ex post* capital market performance developed under heading 3 of this chapter has been motivated by developments, past and present, which, I believe, have suggested the possible need for extensions to financial reporting practice and which have indicated possible directions for such change. To get an idea about where the proposed system is 'coming from', I spend a little time discussing these developments.

In recent years, there has been a heightened interest in the financial returns to investors from equity investment, which has centred around the idea of 'shareholder value'. This development has been intimately associated with a variety of different approaches to value-based management based on residual income and cash flow valuation models, among the best known being the Stern Stewart EVA[TM] method based on residual income[2] and the Holt CFROI[TM] approach based on the cash flow valuation model.[3] In relation to *ex post* capital market performance analysis, Stern Stewart's EVA[TM] approach makes use of the market value added concept (or MVA), based on the difference between (adjusted) equity book values and company market capitalization, as a basis for assessing current and expected future financial performance.[4] A cash flow metric arising from Holt's CFROI[TM] approach (see Holt's DualGrade® corporate performance scorecard as discussed in Madden[5]) involves the division of current market capitalization between the present value of expected cash flows from current operations and the present value of expected net cash flows from future investment. In both cases, the resulting numbers have been used to rank companies in terms of their ability to generate shareholder value.

While sharing an interest in analysis of shareholder value performance with these approaches, my specific concern in this chapter is more with the reporting of (rather than the analysis of) *ex post* capital market performance. In other words, the fundamental issue of interest here is how financial reporting might be developed in a way that reinforces a focus on analysis of shareholder value creation. The reporting system which I develop is based on the view that security returns, or total shareholder returns (TSR) as they are widely referred to in the financial press, are the obvious basis for reporting *ex post* capital market performance (as most people would argue that capital market performance is directly measured by security returns[6]). A problem with TSR, however, is that it is made up of two main components, dividends and capital gains, which are affected by a company's dividend policy and which are not easily related to the actual operations of the business. The question that arises therefore is: can TSR be divided up in an alternative way that could help to explain the drivers of capital market performance?

The concept of 'economic income' suggests that income can be split into cash flow and valuation components, where the valuation component reflects

> The fundamental issue of interest here is how financial reporting might be developed in a way that reinforces a focus on analysis of shareholder value creation.

> A problem with TSR, however, is that it is made up of two main components, dividends and capital gains, which are affected by a company's dividend policy and which are not easily related to the actual operations of the business.

changes in relation to future cash flow expectations. This concept, widely associated with the work of Hicks,[7] provides the basis for an affirmative answer to the question just posed and is the basis for the proposed reporting system under heading 3. More specifically, it suggests that the TSR can be split between cash flows realized from the operations of the business and a valuation component reflecting changes in the capital market's valuation of future expected cash flows from current and future activities. The proposed approach therefore combines information from the cash flow statement (and other relevant financial flows) with information on changes in the market capitalization of the firm in order to provide a breakdown of TSR which focuses on realized and unrealized performance.

In summary, the system for reporting *ex post* capital market performance which I develop at heading 3 can be viewed as an attempt to respond to the financial reporting challenge which I believe is raised by increased interest in analysis of shareholder value performance. The proposed approach is concerned with reporting capital market performance, in contrast to the focus of well-known consulting firms such as Stern Stewart and Holt with systems for analysing capital market performance. While 'reporting' and 'analysis' of capital market performance are closely related concerns (in particular, because reporting systems should be developed ideally with an interpretative framework in mind), a reporting system should be based on reliable and verifiable data which allow investors to come to their own conclusions (using additional information and knowledge) about the future prospects and performance of a business.[8] The well established concept of 'economic income', applied to the widely accepted capital market metric TSR, provides the basis for the proposed attempt to satisfy this perceived reporting requirement.

3. Capital market performance and the shareholder income statement

The 'Shareholder Income Statement' (SIS) combines cash flow and other financial flow information with market capitalization information for a period in order to split TSR (or its money equivalent) into an operating cash flow component and a valuation component. The following analysis is divided into two main sub-sections. First, I present what I term the 'Statement of financial flows' (SFF) which combines information from cash flow statements published in company financial statements with additional non-cash financial flows in a manner which facilitates the production of the SIS. While the SFF can be viewed as a companion financial statement to the SIS, it is also a stand-alone financial statement which highlights financial flow data useful for fundamental cash flow valuation purposes. It therefore provides a link between the fundamental cash flow valuation perspective emphasized in much of the shareholder value and corporate finance literature and the *ex post* shareholder income measurement perspective based on observed security values developed in this chapter. I then show in the following subsection how data from the SFF can be combined with share value and other data to generate a SIS and discuss implementation of the SIS approach to capital market performance reporting.[9]

Statement of financial flows (SFF)

The SFF is structured to provide information which is relevant for both *ex ante* company valuation and *ex post* shareholder value performance evaluation. A multiperiod example of the SFF based on accounting data for BT plc for the period 1997–2001 is given in Table 6.1. It should be noted that the SFF combines both cash flow and non-cash flow data. The statement is divided into three sections concerned with operating, investment and financing flows.

The operating flow section uses cash flow from operations data from the published cash flow statement based on UK GAAP.[10] A simple distinction is made between operating cash flow generated by primary operations (which refers to core operations and subsidiaries) and cash flows from associates, joint ventures and financial investments. Taxation paid is deducted to obtain the 'after-tax' Cash Flow from Operations figure.[11]

The investment section of SFF incorporates all (cash and non-cash) investments and disposals. In particular, investment in primary assets provides information on *all primary assets* acquired and disposed of by the firm. Therefore, 'Investment in Assets of Subsidiaries' equals the acquisition price of the shares of the subsidiary *less* cash and financial assets held by the subsidiary (financial assets of acquired subsidiaries are included under 'Investment in Financial Assets') *plus* all long-term and short-term debt outstanding in the subsidiary undertaking (debt of acquired subsidiaries are included in the financing section of the SFF). Also, in contrast to published cash flow statements where the change in cash is the 'bottom line', the SFF includes changes in cash and changes in non-cash, highly liquid assets as part of the investment activities of the business.[12]

The third section of SFF reports financing information. Note that SCFO (cash flow from operations after interest and tax, as in Table 6.1 line 14) is an equity financing inflow and dividends are an equity financing outflow. Note also that non-cash changes in equity and debt capital are included in the overall financing flow. Finally, note that the SFF is based on an identity between total investment and total financing, in marked contrast to cash flow statements produced under GAAP.[13]

The main difference between the SFF and published cash flow statements is the inclusion of non-cash investment and financing transactions in the former which are excluded from the latter. The reason for this difference is that the SFF aims to provide information relevant for capital market and shareholder value performance analysis (while published cash flow statements are concerned primarily with liquidity analysis). As will be shown below, it is necessary for the SFF to incorporate these transactions so it can provide the necessary financial flow data for the SIS. Furthermore, the SFF provides *ex post* measures of variables that are important for *ex ante* valuation analysis. For example, the difference between CFO after tax and investment in Table 6.1 can be regarded as equivalent to the concept of 'free cash flow' widely employed in the company valuation literature.[14] In summary, the SFF captures the core company transactional data required for effective shareholder value analysis.

> The main difference between the SFF and published cash flow statements is the inclusion of non-cash investment and financing transactions in the former which are excluded from the latter.

Total shareholder income and the shareholder income statement

Given the information provided by the SFF, it is now a relatively straightforward task to move to the SIS. First, I provide a very brief algebraic presentation of how the cash flow and the valuation components of total shareholder income (the 'bottom-line' of the SIS) can be calculated from market capitalization and SFF data. Second, I apply this analysis to produce multiperiod SISs for BT for the period 1994–2001. Finally, some further issues in relation to implementing the SIS are considered.

Cash flow and valuation components of total shareholder income

Some simple algebra helps to explain how total shareholder income (TSI: the money equivalent to TSR) can be split into a cash flow component and a valuation component. First, a money version of the usual definition of TSR implies that TSI can be expressed as follows:

TABLE 6.1

Statement of financial flows for BT plc, 1994–2001 (all figures £m)

	1994	1995	1996	1997	1998	1999	2000	2001
Operating flows								
CFO from primary activities	4914	5113	5829	6192	6076	6037	5854	5897
CFO from financial assets	200	147	207	196	168	111	286	293
Tax paid	−605	−1175	−784	−1045	−1886	−630	−1311	−669
CFO after tax	4509	4085	5252	5343	4358	5518	4829	5521
Investment flows								
Net payments for tangible fixed assets	−1993	−2400	−2399	−2699	−2893	−3077	−3425	−4316
Investment in assets of subsidiaries	−25	−6	−26	−115	−121	−762	−4220	−10970
Other	−587	0	0	−137	−1380	−1295	−2546	−6992
Investment in primary activities	−2605	−2406	−2425	−2951	−4394	−5134	−10191	−22278
Investment in financial assets	−813	96	−1529	−535	2043	1609	855	−526
Total investment (INV)	−3418	−2310	−3954	−3486	−2351	−3525	−9336	−22804
Financing flows								
CFO after tax	4509	4085	5252	5343	4358	5518	4829	5521
Interest paid	−384	−471	−332	−402	−328	−439	−449	−1020
Non-equity dividends paid	−15	−18	−20	−14	0	0	0	0
Shareholder cash flow from operations (SCFO)	4110	3596	4900	4927	4030	5079	4380	4501
Dividends paid to ordinary shareholders (DIV)	−999	−1065	−1138	−1217	−3473	−1186	−1364	−1432
Shareholder cash flow from ops. retained	3111	2531	3762	3710	557	3893	3016	3069
Share capital issued (SCI)	57	118	189	211	192	174	559	185
Total shareholder financing (SFIN)	3168	2649	3951	3921	749	4067	3575	3254
Total debt (and preference share) financing (DFIN)	249	−335	−3	−435	1602	−542	5761	19550
Total financing (FIN)	3417	2314	3948	3486	2351	3525	9336	22804

$$TSI = DIV + \Delta MVS - SCI$$

where TSI is total shareholder income for the period, ΔMVS is the change in market value of share capital during the period (i.e. the change in total market capitalization), DIV is the total dividend paid during the period and SCI is new share capital issued during the period.

Adding and subtracting shareholder cash flow from operations (i.e. SCFO in the SFF) and rearranging gives:

$$TSI = SCFO + [\Delta MVS - (SCFO - DIV + SCI)]$$

This expression says that TSI can be expressed as the sum of SCFO and a second term which can be interpreted as the valuation component of TSI. To see this, it is useful to note that the identity between total financing and total investment flows in the SFF implies that:

$$SFIN = INV - DFIN$$

(where SFIN denotes shareholder financing and DFIN denotes debt financing as shown in Table 6.1) and that the SFF also implies:

$$SFIN = (SCFO - DIV + SCI)$$

It follows that:

$$TSI = SCFO + [\Delta MVS - SFIN]$$

Hence, the second term in our expression for TSI represents the difference between the change in the market value of the equity share capital and the amount of shareholder financing in the firm during the period. This is reasonably interpreted as the valuation gain to shareholders during the period because it represents that part of the change in the market capitalization of the firm's equity which is neither due to reinvestment of retained shareholder cash flow from operations (SCFO – DIV) nor due to newly raised share capital, SCI. Alternatively stated, it is that part of the change in the market value of the firm's equity which is not simply caused by the shareholders' share (as opposed to the debt financed share) of investment in the firm (INV – DFIN).

In summary, I have shown that TSI can be expressed as follows:

$$TSI = SCFO + VCSI$$

where VCSI = $[\Delta MVS - SFIN]$ represents the valuation component of shareholder income (see line 2 of Table 6.2). This dichotomy of TSI is the basis of the SIS which is illustrated for the case of BT plc.

Implementing the shareholder income statement

Table 6.2 provides SISs for BT plc for an eight-year period 1994–2001. For each year, the first part of the table shows: (i) the division of TSI between the realized SCFO component and the unrealized VCSI component, (ii) the determination of VCSI as the difference between the change in market capitalization, ΔMVS, and shareholder financing, SFIN, and (iii) the 'traditional' division of TSI between dividends (net of new equity contributions), DIV – SCI, and capital gains represented by the change in market capitalization, ΔMVS. The second part of the table provides the same information for TSR, where the market value of equity at the beginning of the year is used as the denominator for calculating all percentages.

TABLE 6.2

Shareholder income statements for BT plc, 1994–2001 (all figures £m)

Total shareholder income (TSI)	1994	1995	1996	1997	1998	1999	2000	2001
Shareholder cash flow from operations (SCFO)	4110	3596	4900	4927	4030	5079	4380	4501
Valuation component of shareholder income (VCSI)	–6154	–2656	–5080	1145	12609	19670	7477	–46101
Total shareholder income (TSI)	–2044	940	–180	6072	16639	24749	11857	–41600
Market value of ordinary shares at year-end	24378	24371	23242	28307	41665	65402	76454	33571
Market value of ordinary shares at year-start	27364	24378	24371	23242	28307	41665	65402	76454
Change in market value of share capital	–2986	–7	–1129	5066	13358	23737	11052	–42883
Shareholder financing (SFIN)	3168	2649	3951	3921	749	4067	3575	3218
Valuation component of shareholder income (VCSI)	–6154	–2656	–5080	1144.5	12609	19670	7477	–46101
Dividends, net of share capital issued (DIV – SCI)	942	947	949	1006	3281	1012	805	1283
Change in market value of share capital	–2986	–7	–1129	5066	13358	23737	11052	–42883
Total shareholder income	–2044	940	–180	6072	16639	24749	11857	–41600

TABLE 6.2 *CONTINUED*

Total shareholder returns (TSR)	1994	1995	1996	1997	1998	1999	2000	2001
Shareholder cash flow from operations	15.0%	14.8%	20.1%	21.2%	14.2%	12.2%	6.7%	5.9%
Valuation component of shareholder income	−22.5%	−10.9%	−20.8%	4.9%	44.5%	47.2%	11.4%	−60.3%
Total shareholder return	−7.5%	3.9%	−0.7%	26.1%	58.8%	59.4%	18.1%	−54.4%
Change in market value	−10.9%	0.0%	−4.6%	21.8%	47.2%	57.0%	16.9%	−56.1%
Shareholder financing (SFIN)	11.6%	10.9%	16.2%	16.9%	2.6%	9.8%	5.5%	4.2%
Valuation component of shareholder income	−22.5%	−10.9%	−20.8%	4.9%	44.5%	47.2%	11.4%	−60.3%
Dividends less share capital issued	3.4%	3.9%	3.9%	4.3%	11.6%	2.4%	1.2%	1.7%
Market value change	−10.9%	0.0%	−4.6%	21.8%	47.2%	57.0%	16.9%	−56.1%
Total shareholder return	−7.5%	3.9%	−0.7%	26.1%	58.8%	59.4%	18.1%	−54.4%

As briefly discussed at heading 2, the aim of SIS is not to provide an analysis of a firm's capital market performance (and particularly, not in relation to some estimate of the firm's 'true' financial performance), as any such analysis would necessarily involve subjective judgements about the future prospects of the firm. Instead, the aim is to provide a relatively objective presentation of two components of TSI or TSR, in order to differentiate realized cash flow performance (represented by SCFO) from performance based on the *market's expectations (and changes in the market's expectation)* of the firm's future prospects (represented by VCSI). The realized cash flow component is straightforward to interpret, the factors driving the valuation component of TSI require some discussion.

What factors then drive VCSI? First, if there is no change in market expectations of future cash flows from existing operations between the beginning and end of the year (and if we ignore for the moment expectations about future investments that the firm might undertake), VCSI will simply reflect economic depreciation (or possibly appreciation) of existing assets as perceived by the market – e.g. assuming even annual cash flows and assets with finite lives, VCSI will be negative and equal to the decline in the present value of future expected cash flows due to the ageing of existing assets. Second, if there are changes in expectations about future cash flows from existing assets, then VCSI will also be influenced by such changes, improved expectations impacting on VCSI positively and deteriorating expectations impacting negatively. Third, expected and unexpected changes in the estimated economic value of future expected investments (and the value of 'real options'), will also impact on VCSI and obviously such an impact can be positive or negative. Fourth, expected and unexpected changes in the cost of capital used to discount future cash flow expectations will impact on market valuations and VCSI. Finally, it is possible that market irrationality (independent of cash flow and discount rate expectations) might drive share prices and hence VCSI.

The VCSI data for BT plc presented in Table 6.2 can obviously be interpreted in a wide variety of ways in terms of the drivers discussed above, and different investors are likely to have different views on the appropriate interpretation. Some general comments about the data based on the factors which may impact on VCSI, however, may be useful to highlight questions which the SIS raises. For example, the very poor VCSI performance and poor overall TSR performance in 1996 was associated with relatively strong SCFO compared at least to 1994 and 1995. To the extent that improved SCFO may indicate improved future prospects, it would have been relevant for investors to ask what factors explain the poor VCSI for that year (part of the negative VCSI, assuming a rational market, would presumably represent expected economic depreciation in BT's 'depreciating assets' but this is unlikely to be as high as 20.8% of opening market equity value). Interestingly, in the following year, 1997, similar SCFO performance was associated with positive VCSI and a strong overall TSR. Given BT's ownership of substantial 'depreciating assets', a small positive VCSI of 4.9% in that year may be interpreted as suggesting a substantial improvement in market expectations about future cash flows (for example, assuming economic depreciation based on market expectations at the beginning of the year of 10%, a VCSI of 4.9% suggests improved cash flows expectations of 14.9% *ceteris paribus*). The massively positive VCSI in 1998 and 1999 appear to have been driven by (with the benefit of hindsight) highly over-optimistic expectations at the time about BT's future investment opportunities as a global telecoms business. While it is debatable whether or not such expectations were rational at the time, the SIS clearly indicates that these huge increases in market capitalization were not associated on average with improved realized cash flow performance.[15]

The example in Table 6.2 provides an indication of the relative ease with which basic SIS data can be presented from published financial statement data (organized in the form of the SFF) and observed share prices. While the division of shareholder income or returns into cash flow and valuation components is the fundamental information provided by the SIS, further subdivisions of TSI might provide a more useful representation of the firm's capital market performance. These and other issues in relation to the possible implementation of SIS based financial reporting are now considered.

Further issues in implementing SIS based financial reporting

The division of the SCFO according to business segments represents an obvious direction for disaggregating this component of TSI. The subdivision of the VCSI component according to business segments, however, is not possible because it is not possible to allocate the market value of the firm to different segments in a reliable manner. Thus, while the division of cash flow from operations between major business segments would be a useful additional disclosure in the SIS, a corresponding division of the valuation component of TSI would not appear to be a practical reporting option. But VCSI represents the core component of TSI which investors want to 'understand' and it is therefore important to consider how VCSI can be broken down in a meaningful way. Information provided in existing financial statements, and possibly new accounting disclosures, could be used for this purpose.

First, working capital accruals used in the preparation of the profit and loss account, and usually disclosed in the footnotes to the cash flow statement, can be used to identify components of VCSI which represent non-cash operating funds flows. These accruals represent useful information on 'near cash' transactions which can be viewed as reliable and verifiable components of VCSI. For example, the change in debtors (accounts receivable) resulting from the operations of the business during the year (i.e. excluding any change resulting from company acquisitions or divestitures) can be viewed as part of the VCSI for the period. To see this, note that a credit sale during a period is not part of SCFO for that period but can be viewed as part of the closing equity market value and hence a positive element of VCSI for the period. In the following period, when it is collected, it will be a positive element of SCFO but will be a corresponding negative element of VCSI for that period (i.e. the mere collection of debtors has no impact on TSI). The VCSI for any period will therefore be reduced by the collection of opening debtors and increased by closing debtors. Similarly, change in creditors (accounts payable) and stocks (inventories) can be viewed as part of this relatively reliable and objective component of VCSI which I term the working capital accrual (WCA) component of VCSI.[16]

After identifying the WCA component of VCSI, the remaining (VCSI – WCA) represents (assuming a rational market) change in the present value of future expected cash flows between the beginning and end of the period (excluding, of course, future expected cash flows based on transactions that have already been carried out and reflected in the WCA component of VCSI). As already discussed, some change in value will be expected by the market at the beginning of the period, representing expected economic depreciation of assets due to the passage of time. It is possible that, in some circumstances, the depreciation expense in the published profit and loss account will be a reasonable estimate of this figure, although of course this may not be the case! A second desirable element of VCSI that might be estimated with some plausibility is therefore what I term economic depreciation (EDEP).

We are now left with (VCSI – WCA – EDEP). A third element of VCSI which could be identified are gains or losses in the value of financial assets and liabilities held by the company (i.e. assets and liabilities not related to their primary activities) for which reasonable economic valuations are possible. For traded financial assets and liabilities, this may be straightforward, although for non-traded items (such as pension fund liabilities) value estimation (as in existing published accounts) is required. Denoting these gains or losses on net financial assets as GLNFA, we are now left with (VCSI – WCA – EDEP – GLNFA).

The remainder of the VCSI can be explained by changes in market expectations about future cash flows from existing operations, changes in the cost of capital and changes in the present value of future expected investment opportunities (including real options), assuming a rational and efficient capital market. Clearly, it is not likely that management's estimates of these elements of VCSI will correspond to the market's estimate (only with managerial omniscience and strong form market efficiency would this be the case) and it would probably not be feasible (or desirable) to require a company to disclose its own estimate of these VCSI components. While this might appear at first to be a limitation of capital market performance reporting, I would argue further disaggregation of VCSI entails a shift from capital market performance reporting to capital market performance analysis. This brings us back to the issue of the usefulness and limitations of capital market performance reporting raised in my Introduction and explored briefly in the final section of the chapter.

In summary, implementation of the SIS approach to financial reporting could be enhanced by providing more detailed breakdowns of the cash flow and valuation components of TSI. The cash flow component might be naturally broken down according to business segments but such a breakdown is not possible for VCSI market value and cannot be allocated across segments in a reliable way. Instead the following breakdown of VCSI was suggested:

> Implementation of the SIS approach to financial reporting could be enhanced by providing more detailed breakdowns of the cash flow and valuation components of TSI.

$$VCSI = WCA + EDEP + GLNFA + X$$

where all elements are as previously defined and X represents a crucial residual driven by market expectations (and changes in market expectations) about operating and investment activities and the cost of capital.

The breakdown of X, I would argue, is primarily the concern of shareholder value analysis rather than capital market performance reporting.

4. Is the SIS approach to capital market performance reporting worthwhile? Some concluding comments

In this chapter I have outlined an approach to capital market performance measurement based on the division of TSR or TSI into a realized cash flow element and an unrealized valuation component. I would argue that the proposed reporting system represents a natural application of the concept of 'economic income' to the analysis of corporate financial performance and has the benefit of clarifying the presentation of corporate capital market performance. In order to qualify as a possible candidate for extending financial reporting practice, however, it would be helpful to establish that the approach has potential benefits that outweigh potential costs and/or that the proposal satisfied some societal pressures for change in accounting practices. As a step towards considering these concerns, I suggest the following possible impacts from implementation of SIS-based reporting by companies:

1. greater social visibility of TSR and shareholder value as objectives for business;

2. greater pressure on companies to explain or even challenge their capital market performance;

3. reduced interest in the bottom line of the published profit and loss account but continued interest in the measurement of working capital accruals and

depreciation as an aid to decomposing and interpreting the valuation component of TSI;

4. continued interest in measuring market values of corporate assets and liabilities and estimating economic values for corporate assets and liabilities to facilitate decomposition of the valuation component of TSI; and

5. increased recognition of cash flow and other financial flow data as captured in the proposed Statement of Financial Flows as the core information provided by internal company accounting system.

The first two potential impacts are closely related and really concern the economic and social impact of an increased focus on capital market performance reporting. Broadly, it is reasonable to expect a focus on TSR in financial statements to reinforce 'shareholder value' as an espoused managerial goal and possibly to impact on managerial decision and control processes. Linked to this increased visibility of TSR performance, one might expect greater managerial discussion of their perceptions of the accuracy and fairness of TSR as a measure of economic returns for a particular period. This could encourage companies to voluntarily disclose informally more forward-looking information about their plans and expectations. Interestingly, while an increased focus on TSR in financial reporting might be expected to increase managerial perceptions of the importance of making decisions that add shareholder value, it might also be expected to raise questions from the users of the information about the sources of shareholder value and their social legitimacy. In short, if financial reporting practice is extended to highlight shareholder value generation (and not just historic cost accounting profits), then companies may have a greater need for convincing stories to explain poor TSR performance or to justify good TSR performance.

The next two possible impacts of capital market reporting, numbered 3 and 4, are more focused on the consequences for financial reporting itself than the broader societal impacts. Interestingly, these potential impacts are broadly consistent with current concerns to improve the quality of financial reporting. For example, concern for the quality of accounting accruals (for instance, in relation to the recognition of sales) linked to the accounting scandals at Enron, WorldCom and others and concern for improvements in estimating the value of financial assets and liabilities (for example, in relation to pension accounting) heightened by the weakness in global stock markets are consistent with the objective of a SIS-based reporting system to provide as much (reliable) information as possible on the composition of the valuation component of shareholder income, VCSI. In general, therefore, developments in financial reporting practice aimed at providing 'reasonable' economic valuations of specific assets and liabilities held by a business (and estimates of value transfers resulting from share-based payment systems) increase the potential for decomposing VCSI and highlighting the residual 'unexplained' VCSI based on market expectations of future performance.

The final, fifth, possible impact suggests that a focus on SIS-based reporting might be expected to raise the profile of cash flow data, together with non-cash financial flow data (for example, information on the use of shares to acquire other companies), as vitally important to a reporting approach centred on the analysis of TSR. I have shown that a statement that reports both cash and non-cash transactions, the SFF, pulls together the accounting information required to divide TSR into its cash flow and valuation components. The structure of the SFF emphasizes that it is useful to consider shareholder cash flow from operations as an important source of shareholder financing during the period (in contrast to published cash flow statements which view *only* share capital issued for cash as equity financing). Capital market reporting based on SIS would therefore emphasize the importance of reporting financial flows but the limitations of the existing cash flow statement as a guide to valuation analysis.

In conclusion, I suggest that an extension of financial reporting to incorporate capital market performance reporting based on a Shareholder Income Statement could be a useful development potentially leading to a greater managerial focus on corporate value creation rather than traditional accounting profitability. Interestingly, many of the issues being discussed in relation to the improvement of existing published financial statements are relevant to development of the SIS as a reporting tool. While the TSR focus of the SIS does not provide a panacea in relation to the problems of financial reporting, I would argue that it deserves attention as a potential direction for developing financial reporting practice and that further analysis of the impact of an increased focus on TSR in financial reporting is warranted.

Notes

1   This chapter is based on a paper titled 'A Normative Model for Shareholder Value Accounting' and has benefited from presentations at the 2000 European Accounting Association Annual Congress in Munich, the 2001 British Accounting Association Annual Conference in Nottingham and the 2001 Financial Reporting and Business Communication Conference at Cardiff Business School and seminars at the London Business School,

Lancaster University and Essex University. I would particularly like to thank the editor of this book, Andrew Black, for many interesting discussions on accounting and shareholder value. I would also like to thank Tony Arnold, Neil Garrod, John Grinyer, Gerry Lawson, Brendan McSweeney, Jan Mouritsen, Christopher Napier, John O'Hanlon, Ken Peasnell, Stephen Penman, Peter Pope, Joshua Ronen, Andy Stark, Richard Taffler, Martin Walker and Bob Wearing for helpful comments on the earlier version. Of course, any crimes committed herein are the responsibility of the author. Data used in this chapter have been taken from Datastream International.

2 Stewart, G. B. (1991) *The Quest for Value*. Harper Business.

3 Madden, B. (1999) *CFROI™ Valuation: A Total System Approach to Valuing the Firm*. Butterworth Heinemann. Perhaps the best approaches are those of Stern Stewart's EVA and McKinsey's Economic Profit and cash flow (e.g. the Holt CFROI approach) valuation models (Copeland, T., Koller, T. and Murrin, J. (1994) *Valuation: Measuring and Managing the Value of Companies*. John Wiley & Sons).

4 See O'Hanlon, J. and Peasnell, K. (1998) 'Wall Street's Contribution to Management Accounting: The Stern Stewart EVA®, Financial Management System'. *Management Accounting Research*, 9, pp. 421–44 for a discussion of MVA and other aspects of the Stern Stewart value management system.

5 Madden, op. cit.

6 See, for example, 'The Trouble with Misinterpreting TSR', *Financial Times*, 21 January 2002, p. 18.

7 Hicks, J.R. (1946) *Value and Capital*. Oxford: Clarendon Press.

8 The Holt CFROI system with its focus on cash flow valuation is a fairly natural analysis system to link to reporting system proposed in this chapter. However, any valuation methodology can in principle be used to attempt to explain the valuation component of TSR highlighted by the proposed reporting system.

9 The use of cash and financial flow data as the basis for the shareholder income statement in this chapter can be viewed as building on a UK accounting research literature in the 1980s concerned with the use of cash and funds flow data as the basis for market value based income measurement (Lawson (1985) 'The measurement of corporate performance on a cash flow basis' *Accounting and Business Research*, 15(58): pp. 99–108; Lee, T.A. (1984) *Cash Flow Accounting*, Van Nostrand Reinhold (UK) Co. Ltd; Arnold, A. and Wearing, R. (1988) 'Cash flows, exit prices and British Airways', *Journal of Business Finance and Accounting*, 15 (3):

pp. 311–333; Clubb, C. (1988) 'The potential role of the funds statement in financial reporting', *Omega*, 16(5): pp. 405–419)).

10   Accounting Standards Board (ASB) (1996). Financial Reporting Standard 1 Revised – Cash Flow Statements (FRS 1).

11   Strictly speaking, from a valuation perspective, it could be argued that the impact of interest tax-deductibility ought to be excluded from the tax figure. For presentational ease, this adjustment has not been made here.

12   For the BT example, it has been assumed that cash balances are used to facilitate primary activities and the change in cash has therefore been included as an element of investment in primary activities. Changes in non-cash, highly liquid assets are separately reported as investment in financial assets.

    There are, of course, other potential differences between the investment data reported in the SFS and the investment cash flows reported in cash flow statements. For example, leasing, assets for loans, etc. In general, these items would not appear in the cash flow statement but are relevant financial flows that need to be included in the SFS.

13   See Ijiri, Y. (1978) 'Cash Flow Accounting and Its Structure', *Journal of Accounting, Auditing and Finance*, Summer, pp. 331–48 for an alternative cash flow analysis which is based on this identity and which also emphasizes a valuation perspective.

14   I use the term *equivalent* to 'free cash flow' (FCF) because for a company whose investments includes *non-cash* purchases of assets, the usual definition of FCF as the difference between operating cash flow and the investment *cash flow* is *not* appropriate for *ex ante* valuation. This is simply because future expected FCF defined as the difference between operating cash flow and the investment *cash flow* would include future expected operating cash flows resulting from non-cash investment without deducting the latter. Thus, where a company is expected to make non-cash acquisitions of assets, future estimates of cash flow from operations less all primary asset investment is the relevant aggregate variable to be discounted for valuation of the company's primary assets.

15   Profit for the financial year reported in BT's financial statements for 1998, 1999, 2000 and 2001 were £1,706 million, £2,983 million, £2,050 million and (£1,810 million) respectively. These figures indicate that bottom-line profit was greatly more volatile over this period than shareholder cash flow from operations and more closely related to VCSI (see Table 6.2) during these years than SCFO. It is tempting to conclude that reported profits may have uncritically reflected and/or influenced unwarranted increases in BT's share

price. While it is possible that this was the case, it should, however, be noted that these profit figures were strongly influenced by exceptional items (for example, the 1999 profit of £2,983 million is reduced to £2,236 million after taking out the effect of the profit on disposal of BT's former stake in MCI) and earnings adjusted for exceptional items over the 1994–2000 period as reported by Datastream International, for example, were consistently between £2,000 million and £2,500 million. It can also be argued therefore that neither SCFO nor profit adjusted for exceptional items provide support for the BT price bubble.

16 For the case of a cash purchase of inventory, SCFO is reduced but there is a corresponding increase in VCSI reflecting the conversion of cash into a less liquid asset. When the stock is sold, there is a reduction in VCSI equal to the cost of the stock and either an increase in SCFO equal to sales revenue for cash sales or an increase in VCSI for credit sales. When creditors increase due to a credit purchase of inventory, there is no effect on VCSI as the increase in inventory is offset by the increase in creditors.

7

ACCOUNTING AT ENERGY FIRMS AFTER ENRON:

IS THE 'CURE' WORSE THAN THE 'DISEASE'?[1]

RICHARD BASSETT and MARK STORRIE
Risktoolz

Introduction

The collapse of Enron in December 2001 amid a flurry of accusations of misleading accounting, unreliable financial disclosures and probable criminal behaviour has rocked wholesale energy markets and contributed to a downturn in worldwide equity markets. Are the global market reactions predicated on the notion that Enron was just the tip of the iceberg? Are Enron, WorldCom, Adelphia, Global Crossing and a few others just the first of many corporations to be caught 'cooking the books'? If so, falling equity prices may be a reflection of the expectation on the part of investors of a correction in endemically misleading US corporate accounting and disclosure policies. Alternatively, if the problem is not one of systemic corporate corruption and the vast majority of business people and corporations are honest and responsible, the downturn in the US equity markets may actually reflect fear of too many government interventions in a market already working diligently to right itself.

> **Are the global market reactions predicated on the notion that Enron was just the tip of the iceberg?**

The accounting and disclosure issues that the Enron scandal has created are the focus of this chapter. The ultimate goal is to attempt to answer the following questions: are current equity market woes driven by a fear of more 'Enrons' and 'too little post-Enron action' or by the fear of too much overreaction to Enron? In answering that question, the point of departure is an examination of what Enron itself allegedly did wrong: what exactly were Enron's accounting and disclosure sins that are believed to be lurking in so many other companies?

After a summary of what went wrong at Enron, the focus shifts to the bigger issue of *what is wrong with mandated accounting rules* themselves. We argue that earnings can never be more than opinion and that cash flows are the real basis for corporate valuations. With that in mind, we examine some commonly misleading accounting aggregates and explore the central role played by cash flows in modern corporate finance. We then examine what a cash flow analysis of Enron would have shown in 2001, as compared to the firm's stated and misleading earnings releases.

> **What exactly were Enron's accounting and disclosure sins that are believed to be lurking in so many other companies?**

We then turn to how estimates of future cash flows are reflected in equity prices. Specifically, consideration is given to how Enron's stock price 'processed' information in a manner quite different from the way Wall Street analysts, rating agencies, regulators and other spectators did. We also analyse the political response to Enron, first by evaluating whether the accounting and disclosure problems that beset Enron appear to be systemic in the United States and then, after concluding the problem is *not* a systemic one, by considering some of the problems and risks of political overreaction to Enron.

Accounting and disclosure at Enron

The current debate over the adequacy of accounting and disclosure in the USA crosses both industry lines and company types and derives not just from Enron but also the collapse of WorldCom, Global Crossing and Tyco as well as several other recent public disasters. But Enron was the first and, arguably, far and away the most important and complex. The black cloud it created now hangs over all US corporations, but there is little doubt that energy companies have borne the greatest part of the brunt through the impact on their equity value, debt ratings, costs of funding and liquidity issues. Accordingly, we begin by analysing Enron's sins.

> The primary areas in which Enron misled investors can be separated into four categories.

In brief, Enron's senior management and others engaged in a systematic attempt to use various accounting and reporting techniques to mislead investors. The primary areas in which Enron misled investors can be separated into four categories, most of which pertain to the company's energy market activities:

- *Wash and roundtrip trades.* These are transactions in which there is no real counterparty. Mainly in electricity markets, Enron appears to have essentially been 'trading with itself' in a number of cases, seemingly to inflate its revenues and possibly its asset values without generating any tangible economic benefits.

- *Mark-to-market accounting.* At least in some cases, Enron improperly applied the useful and well-accepted principle of marking certain open energy transactions to their current market values to create false accounting results.

- *Revenue recognition.* Enron apparently booked trading revenues on many energy transactions when the deals were first consummated instead of waiting for the actual economic profits to be earned over the life of the transaction.

- *Special purpose entities.* Enron used at least certain 'special purpose entities' inappropriately to facilitate improper wash trades and mark-to-market accounting. In addition, Enron appears to have used these types of structures outside its energy activities to hide its total indebtedness and to inflate certain asset values.

To illustrate how Enron could have used the above techniques to enhance earnings and inflate its balance sheet, we have constructed a simple example. Suppose Enron enters into a seven-year weather derivatives transaction with a firm at an agreed price of $120 million when the 'true' value of the same transaction is $100 million.[2] Suppose the counterparty firm is a special purpose entity (SPE) owned by Enron and established solely for the purpose of conducting transactions with Enron. Then, the transaction is a wash trade – the total cash flows and risks to Enron when considered across the company and the SPE are unaffected by the transaction. The SPE thus does not care whether the $120 million price is correct – it is taking no risk. Enron, however, could book a profit of $20 million to reflect the immediate realization of the increase in the contract's value above its fair value. Note that because this $120 million is an actual transaction price, this profit would be based on the market value of the transaction and not just on its mark-to-market revaluation.

The above transaction makes sense only under certain circumstances. First, the SPE must be essentially a part of Enron. Otherwise, the shareholders of the SPE will never agree to the terms of the initial transaction. Because derivatives transactions are a zero-sum game,[3] an immediate gain of $20 million for Enron implies an immediate loss for the SPE. Second, Enron must not be consolidating the financial statements of the SPE into its own balance sheet; otherwise, the $20 million gain for Enron would just wash with the $20 million loss the SPE takes.

Finally, this transaction makes sense only for highly illiquid and customized transactions in which the 'true' value of the deal is not easily observable. If no one else was actively trading seven-year weather derivatives, Enron's internal or external auditor or internal risk managers might well have accepted that this was a reasonable market price. But if a liquid market quote had revealed the true value of an otherwise identical trade to be $100 million, then the $120 million valuation likely would have been questioned. The next step would be for Enron to extrapolate from this single trade to revalue its whole book of seven-year weather derivatives. If this book or portfolio had a prior value of $1 billion, the whole book could now be marked to market at $1.2 billion on the basis of the $120 million price of the transaction between Enron and the SPE. This would create a *notional* profit of $200 million for Enron.

This illustrative transaction would create an accounting profit of $200 million for Enron, but it would actually be cash negative. Enron or others would normally incur a minimum of two cash costs to achieve that notional profit – a bonus to the people involved in creating the notional profit and the transaction costs of the deal itself. In an accounting framework this could be depicted as a success at a certain point in time, usually at the end of an accounting period.

However, in an economic, or cash flow, framework, that transaction would be value destroying. Although the only people harmed by this fiction are the Enron shareholders, not the overall market, behaviour that rewards people for accounting fiction instead of economic value creation would send a signal to others at Enron to create further transactions with similar value-destroying characteristics.

The Powers Report, commissioned by the Enron board of directors to investigate the activities of Enron's former chief financial officer, Andrew Fastow, describes the accounting-driven behaviour at Enron as follows:

> Many of the most significant transactions apparently were designed to accomplish favorable financial statement results, not to achieve bona fide economic objectives or to transfer risk. Some transactions were designed so that, had they followed applicable accounting rules, Enron could have kept assets and liabilities (especially debt) off its balance sheet; but the transactions did not follow those rules.

Other transactions were implemented – improperly, we are informed by our accounting advisers – to offset losses. They allowed Enron to conceal from the market very large losses resulting from Enron's merchant investments by creating an appearance that those investments were hedged – that is, that a third party was obliged to pay Enron the amount of the losses – when in fact that third party was simply an entity in which only Enron had a substantial economic stake. We believe these transactions resulted in Enron reporting earnings from the third quarter of 2000 through to the third quarter of 2001 that were almost $1 billion higher than should have been reported.[4]

The Powers Report continues:

> *Asset Sales.* Enron sold assets to LJM [an SPE controlled by Andrew Fastow] that it wanted to remove from its books. The transactions often occurred close to the end of the reporting period . . . Enron bought back five of the seven assets after the close of the financial reporting period, in some cases within a matter of months; the LJM

partnerships made a profit on every transaction, even when the asset it had purchased appears to have declined in market value.[5]

Those quotes reveal the accounting mindset that continues to dominate discussions about Enron. Notably, 'Some transactions were designed so that, had they followed applicable accounting rules, Enron could have kept the assets and liabilities (especially debt) off its balance sheet; but the transactions did not follow those rules.' In other words, all this deception could not have worked if Enron had followed the accounting rules. However, had it followed the rules, Enron would still not have achieved a bona fide economic result. The company would still have achieved only an accounting result. That is indicative of how the rules-based system that guides US GAAP (generally accepted accounting principles) has conditioned people to look not at whether the information presented to the market is a true and fair characterization of the condition of the company, but at whether it complies with the rules. By contrast, if the overriding guidance had been principles-based – as in some other countries such as the UK – it is more likely that managers and professionals would simply have seen Enron's behaviour for what it was, a deceptive and fraudulent practice. More important, if the measure of success is not adherence to accounting rules and government regulation but adherence to investor concerns, we would measure success in terms of delivering the highest sustainable risk-adjusted returns, not merely in terms of a pure compliance standard.

Accounting versus cash flows

Accounting is not an exact science. Current accounting standards are a combination of rules and guidelines that run to many thousands of dense pages. A great deal of the complexity inherent in current accounting practice is the result of legislation at the state, federal and international levels concerning taxes, the regulation of capital markets, corporate governance, social programmes, health and safety and environmental and pension issues, among many others. For accounting standards to incorporate all the variables inherent in this constantly changing landscape while still providing a framework that can fulfil its original role of reporting historical information to investors is difficult.

Different companies have different needs, and, as a result, all accounting rules cannot be universally applied in lockstep to all firms. That is why the US rules are referred to as 'generally accepted' accounting principles. For example, a rule that all fixed capital assets must be depreciated over ten years would not suit a steel mill for which 20 years may be more appropriate, and depreciating laptop computers over 10 years would be equally unrealistic. From an economic (i.e. cash flow) viewpoint, depreciation is a non-cash charge and does not affect cash flow, whereas from an accounting viewpoint, depreciation choices can make a significant difference to the accounting 'bottom line'. Depreciation schedules are one simple example of an area in which companies and accounting practitioners are left to make some reasonable judgements. Managers and auditors know that in making most of those judgements they will alter the earnings results, and many will alter the balance sheet as well. However, most of those judgements will not alter the cash flow of a business. Hence the increasingly well-known phrase, first recorded in the 1890s: *Earnings are an opinion, cash flow is a fact.*

A sample list of standard accounting issues and how those issues affect earnings and cash flows is given in Table 7.1.[6] Most of those issues require managers and auditors to make judgements, and some of those judgements are based on assumptions about the future, for example outcomes of litigation,

TABLE 7.1
Impact of accounting variables on earnings and cash flows

Issue	Change in earnings	Change in cash flow
Depreciation – at least three choices and variations within them	Yes	No
Revenue recognition – on long-term contracts, prepayments, advances, etc.	Yes	No
Mark-to-market – straightforward in liquid markets, but in illiquid markets requires application of formulas and a range of assumptions	Yes	No
Affiliated transactions – transfer pricing and royalties, implications for tax and international issues	Yes	Possibly, because of tax issues
Pensions – the asset and liability sides can both be overstated or understated; requires a judgement on future returns of the fund and future liabilities of the fund	Yes	No
Valuation of foreign assets – considerations of useful life, exchange rates and taxation issues	Yes	No

TABLE 7.1 CONTINUED

Issue	Change in earnings	Change in cash flow
Securitization of receivables or other items – revenue, risk, horizon and liability issues	Yes	Yes
Foreign exchange – beginning, mid and end periods are all usually different and the managerial decisions about how and when to recognize gains and are often material	Eventually, but the changes in the balance sheet may be more significant	Yes in terms of repatriation of cash but not necessarily losses in terms of local currency
Treatment of stock options – expensing, valuing, recording	Yes	No
Goodwill – the accounting rationale for the difference between the book and the economic value	Yes	No
Amortization of goodwill	Yes	No
Income taxes – deferred, in dispute, tax credits	Yes	Yes
Litigation – estimates and provisions of liability and outcomes	Yes	Not until realized
Customer returns and product defects	Yes	Not until realized
Leases – capitalized versus operating	Yes	No
Allowance for bad debts – customers	Yes	No
Provisions and write-downs – in banks for loan losses	Yes	No, the money is already gone
Reserves – in insurance companies	Yes	Possibly
Product liability and other contingent liabilities	Yes	No
Impairment of long-lived assets – i.e. you paid too much and now you need to write it down	Yes	No, you already paid the money; this is just the accounting reconciliation of failure

health and pension liabilities, foreign asset values and environmental costs. Those assumptions are virtually always detailed in the notes to the annual report and in various regulatory filings and have been for decades. The difficulty is that, as the complexity of legislation and regulation has increased, this analysis has become more difficult and time-consuming. The unfortunate consequence is the continuing use and growth of certain types of investor shorthand, of which the most prominent are price-to-earnings (P/E) multiples; earnings per share (EPS) numbers; and earnings before interest, taxes, depreciation and amortization (EBITDA).

The shortcomings of P/E and EPS as true measures of value have been well documented over the past 40 years.[7] EBITDA warrants more up-to-date attention because of the prominent role it has played in recent years in promoting the telecoms, media and technology sectors and the false assertion that it is a measure equivalent to cash flow. The reliability of EBITDA as a measure was recently summed up by Warren Buffett: 'Among those who talk about EBITDA . . . and those who don't, there are more frauds among those who do. Either they're trying to con you, or they're conning themselves.'[8] Buffett, like many other investors, recognizes that the variability of earnings makes EBITDA an unreliable measure. Using Enron's figures as an example, EBITDA is contrasted with free cash flow (i.e. cash available to a company that is not required for operations or for reinvestment) in Table 7.2. The wide disparity in the results serves to remind us that accounting is the starting point of an investment analysis, not the end point.

> Buffett, like many other investors, recognizes that the variability of earnings makes EBITDA an unreliable measure.

TABLE 7.2
Enron's EBITDA versus free cash flows ($m)

	1997	1998	1999	2000
EBITDA	615	2,205	1,672	2,808
Free cash flow	(5,717)	1,986	(1,108)	(5,256)

Modern corporate finance and discounted cash flow analysis

Academics and market practitioners have dramatically advanced our understanding of how markets work and investors behave, which makes it dismaying that the contributions of financial economists have played little or no role in the current public debate. Contributions by Nobel Prize-winning economists such as Harry Markowitz (diversification theory),[9] William Sharpe and John Lintner (the capital asset pricing model)[10] and Merton Miller and Franco Modigliani (the relation between the value of a firm and its capital structure)[11] have been largely ignored in the public post-Enron debate. Yet, as we will discuss later, the markets performed much as financial economists would have expected by consistently reducing the value of Enron, WorldCom and other corporations to reflect their worsening future prospects, deteriorating cash generation, and increasing risks.

Financial economists observe and measure market behaviour over long periods of time and have developed and tested a range of tools for analysing investments with explicit measures of risk and return. The financial economics definition of the value of a business or an investment is *the present value of a stream of expected future cash flows discounted at an appropriate rate.* That is not the same as a stream of earnings, a multiple of the balance sheet or a multiple of past results. Valuation is future-oriented and based on expected results – keep in mind that investors cannot earn last year's dividends or cash flows, only those of future years. That is not just an academic measure; it is also a description of how the market actually values investments. To take an example, Warren Buffett, when asked how to value a company at the April 2002 Berkshire Hathaway Annual Meeting, gave the same answer he has been giving for decades: 'You just want to estimate a company's cash flows over time, discount them back, and buy for less than that.'[12]

Every mainstream corporate finance textbook chooses discounted cash flow (DCF) analysis as its preferred measure for valuation or investment analysis.[13] However, there is no alchemy in this formulation that turns those who apply it into stock market geniuses – forecasts always require judgements, and some people are better at forecasting than others. However, DCF analysis does provide us with a valid economic framework within which to consider our forecasts of an investment or company's expected future returns so that we can price the opportunity. A DCF analysis has two requirements: establishing a financial framework for the analysis and generating the inputs to populate the framework.

> A DCF analysis has two requirements: establishing a financial framework for the analysis and generating the inputs to populate the framework.

Setting the framework requires a reasonable understanding of finance and includes:

- creating a free cash flow format (the first step is normally translating the income statement and balance sheet information into free cash flow);

- estimating an appropriate discount rate (the minimum expected risk-adjusted rate of return);

- selecting a forecast horizon (the length of the forecast reflects the company's competitive advantage, and the forecast horizon will affect the value);

- selecting a residual or terminal value method (the most conservative – normally perpetuation – is usually the most appropriate given the total percentage of the value that this calculation represents); and

- choosing a capital structure – that is, the mix of debt and equity – ideally by iterating to an 'optimal' capital structure and reflecting this target capital structure in the estimate of the discount rate.

The art of the analysis comes in making the forecast of sales, costs, fixed and working capital investments and taxes. In the past 20 years the growth of computer models has made the first part of this process comparatively easy.[14] The second stage of the analysis, however, involves the quantification of strategic assumptions. A standard strategic analysis can often be gleaned from an analyst's report, or a five-year forecast can simply be taken from a Value Line tear sheet and used for a 'quick and dirty' valuation. Do investors use those approaches? We think that WorldCom provides a clear example of the difference between, on the one hand, investor expectations and the cash-flow-driven analyses that drive equity markets and, on the other hand, the accounting reports that drive regulators and rating agencies. For example, in January 1999, WorldCom stock was worth $75 per share. On the day before the firm announced a $3.9 billion restatement of revenues, the shares were worth $0.83. While the announced earnings restatement dramatically altered WorldCom's reported earnings and EBITDA, *the accounting restatement did not change its cash flows by a single dollar*.

Similarly, the incremental announcements of more wrongdoing at WorldCom look suspiciously like efforts by the insolvency practitioners to overstate the difficulties of the firm as virtually none of these make a material difference to the cash balances or cash generation of the remainder of WorldCom. The market reality is that investors had been anticipating and reacting to the value destruction in WorldCom's operating strategy for years before the accounting restatement or the arrival of the insolvency 'experts'.

TABLE 7.3
Enron's cash flow analysis ($m)

	1998	1999	2000
Revenues			
Natural gas and other products	13,276	19,536	50,500
Electricity	13,939	15,238	33,823
Metals	0	0	9,234
Other	4,045	5,338	7,232
Total revenues	31,260	40,112	100,789
Less non-cash revenues	(1,984)	(2,533)	(4,794)
Cash revenues	29,276	37,579	95,995
Cash cost of sales	26,381	34,761	94,517
Cash gross margin (deficit)	2,895	2,818	1,478
Operating expenses	2,473	3,045	3,184
Cash operating income (loss)	422	(227)	(1,706)

Cash flows at Enron

Table 7.3 was constructed from Enron's public cash flow statements in its *2000 Annual Report*[15] and from several of the firm's 2000 filings with the SEC. Then, from a reading of the notes in the annual report, we made judgements based on the information provided about cash and *non-cash revenues* and transactions. The impact of non-cash revenues recorded and accepted by Enron's independent auditor, Arthur Andersen, LLP, are highlighted in grey in Table 7.3.[16]

Further, for the years ending 31 December 1998, 1999 and 2000, Enron disclosed pre-tax gains from sales of merchant assets and investments totalling $628 million, $756 million and $104 million, respectively, all of which are included in 'Other revenues'.[17] Proceeds from those sales were $1,838 million, $2,217 million and $1,434 million, respectively. In each year, the gains on sales from merchant assets and investments *exceeded the whole of Enron's annualized earnings figures!* The combination of the notes and the reported statements would lead to the results given in Table 7.4.

TABLE 7.4
Enron's net income and cash flows ($m)

	1998	1999	2000
Net income	703	893	979
Enron cash flows	(205)	(815)	(2,306)

The steady growth in net income from year to year may look good to accountants, but investors follow cash flow. The more erratic and deteriorating cash position at Enron gave a truer picture of the firm's performance. Investors could also have read in Note 1 from Enron's *2000 Annual Report* the following:

> *Accounting for Price Risk Management.* Enron engages in price risk management activities for both trading and non-trading purposes. Instruments utilized in connection with trading activities are accounted for using the mark-to-market method. Under the mark-to-market method of accounting, forwards, swaps, options, energy transportation contracts utilized for trading activities and other instruments with third parties are reflected at fair value and are shown as 'Assets and Liabilities from Price Risk Management Activities' in the Consolidated Balance Sheet. These activities also include the commodity risk management component embedded in energy outsourcing contracts. Unrealized gains and losses from newly originated contracts, contract restructurings and the impact of price movements are recognized as 'Other Revenues.' Changes in the assets and liabilities from price risk management activities result primarily from changes in the valuation of the portfolio of contracts, newly originated transactions and the timing of settlement relative to the receipt of cash for certain contracts. The market prices used to value these transactions reflect management's best estimate considering various factors including closing exchange and over-the-counter quotations, time value and volatility factors underlying the commitments.[18]

In 2000 and 2001 this note attracted the attention of some analysts who recognized that there was a risk that the values of some of Enron's positions could have been overstated. As noted previously, one reason for that attention was the lack of any real market for some of the financial instruments in which Enron traded. Enron's own assumptions, estimates, calculations, and questionable wash trades thus allowed it to manufacture valuations.

In addition, as the note suggests, unrealized gains or losses on newly recognized transactions were booked by Enron to 'Other revenue'. Even for a *fairly* priced derivatives transaction, such up-front 'gains' would actually represent a risk premium paid to Enron for bearing the risk that the transaction could move substantially against it. Nevertheless, Enron still treated those risk premiums as gains when transactions were first initiated.

Stress-testing the balance sheet

If an analyst becomes uncomfortable with discrepancies between reported accounting profits and the risk that there is no underlying operating cash generation in some transactions, he normally turns to the balance sheet to 'stress-test' the result. Stress-testing the balance sheet – particularly one composed largely of financial assets – is done from a cash liquidation viewpoint.

> Stress-testing the balance sheet is done from a cash liquidation viewpoint.

Adopting that stance together with a more principles-based accounting philosophy as opposed to a pure compliance philosophy should have led to a different interpretation of Enron's numbers. First, Note 1 implies that the value of the $9 billion in current assets listed as 'Assets from price risk management activities' may have been overstated by as much as 25%, or approximately $2 billion.

Second, it would have been reasonable to assume that in a position of financial distress the $7.1 billion of long-term investments in the form of advances to unconsolidated affiliates would become unrecoverable. (Such assets are probably largely illiquid.) Accordingly, the cash value could have been marked down by as much as 50% of book value, to approximately $3.5 billion. Indeed, early in 2001 analysts were questioning Enron's management on the value of those assets, as there was a suspicion that a significant portion of them was in failed dotcoms, fibre-optic capacity or other technology-related investments for which 90% drops in value during 2000 were not uncommon. Enron remained true to its accounting view of the world, however, and resisted market suggestions to write those positions down. But the market, in turn, remained true to its economic view of risk and return and wrote down the value of Enron's stock to reflect the deterioration in those and other assets.

Third, $9.7 billion in long-term investments was 'Assets from price risk management activities'. Those were the assets most likely to have been overstated because of false mark-to-market or wash trades. Those assets also were presumably less liquid than other assets and probably represented the highest proportion of assets in which no other firm was making a market. In the extreme case of a short-term asset liquidation, the cash realized could have been as much as 50% less than the amount stated on the balance sheet ($4.9 billion). As a rule of thumb, assuming a 50% discount for the liquidation value of contracts in which the firm is essentially the sole market maker is reasonable.

Fourth, Enron booked $3.5 billion of 'goodwill'. Goodwill is largely a meaningless number to anyone other than an accountant as it represents cash that has gone out of the door to purchase a company for more than its net asset value. As virtually no company has a value that is equal to or less than net asset value, merger and acquisition (M&A) transactions almost always create goodwill. As studies by McKinsey, BCG, KPMG and Deloitte have shown, more than 65% of M&A transactions fail to

> Goodwill is largely a meaningless number to anyone other than an accountant as it represents cash that has gone out of the door to purchase a company for more than its net asset value.

deliver value to the buyer.[19] Given this backdrop of probable economic failure, listing goodwill as an asset, particularly in a distress situation, produces highly suspect figures for goodwill, which is in itself a somewhat spurious concept. Notwithstanding the evidence, in the United States the buyer in a corporate transaction can list goodwill on its balance sheet as an asset. Managers at Enron, WorldCom and Global Crossing clearly thought this important because it inflated their balance sheets. However, while accountants, regulators and rating agencies care much about this, markets do not pay much attention to those figures. Table 7.5[20] shows the scores of billions of dollars written off the asset values of JDS Uniphase, AOL, Lucent and Vivendi in recent years. In each of those cases and others, the fall in the equity value reflecting the loss of goodwill always occurred far in advance of the actual accounting write-down.

TABLE 7.5
Goodwill write-offs and changes in market capitalization*

Company	Market capitalization	Goodwill write-off	Change in market capitalization	Change in market capitalization
	($bn)	($bn)	($bn)	(%)
AOL	103	54	3.18	3
JDS Uniphase	12	50	0.82	6.8
Lucent	22	10	0.73	3.3
Vivendi	35.5	13	2.84	8

*Note: changes in market capitalization are from one day before write-off to one day after the announcement.

JDS provides the strongest indication that the market recognizes value destruction faster than do accountants, rating agencies or investment bankers. At the time of the firm's $50 billion write-down, its market capitalization was only $12 billion, less than one-sixth the book value of the equity; the change in value at the announcement of the $50 billion write-down was less than $1 billion. Enron, with its accounting-oriented mindset, strongly resisted making these write-downs, but the market did so by reducing the firm's share value. In our view, goodwill should have a zero cash value in a distress situation. So we would reduce the $3.5 billion in goodwill on Enron's balance sheet to zero. Finally, the cash value of the $5.6 billion of 'Other' could have been overstated by as much as 25%, depending on the assumptions used to value 'Other'. From 1997 to 2000 it appears that less than 25%, or $1.4 billion, of the 'Other' actually had a cash value. A reduction of only $1.4 billion thus may be too generous.

The five points above certainly do not constitute an exhaustive balance-sheet stress test, notably because we have not considered liabilities at all. But even with that simple analysis, it is easy to see where pessimistic assumptions about Enron's balance sheet could have led to a reduction in assets of $15 billion that would have eliminated 100% of its equity book value and made the firm technically insolvent long before the company filed for Chapter 11 bankruptcy.

The role of the equity market

Some observers may contend that the analysis of Enron's cash flows in the prior section is easy to do *ex post* but would have been hard to undertake *ex ante*. Hindsight, after all, is 20/20. Some observers argue further that the DCF approach is really just one of many valuation methods. But, in fact, there is a compelling reason to believe that the most important processor of information about corporate performance – the stock market – does indeed reflect a cash-flow-based approach. Indeed, movements in Enron's share price strongly suggest that the equity market saw through many of Enron's accounting machinations many months before its illegal operating and accounting practices were formally acknowledged. While the accountants, regulators and rating agencies were on the sidelines, the equity market was anticipating a steep fall in Enron's fortunes. By 14 August 2001, Enron's market capitalization had declined by almost 40% from $62 billion to $38 billion. By contrast, other stocks in the US energy sector were basically unchanged to slightly higher for the year to date. By the date of the accounting restatement – 8 November 2001 – the share price was down 90% (market capitalization down $56 billion) from 1 January 2001. When Enron lost its investment-grade credit rating in late November 2001, the equity was virtually worthless.

> Movements in Enron's share price strongly suggest that the equity market saw through many of Enron's accounting machinations many months before its illegal operating and accounting practices were formally acknowledged.

Throughout 2001 investors in Enron appear to have been more concerned about the firm's future prospects than about current results. Enron continued to post double-digit growth and EPS numbers throughout 2001, but the share price continued to fall. Investors appear to have been particularly concerned about the following Enron-specific issues:

- the firm's cash-negative position, despite Enron's reported double-digit earnings growth in each quarter of 2001;

- declines in sales profit margins from 5% to 1% over the prior five years;

- the potential overvaluation of some assets on Enron's balance sheet and suggestions that debt was understated;

- the possibility of conflict-of-interest issues with the firm's SPEs; and

- the overall risk/return characteristics of the business, given the failures in dot-coms and fibre-optic markets, suggesting that the firm was actually making investment returns below its cost of capital and had been for some time.

Yet while the market was sending clear signals of concern about Enron and its future prospects, Enron's external auditor, Andersen, did not qualify any of the quarterly reports or resign as the company's auditor. Nor did the SEC launch an informal inquiry into third-party transactions until 22 October 2001, or a formal inquiry until 31 October 2001. The rating agencies, moreover, did not downgrade Enron below investment grade until 28 November 2001, only days before its bankruptcy.

Equity investors were focused largely on future prospects while regulators appeared to be focused on past events and how they were reported. Enron's management continued to be 'laser-focused on earnings per share',[21] while investors reduced the value of the shares. In short, there is strong reason to believe that, despite Enron's attempts to fool the market, the firm had not entirely succeeded in that endeavour.

> Equity investors were focused largely on future prospects while regulators appeared to be focused on past events and how they were reported.

The political reaction and 'corporate reform'

'When Dr Johnson said that patriotism was the last refuge of the scoundrel', an American senator once remarked, 'he overlooked the immense possibilities of the word "reform".'[22] Despite the sound performance of equity markets in accurately processing the information available and pricing the risk in Enron or WorldCom, while the compliance-driven accounting and disclosure rules failed to reflect those risks, the political focus has remained squarely on the measures and bodies that failed, instead of on reinforcing the measures and groups that processed the available information in the most timely fashion – that is, the equity and debt markets. On the day after WorldCom's $3.9 billion revenue restatement announcement (27 June 2002), the SEC issued an order that required officers at almost 1,000 of the largest publicly traded companies to file sworn statements attesting to the truthfulness of their accounting and disclosure policies by 14 August 2002. In addition to increasing market volatility and imposing huge legal and accounting costs on shareholders, that misguided action effectively entrenches the measures and positions of the bodies that failed the shareholders of Enron, WorldCom and others. Perversely, accounting is now more important than ever, and auditors will be significant beneficiaries of the 'reform' as the cost of audits and internal management increases, all at the expense of shareholders.

Further, that action reinforces the widespread perception among many politicians, commentators and the general public that the problems at Enron, WorldCom and other companies are somehow 'systemic' in nature – that is, broadly representative of a much bigger problem endemic to US corporate governance. Can this proposition be supported?

Is there a systemic problem in the United States?

The notion that corporate irresponsibility is relatively more widespread in the United States than elsewhere is based more on assertion than on any hard empirical evidence. Indeed, many observers would consider existing US laws to already be on the conservative side compared with other international corporate law regimes. One recent study,[23] for example, examined the accounts of more than 70,000 companies from 31 countries from 1990 to 1999, specifically to evaluate the relations between accounting practice, legal protections and quality of investor protection. The authors of that study concluded that the United States and Great Britain experienced the lowest deviations between corporate cash flows and reported earnings. In other words, in comparison with companies in the other 29 countries, companies in the United States and Great Britain appear to engage the least in 'earnings management'. In addition, on the question of the rights afforded to outside investors, the United States, Great Britain, Canada, Hong Kong, India, Pakistan and South Africa all scored top marks. Although there is always room for improvement, that study and a number of similar ones[24] suggest that the problem may not be quite as widespread in the United States as some commentators would have us believe. When considering the implications of actions such as the recent SEC requirement for sworn statements by company CEOs and CFOs, it is useful to think about the reporting requirements a typical Fortune 1000 company *already faces*. On average, each of those companies has more than 100 legal entities or business units and operates in more than 50 countries. The ownership interest in each entity is often less than 100%, which means that decisions about certain accounting issues are not solely the domain of the US partner – and all of the other countries have different accounting standards. Even the translation from the Canadian or English GAAP to the US GAAP is a non-trivial task.

As noted earlier, hundreds if not thousands of judgements are made about revenue recognition, cost allocations, capital structures and other issues in each of those individual entities and again at a consolidated, or holding company, level. Frankly, the notion that a CEO or CFO at a large company could reasonably 'certify' a company's accounts on pain of imprisonment could be propagated only by someone with no practical knowledge of accounting and reporting or no practical understanding that that type of order costs real time and substantial money, all of which achieves, at best, a spurious result. Because the new disclosures are being required under the pain of severe personal penalties for non-compliance, the most likely result will be a significant number of restatements as CEOs and CFOs move from an accounting stance that may have been overly optimistic to one that is likely to be overly cautious. That does not mean that they lied or misrepresented their accounts before; it is simply a recognition that accounting requires, by definition, managerial choices, and the bias of those choices will have shifted. Regulatory moves such as the required SEC disclosures have already imparted significant volatility to US equity markets. Companies will be extremely cautious about what they say, and that could further undermine investor confidence in the future performance of the firms – for no good reason. Unfortunately, that in turn could reinforce claims that there is a systemic failure in corporate governance and have the undesirable result of reinforcing in the public mindset the idea that political intervention is the only answer.

Voluntary versus political responses

Legislative or regulatory efforts to mandate 'more responsible corporate behaviour' are not the only way to restore confidence in corporate America. In fact, many proposals – including the Sarbanes-Oxley Corporate Reform Act of 2002 – will probably achieve the opposite result. At a series of SEC round-table functions held prior to passage of the Sarbanes-Oxley Act,[25] the clear and overriding opinion of the participants was that it was the job of market participants, not government, to make credible changes. Numerous changes were, in fact, under way even before the Sarbanes-Oxley Act was passed. Consider some examples:

- Many corporations had already passed resolutions restricting the granting of contracts to their auditors for non-audit-related consulting work.

- The boards of the New York Stock Exchange and the National Association of Securities Dealers Automated Quotation System proposed changes, received feedback and adopted a series of new rules on the independence of corporate directors, the operation and organization of audit committees, and other pro-shareholder-power-oriented initiatives.[26]

- Many securities firms had already adopted the practice of declaring on their reports when they acted for a company in an investment banking or other capacity.

- The rating agencies, notably Standard and Poor's, had already moved to bring their data on company accounts closer to a cash flow result. Moody's went further with its purchase of KMV for a reported $200 million. KMV models and databases are intended to aid in the credit-rating process by providing explicit guidance, based on equity market movements, to debt issuers and lenders on expected default rates.[27]

In short, the market was already working to heal itself in response to its constituents: shareholders. By contrast, the Sarbanes-Oxley Act contains provisions that will measurably harm investors:

- The act will reduce the *quality* of reports in favour of increasing the quantity. Because accounting is not a precise science and judgements must be made, for executives to avoid any personal risk, the *quality* of the information they provide in their filings may be reduced and the language may become even more guarded to reduce the threat of legal action against senior executives, all of which will increase the quantity of reporting and make the reports less accessible to the average reader.

- The legislation will exacerbate the divide between shareholders and the managerial custodians of their businesses. Managers may be forced to choose between the desires of shareholders for information and shareholders' demand for ongoing improvements in operating performance. The severity of the regulatory demands with their threats of jail and personal bankruptcy are tilting the scales in favour of form filing over value creation. Inevitably, senior managers will spend less time running the business and more time with their lawyers than with their shareholders.

- The new accounting oversight body will impose direct costs on publicly traded companies, as well as indirect costs through increased and unnecessary compliance costs and the cost in management time – all of which will ultimately be shouldered by the shareholders. In addition, efforts by US companies to compete with one another through creative voluntary disclosures will stagnate in the face of a super-regulator dictating accounting policy. In other words, the current compliance-based system will become *even more compliance based*, despite the obvious benefits presented earlier of a more principles-based approach.

- Global capital flows into the United States will be inhibited by the new law. The vagaries of accounting interpretation and ambiguities in the American legal system will surely lead prudent non-US issuers to review the status of their US listings. The overwhelming business opinion outside the United States before the passage of this act was *already* that the US legal system is highly politicized and actively discriminates against non-US defendants (note US asbestos, trade and environmental rulings). According to the International Relations Department of the NYSE, more than 10% of the securities on the exchange – $1.2 trillion of securities – are from non-US firms. In light of Sarbanes-Oxley, all non-US-domiciled company boards should reconsider the value of any US listing as the legal risk and shareholder costs to maintain those listings are probably too high to justify continuing them.

- The act is also the twenty-first-century equivalent of economic imperialism, as it arbitrarily dictates the standard of behaviour to non-US accounting bodies, foreign-owned companies and non-American executives.

The worst aspect of the Sarbanes-Oxley Act is that it will, through section 401 on disclosures, actually reduce the ability of companies to

> The worst aspect of the Sarbanes-Oxley Act is that it will, through section 401 on disclosures, actually reduce the ability of companies to provide reasonable guidance on their future prospects to investors and potential investors.

provide reasonable guidance on their future prospects to investors and potential investors. The fear of being sentenced to a prison term of up to 25 years will be a major disincentive to providing any information that could be refuted later. Valuing the firm by forecasting the cash flows and discounting them back at an appropriate rate to a present value just got harder. Investors will have less information about the long-term prospects of a firm, which will in turn reduce their ability to price investments, thus making investors more focused on short-term results, increasing the volatility of stock prices, and, most perversely, increasing the power of Wall Street analysts.

Conclusion

In the pursuit of short-term accounting targets and annual bonuses, Enron executives harmed the wholesale energy markets, damaged the credibility of the derivatives markets, and handed the friends of regulation a powerful political weapon – 'corporate sleaze'. That has had the combined effect of reducing the attractiveness of new energy projects and increasing US dependence on external providers of energy. It has damaged the credit ratings of all energy traders and precipitated ratings downgrades and liquidity problems that undermine efficiency in energy trading and therefore consumer prices. Fortunately, this situation may be short-lived as the markets and the reality of US energy demands reassert themselves. Unfortunately, this is at best a 50/50 proposition, as the rating agencies, in particular, are as concerned about their own reputations as they are about energy providers. What may not be short term is the damage done to trust in business leaders and the regulatory overreaction inflicted on the broader markets. That combination is likely to *permanently* increase market volatility and the cost of capital for all US firms to the detriment of everyone with a pension plan, savings plan, insurance, or direct investment portfolio.

Notes

1 Excerpted from: Culp, Christopher L. and Niskanen, William A. (eds) (2003) *Corporate Aftershock: The Public Policy Lessons from the Collapse of Enron and Other Major Corporations.* Copyright © 2003 Christopher L. Culp and William A. Niskanen. This material is used by permission of John Wiley & Sons, Inc.

2 Assume here that 'fair value' is what the transaction would be worth if negotiated freely on the open market between two competitive firms. For the purpose of this example, suppose fair value is uncontroversial and readily available.

3 In other words, the net present value of any derivative contract at initiation is equal to zero.

4 Powers, William C., Jr., Troubh, Raymond S. and Winokur, Herbert S., Jr. (2002) 'Report of Investigation by the Special Investigation Committee of the Board of Directors of Enron Corp', 1 February, p. 4.

5 Ibid., p. 11.

6 The accounting issues listed in this table are generalized and based on the US GAAP; in other jurisdictions, other treatments may produce a cash event, primarily because of tax issues.

7 See, for instance, Alfred Rappaport, *Creating Shareholder Value: A Guide for Managers and Investors* (New York: Free Press, 1998).

8 Warren E. Buffett, Speech delivered at the Berkshire Hathaway Annual General Meeting, as reported in Selena Maranjian, 'Notes from Omaha', *Motley Fool*, 7 May, 2002.

9 Markowitz's seminal work can be found in Markowitz, Harry M. (1952) 'Portfolio Selection', *Journal of Finance*, 7, No. 1, pp. 77–91; and Markowitz, Harry M. (1959) *Portfolio Selection: Efficient Diversification of Investments.* New Haven, CN: Yale University Press.

10 See Sharpe, William F. (1964) 'Capital Asset Prices: A Theory of Market Equilibrium under Conditions of Risk', *Journal of Finance*, 19, No. 3, pp. 425–42; and Lintner, John (1965) 'The Valuation of Risk Assets and the Selection of Risky Investments in Stock Portfolios and Capital Budgets', *Review of Economics and Statistics*, 47, February, pp. 13–37. Lintner did not receive the Nobel Memorial Prize in economic sciences.

11 Franco Modigliani and Merton H. Miller's seminal contributions in the area of corporate finance, capital structure and dividend policy can be found in Modigliani, Franco and Miller, Merton H. (1958) 'The Cost of Capital, Corporation Finance, and the Theory of Investment', *American Economic Review*, 48, No. 3, pp. 261–97; Modigliani, Franco and Miller, Merton H. (1961) 'Dividend Policy, Growth, and the Valuation of Shares', *Journal of Business*, 34, October, pp. 235–64; and Modigliani, Franco and Miller, Merton H. (1963) 'Corporate Income Taxes and the Cost of Capital', *American Economic Review*, 53, No. 3, pp. 433–43.

12 Buffett, loc. cit.

13 See, for example, Myers, Stewart C. and Brealey, Richard A. (2003) *Principles of Corporate Finance,* 7th edn. New York: McGraw-Hill.

14 We have provided a pdf file with a full set of Enron financial statements that allow interested parties to review the historical performance as well as the forecasts that we developed for our analysis. This file is available at www.risktoolz.com/enron.

15 See Enron Corp., *2000 Annual Report,* 2001.

16 Prepared from information provided in ibid. and selected filings by Enron with the Securities and Exchange Commission, and the assistance of Charles Conner, formerly an executive at Enron. The data were synthesized by Charles Conner, Mark Storrie and Richard Bassett.

17 Enron Corp., *2000 Annual Report*, Note 4.

18 Ibid., p. 36.

19 See, for example, Sirower, Mark L. (1997) *The Synergy Trap: How Companies Lose the Acquisitions Game.* New York: Free Press.

20 The data in Table 7.5 were derived from market data provided through links to the respective exchanges for the individual share price performance of the companies noted.

21 Enron Corp., p. 2.

22 Quoted in Parris, Matthew (2002) 'Another Bold Initiative? No Change There Then', *Sunday Times,* 10 August, p. 22.

23 Leuz, Christian, Nanda, Dhananjay and Wysocki, Peter D. (2001) 'Investor Protection and Earnings Management: An International Comparison', Working Paper, Wharton School of the University of Pennsylvania, University of Michigan Business School, and MIT Sloan School of Management, August.

24 See, for example, LaPorta, Rafael F. *et al.* (2000) 'Investor Protection and Corporate Governance', *Journal of Financial Economics,* 58, Nos. 1–2, pp. 3–27.

25 SEC round-tables, announced in 2001, addressed disclosure, regulation and related market issues. Transcripts are available on the SEC website, www.sec.gov.

26 The complete lists of actions are available on their websites, www.nyse.com and www.nasdaq.com. See also Chapter 2 in this book.

27 The authors are not suggesting support for the KMV model; they are simply noting the reaction of one of the rating agencies that recognized the superiority of market information to filed reports.

section III:

QUESTIONS OF DELIVERY

8

A CLIENT'S PERSPECTIVE ON VALUE-BASED MANAGEMENT

A CASE STUDY

DAVID GEE[1]

Introduction

Most of the ABC Corporation's[2] 25,000 employees felt they were working for a good company. By the mid-1990s, it had grown, both organically and by a series of acquisitions, into a true multinational, with several important brand names in a large portfolio of consumer products. ABC's annual reports showed steady, if unspectacular, growth in sales and profits. Within these results, there always seemed to be divisions that had done particularly well or had introduced promising new products: though the annual report typically also revealed a few that had 'failed to match previous expectations' or were 'facing more intense competition'. Often, a charge for 'restructuring' had been sufficiently material to be disclosed separately – implying some job losses, though efforts were always made to keep any compulsory redundancies to a minimum.

In 1996, ABC appointed a new CEO, Rick Thompson, whose long career in the corporation had spanned the main product divisions and whose achievements included the integration of two major acquisitions. Acutely aware that ABC's TSR (total shareholder return) put it towards the lower end of the third quartile of its peer group, he was determined to improve matters by making increased shareholder value the organization's key objective.

Acutely aware that ABC's TSR (total shareholder return) put it towards the lower end of the third quartile of its peer group, he was determined to improve matters by making increased shareholder value the organization's key objective.

At this point I myself was working in ABC's head office finance department; my main responsibility was to coordinate the long-range planning process (usually over five years), value individual business unit (BU) plans and evaluate potential acquisitions or divestments. In this capacity I was in frequent contact with the CFO, although I had few dealings with the other main board directors.

Better performance measures

In the weeks following his appointment as CEO, Thompson sought the views of many of ABC's managers on how the corporation's TSR could be improved. My turn came a few days after I had attended a seminar by Stern Stewart propounding the benefits of EVA™ (Economic Value Added). With me at that seminar was a colleague whose main responsibility was the head office scrutiny of major capital expenditure projects; we had both formed the opinion that

EVA™ was, in principle, a sound measure and that a focus on increasing EVA™ was less likely to produce unwanted effects than ABC's then current focus on trading profit. The principal unwanted effect was that ABC spent over 10% of sales on marketing; it was all too easy to cut marketing in order to meet a profit target. We were, however, concerned that the absence of any EVA™ adjustment for past inflation or internally generated brand values could give misleading results for a long-established business such as ABC. We also felt that any attempt to include more than one or two of Stern Stewart's 150-plus potential accounting adjustments would be strongly resisted by BU finance directors. We discussed such thoughts with Rick Thompson, who asked us to devise a measure that would fairly reflect true economic performance, would encourage managers to make the right decisions and would not be too complicated to implement.

Following that meeting, I devised several possible variations on EVA™, using the corporation's database to calculate the past five years' results and project the next five years for each BU on each of these variations on EVA™. After meetings with other key finance people, it was agreed that the key measure would be called 'economic profit' (EP) and would be defined as:

> It was agreed that the key measure would be called 'economic profit' (EP).

- trading profit, plus or minus adjustments that regarded marketing and restructuring costs as if they were capital and amortized over three years;

- less tax at the standard rate for the country where the BU operated;

- less a capital charge at the WACC (weighted average cost of capital) for the country where the BU operated levied on its average operating assets – i.e. tangible fixed assets, working capital and the unamortized balance of the marketing and restructuring adjustments. ('Average' meant the average of all relevant month-end amounts: working capital in most BUs showed big seasonal variations.)

Even as this measure was approved and introduced, we recognized that it failed to meet one of the CEO's criteria – that it should reflect true economic performance. This was because ABC's enterprise value (EV, i.e. equity market capitalization plus debt) was about four times the book value of operating assets. Thus it was conceivable – even likely – that while all BUs would show a positive EP, external analysts would report that the corporation was earning less than its cost of capital. In our meetings we had analysed the enterprise value approximately as in Table 8.1.

I think Thompson may have preferred a measure in which the asset base

TABLE 8.1
Analysis of enterprise value

Book value of operating assets	25%
Intangible assets [a]	50%
Other [b]	25%
Enterprise value	100%

[a] Mainly the unamortized balance of goodwill on acquisitions.

[b] Logically, this balancing item should comprise an inflation adjustment to fixed assets (shown at depreciated historical costs), increases in the value of intangibles since acquisition and the value of self-generated brands, patents, know-how and the skills of the workforce.

included all the above, and which would have resulted in lower, more realistic EP. The problem, however, was that there was no objective means of allocating the 'other' element by BU. But if it was excluded, there would not be a level playing field between recently acquired BUs with high intangibles and those that had been in the corporation for decades with low intangible values. It was felt that a solution to this problem might be found on the basis set out in Table 8.2.

TABLE 8.2
Enterprise value: another approach

Book value of operating assets	25%
Current brand values (rounded up to include other intangibles)	75%
Enterprise value	100%

Potentially, this might result in an alternative measure, linked to economic profit (EP) as already defined, as follows:

> EP – additional capital charge at WACC on current brand
> value + / – change in current brand value over the period[3]

I searched for some system of capitalized notional royalties on sales as a basis for estimating brand values, and several BUs participated in a pilot study. Although the CFO was, and I believe still is, keen to introduce something like this 'improved' measure across the corporation, this has not yet happened, partly because of other priorities.

Arrival of the consultants

Not long after my meeting with Rick Thompson, I learned that the corporation had engaged a highly respected consultancy, Strat-Pro,[4] which specializes in assisting managements to install the best processes for identifying, evaluating, prioritizing and delivering value-enhancing strategies.

I am not sure whether it was Thompson or Strat-Pro who first used the phrase 'managing for value' (MFV), but do recall that, initially, there was some confusion between that term and value-based management. However, it soon became clear that, at least in the corporation if not universally, VBM is one segment of MFV. There were four other segments within MFV, which may be summarized as higher performance expectations; a keener, more focused business culture; making managers act more like owners; and linking remuneration more closely with performance. These segments, particularly the last two, seemed to echo what I had heard at the Stern Stewart seminar.

One of the first things I learned was that every Strat-Pro client must have a clear objective in terms of shareholder value – for example, to be in the top quartile of a defined peer group as measured by TSR, or to create a specified amount of shareholder value in a defined period. Strat-Pro could point to clients who had doubled shareholder value within only three years; there was a clear implication that it could help ABC to do the same. Neither consultants nor client wanted to be committed to a public objective that stood little chance of being achieved. Nevertheless, despite the obvious risks in stating the objective in absolute terms, the board preferred a simple direct message that could cascade down through the organization. Thus, ABC's governing objective was announced as 'to double shareholder value in five years'.

Initial attitudes, expectations and questions

Strat-Pro was confident this objective could be achieved. After all, it was not as stretching as its other clients had achieved, even though it was more than anything ABC had managed in living memory.

The MFV programme, then, would change attitudes and beliefs throughout the organization. Senior staff, both at headquarters and in the business units, reacted with a mixture of excitement at the prospects of much better business performance – *with rewards linked to it!* – and fear that new skills would have to be learned and that jobs would be less secure. There was also significant scepticism: could an organization that depended almost entirely on slow-growing markets ever achieve the required objective TSR growth rate of 15% p.a. compound?

A typical question at this time would be: 'Our latest business unit plan shows trading profit growing at 8% p.a.: what profit growth rate do we need to meet the objective?' Although we, at the centre, tried to give helpful and numerical answers to such questions, a full answer required an understanding of the way cost of equity, market consensus projections and the impact of 'good surprises' were linked – which we did not yet have. (But one good surprise was that the mere announcement of Strat-Pro's appointment and the TSR objective led to a rise of 10–20% in ABC's share price: a good start!)

The board made it clear that the whole MFV programme was so comprehensive that it would take two to three years to implement fully. Initially, only the five largest BUs – which nevertheless accounted for about three-quarters of total corporation value – would be involved. I suspect that many smaller BUs hoped they would *never* be affected – an attitude derived from the fear (largely groundless) that the main way to achieve the objective would be via massive redundancies.

The Strat-Pro approach

Strat-Pro's approach was firmly based on the following logical chain:

> Superior objective → superior analysis → superior strategy →
> superior financial performance → superior shareholder value

ABC now had its 'superior objective'. Work began immediately on 'superior analysis' in the form of a 'Corporate Position Assessment' which set out to identify 'values at stake' at the corporate level. While MFV was for everyone, VBM had a strong bias towards the finance function. A forceful ABC cost accountant, Tom Brown, was promoted to head a small VBM team to work closely with Strat-Pro and succeeded in setting demanding timetables for other departments to implement VBM. As the programme evolved, the work of his VBM team became increasingly one of training others who, in turn, trained staff in the smaller BUs. Presentations and seminars, typically led by Strat-Pro and Brown, stressed that value was more likely to be created by 'doing better things, not just doing things better'.

Early in the programme, Strat-Pro proposed more structured agendas for board and committee meetings on a new annual cycle that integrated previously separate annual budget and five-year plan cycles. In practice, this was only partially implemented: nevertheless, these changes did have the beneficial result that the executive directors' time was used more effectively and that there was a much clearer distinction between their strategy selection role and their performance-monitoring role.

Overturning established DCF methodology

Some background information on ABC's practices is relevant at this point. Throughout the corporation, discounted cash flow (DCF) methodology had been used for many years for capital and development projects and for evaluating potential acquisitions or disposals. There was a system of DCF 'hurdle rates' for each country, taking account of local country risk and inflation. These hurdle rates were set higher than the WACC (weighted average cost of capital) for the country concerned in order to compensate for double-counting of benefits in what were submitted as separate projects, 'non-earning' but essential projects, and traditional optimism about benefits. This was considered 'safer', bearing in mind that the procedure was used by thousands of finance staff with varying levels of experience, in dozens of BUs. When evaluating potential acquisitions, which was normally a head office responsibility, the discount rate was normally set at the relevant WACC for the 'base case'; the higher 'hurdle rate' applied only to projected volume synergies. Discounting was normally as at mid-year rather than year-end to reflect more accurately the average date on which cash was generated.

Using WACC rather than the higher hurdle rates, head office applied the same DCF methodology from time to time to value the corporation's BUs, and hence to produce an internal estimate of the value per share for comparison with the market price. Typically, the difference was not much more than 10% either way. These occasional valuations were not really used to manage the business in any real sense.

Soon after Strat-Pro's appointment, my boss, the vice-president for corporate development, Bill Everett, and I met a senior Strat-Pro consultant, Jack Wilson. He started by telling us that our DCF methodology was wrong – and not just because of the way we had developed the procedures outlined above. The problem was that the DCF method itself was wrong unless (he conceded) one adjusts the WACC in each year of the cash flow to reflect the business's gearing that results from a project's cash flow. Furthermore, gearing in a wholly-owned subsidiary of ABC Corporation was often more dependent on dividends demanded by, and paid to, the centre than on cash generation. Bill was not a finance person, and told Wilson, in no uncertain terms, we could not operate a system that involved such complication.

Possibly Wilson half-expected this reaction. He explained the 'correct' methodology, which was to discount economic profits and add the initial equity. Wilson further explained that, since economic profit is the 'super-profit' that remains after both shareholders and debt-holders have received as much return as they could expect, it belongs to the shareholders alone. Accordingly, it must be discounted at the cost of equity (which Strat-Pro always abbreviated to K_e).

> Since economic profit is the 'super-profit' that remains after both shareholders and debt-holders have received as much return as they could expect, it belongs to the shareholders alone. Accordingly, it must be discounted at the cost of equity (abbreviated to K_e).

Even supposing we accepted the theory – at that stage we did not – we could not see how to make it work in practice. In particular, the need to include 'initial equity' in the calculation took us back into problems of the financial gearing of the BUs, many of which had no meaningful balance sheet. (In many cases, a BU's assets were financed by inter-company loans and current accounts.) Some time later, I realized that there are, at least in theory, good reasons for preferring the discounted economic profit approach to the more common discounted cash flow. These are:

- a smaller proportion of total value in the distant future;
- more objective estimates of distant years since EP should trend to zero;
- a clear link to the most common internal measure: annual (or monthly) EP is a good financial measure, whereas cash flow is normally too volatile.

The first of these advantages is illustrated in Figure 8.1.

FIGURE 8.1
Cash flow versus assets + economic profit

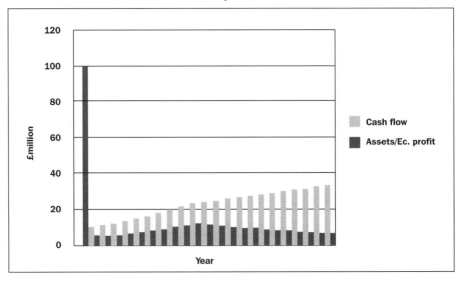

Meanwhile, the important question seemed to me: What exactly did 'doubling shareholder value in five years' mean? Bill and I had, in fact, done some work on this earlier. The key questions were:

1. Did it mean doubling the share price, or were dividends to be taken into account and, if so, on what basis?

2. Were the start and end points for the five years particular days or averages over a week, month or year?

3. What assumptions should be made as to share issues or repurchases?

4. Given that we were going to have to break the corporate objective down into corresponding objectives for regions and business units (for which there were no market values except in a few small partly owned businesses), how would we handle any discrepancy between internal valuations and market values?

Defining 'doubling shareholder value' more fully

Strat-Pro having sent Wilson to the USA on another project, I worked through the questions listed above with Mike Price, his replacement. We (and others who wanted to be involved) concluded that:

1. It should be assumed that shareholders would immediately reinvest their (net) dividends. We assumed the dividend rate would be such that the yield remained constant. The share price at the time of reinvestment would be in accordance with an assumed constant 15% annual TSR growth rate, except for the first two dividends which, as a result of decision 2 below, were already in the past, and the actual share price on the dividend payment date was used. These assumptions enabled us to calculate that a shareholder who started with 100 shares would have something like 115 shares in five years' time. This objective meant that the value of 115 shares had to be double the value of the initial 100 shares (assuming no discounted share issue which would require a further adjustment).

2. The start point would be the average of the daily closing share prices in the previous financial year. Thus the end point would be a similar average five years later.

3. We should assume no share issues or repurchases, except those that were expected to occur as and when employees exercised other share options. It may be noticed that this decision conflicts with decision 1, which would

require additional shares to be available when dividends were reinvested. However, we decided that decision 1 was only a formula for deciding what doubling meant, not an actual projection, and so the inconsistency did not matter.

4. While we needed to be aware of possible discrepancies between values derived from internal projections and market values, this risk was inherent in the choice of an absolute objective rather than a relative one, which would absorb general market movements. Nevertheless, we realized we needed to be sure the problem was not aggravated by inconsistencies from one year to another, or between BUs, in the way values were estimated.

The quest for a standard valuation methodology

It was, therefore, easy to agree that we needed a practicable, standard valuation methodology for use throughout the corporation. The sum of the resulting enterprise values of the BUs, less debt and amounts attributable to minorities, should therefore represent the value of the ABC Corporation's equity. We also needed a fair and easily understood basis for allocating the total corporation value target among the BUs – of which more later. Finally, we needed some means of linking each BU's value target to monthly or annual financial measures of performance in order to show whether progress towards its value target was satisfactory. This last requirement meant that the standard valuation methodology (once specified and agreed!) could be used in reverse to derive target EPs from the target values.

Many issues arose from these apparently simple tasks. The first was that Mike Price and I needed to resolve the question of equivalence of values derived either using DCF or discounted EP. I did a lot of work on the examples and eventually came to the conclusion that the two methods were indeed equivalent, though only if:

■ gearing (or leverage) was zero so that WACC was the same as K_e;

■ we abandoned our mid-year discounting of cash flows; and

■ we ignored the differences between tax charges and tax payments.

We were willing to accept the last two points above as simplifications that would not cause significant errors. As to the first point, Mike explained that gearing could be non-zero as long as WACC was weighted by book values, not – as ABC had always done – market. At the time of our discussions, ABC's total debt was about $500 million, which was reasonable in relation to equity market capitalization of about $3 billion. The book value of equity, however, was only about $250 million. Therefore, 'book WACC' would be calculated with a debt/equity weighting of 67/33, resulting in a WACC far below the rate used hitherto. Since the corporation's governing objective demanded a higher surplus return over WACC, issuing artificially low WACCs around the corporation would have sent completely the wrong message.

Eventually, the compromise reached was to continue to assume a standard gearing ratio of 15/85 in each BU (i.e. similar to the overall corporation target ratio). This enabled us to continue to use WACCs as previously estimated – with country risk and inflation adjustments where appropriate –and issued (typically rounded up to the nearest whole percentage). We also then issued a simple formula to enable each BU to calculate the K_e to be used to discount its projected economic profits: this was K_e = WACC + 1%. We acknowledged that, consequently, when valuing the total corporation, we needed to adjust for the differences between:

- the weighted average of the WACCs used by the BUs and the WACC for the corporation as a whole; and

- the weighted average of the K_es used by the BUs and K_e for the corporation as a whole.

We also instructed the BUs to assume tax at the standard rate for the country where they operated, which meant a further adjustment was needed.

We now had at least the skeleton of an agreed methodology. Since Strat-Pro liked to express everything in terms of equity values, rather than the more familiar (within ABC) enterprise values, in any BU, the equity value was to be calculated as:

- initial equity which, from the decision on gearing and the definition of economic profit, was always 85% of initial operating assets; plus

- the sum of each year's economic profit (in which the capital charge was at the BU's WACC) discounted at the BU's K_e to the planning horizon; plus

- a residual value, based on the theory that economic profit eventually fades to zero.

This framework still left unresolved questions as to the planning horizon and assumptions for calculating the residual value. Realizing that consistency would be more important than spurious accuracy, Bill played a significant role here. He

FIGURE 8.2
Typical business unit value components

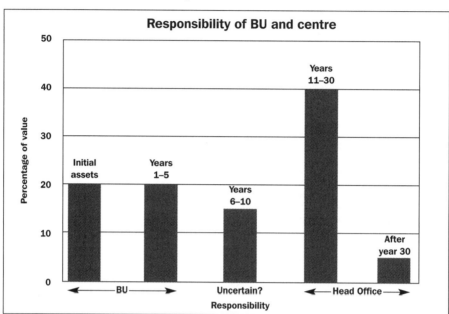

realized that making the planning horizon too short would result in a high proportion of value being left in the residual, which would be seen as calculated in a head office 'black box'. On the other hand, too long a period would force BUs to gaze further into the future than the five years they were used to – and heretofore, the figures for years 3, 4 and 5 had often not been at all robust. The resolution of this issue is shown diagrammatically in Figure 8.2, which illustrates the components of value in a typical manufacturing BU.

With every BU responsible for the value arising from its initial assets and a five-year 'planning period', ABC's head office would issue guidelines on assumptions for a further five-year 'post-planning period'; but BUs would be able to depart from these assumptions if they thought fit. Head office would also issue the assumptions that would determine the value of a 20-year 'transitional period' in which economic profit – *in its true economic sense* – would decline to zero. Since, however, on ABC's definition, EP nearly always exceeded true economic profit (owing to ignoring intangibles in the capital charge), there would still normally be a non-zero residual value at the end of 30 years.

In Figure 8.2's example, the BU would be responsible for a minimum 40% of value and could, if it chose, be responsible for a further 15% in the post-planning period. The BU's assumptions would also, in fact, influence the values

FIGURE 8.3
'Low-asset' business unit value components

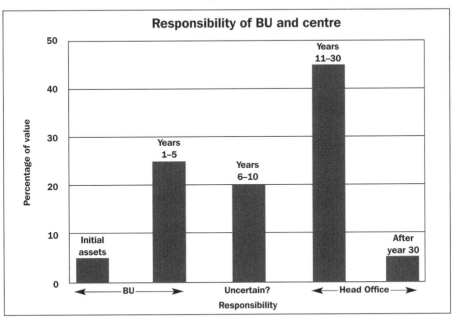

in the transitional period and the residual as these may be regarded as the result of multiplying EP determined by the BU by a numerical factor determined by the centre. This was considered a reasonable balance between the philosophy of MFV – which involved delegating responsibility wherever possible – and the practical issue of keeping at the centre those aspects of valuation that might otherwise be too difficult for the BUs.

Unfortunately, the ABC Corporation had many BUs engaged only in selling or franchising, with few tangible assets. The components of their values were more like Figure 8.3. In this case, the BU would be directly responsible for only between 30% and 50% of value. Since, in practice, most chose not to depart from head office's assumptions for the post-planning period, they were at the lower end of this range; but complaints that the value was understated due to inappropriate assumptions by head office were, thankfully, rare.

An agreed standard valuation methodology

We had started from Strat-Pro's research (or maybe gut-feel) that, in a well-established business such as ABC, competitive advantage should last for about 30 years. This determined the length of the transitional period. However, we searched in vain for a robust formula to link economic profit on ABC's definition ('EP') to true economic profit. In the end, all the BUs were divided into just two categories: those with high trading margins relative to competitors and those with margins below competitors. (This presupposed similar competitors existed in the countries concerned and that we could get adequate data on them – if not, guesstimates were needed.) For the first category, we assumed that EP per unit of volume (in real terms, excluding inflation) would decline by 50%. For the second category, we assumed that EP per unit of volume would remain unchanged. This categorization struck me as an unusually crude component of an otherwise sophisticated methodology. However, a few examples showed that the effect on value of moving a BU from one category to the other was only about 10%.

> In the end, all the BUs were divided into just two categories: those with high trading margins relative to competitors and those with margins below competitors.

As part of the Corporate Position Assessment, Strat-Pro had found and used some historical growth rates for population and per capita consumption in ABC's markets. On the 'consistency is more important than spurious accuracy' principle, we agreed that population growth, in each country of the world, would change steadily from its early 1990s average to 0.5% p.a. in year 30. (In most cases this implied a gradual decline but in some European countries it implied a slow increase from about 0.3% p.a.) We also assumed that, after year 10, growth in per capita consumption would decline to zero by year 30.

By combining the assumptions for population, per capita consumption, real EP per unit of volume and inflation, we had all that was needed to project EP from years 6 (or 11) to 30. All that remained was to build a model that would pull in some history and the five-year planning period from the BUs' databases, extend the data rows through the post-planning period, extend just the EP row through the transitional period, discount the EPs and add them up. We did have some difficulties with projections for depreciation and capital expenditure, as few BUs seemed able to project depreciation on their then-existing assets, so inconsistencies were more likely in terms of the ratio of capital expenditure to depreciation than anything else. In general, however, it worked well.

In practice, only the firm's five largest BUs used the valuation model described above. The smaller BUs, which generally did not seek to depart from head office's assumptions for the post-planning period, were given a much simpler valuation model. In effect, I fed all the assumptions for each BU as to population, per capita consumption, EP 'fade' and discount rate into the original model in order to express the total value beyond year 5 as a multiple of the year 5 EP. This enabled us to issue a very much smaller model that simply retrieved the key asset and EP data for years 1 to 5 and used a look-up table to access the appropriate discount rate and multiple.

One important aspect of the Strat-Pro approach is its concept of 'base business', implementation initiatives and development initiatives, and calculating the value of each of them separately. 'Base business' was defined as the continuation of the business's existing strategy; an 'implementation initiative' comprised the incremental effects of an agreed new or additional strategy; and a 'development initiative' the incremental effects of a strategy not yet agreed. Meetings of the Chief Executive's Committee would discuss development initiatives and decide which (if any) of them should become implementation initiatives. The distinction was important: the value of each BU was regarded as the sum of base business and implementation initiatives but excluding any development initiatives, and managers had performance objectives related to the success of the base business plus implementation initiatives. Development initiatives were regarded as too uncertain to be included.

> One important aspect of the Strat-Pro approach is its concept of 'base business', implementation initiatives and development initiatives, and calculating the value of each of them separately.

As the budget/plan numbers in the corporation's Hyperion financial database were for the sum of base business and implementation initiatives, it was easy for a BU to find its value, using either the original ('ten-year') or much simplified ('five-year') model. However, it also had to use one of these two models, with manual input of the projections, to value any implementation initiative separately. A BU could also use either of these models to value development initiatives.

To return to the claimed advantages of the discounted EP method, we can now see that, in a business where much of the value is in intangibles, the first two advantages – smaller proportion of total value in distant future, and more objective estimates of distant years – are nowhere near as big as Strat-Pro had claimed. However, the EP method is still unlikely to be worse than DCF on the first two criteria; and may be superior to DCF on the third point (clear link to the most common internal measure). Thus I had to agree that the balance of advantage is with the discounted EP method, even if a DCF valuation may be worth doing too – just to check if equivalence applies!

Target setting

We have already seen how the 'doubling of value' objective was translated, via dividend and share issue assumptions, into a numerical objective for the corporation's equity market capitalization (averaged over the fifth then-future year). For the VBM system to work effectively, each BU's management needed not only to know what its value objective was but also to understand its basis and perceive it as a fair target.

Strat-Pro started from a definition of 'cost of equity' as the average annual return a shareholder could expect. This expected return comprised dividends and share price appreciation. We had already made an estimate of the cost of equity (K_e) and made assumptions as to the dividend yield at any time in the five years. By subtracting the dividend yield from K_e we had the expected share price growth rate implied by the market. (This was sometimes called the 'natural growth rate'.) Thus it seemed reasonable to use this growth rate to discount the corporate value objective for year 5 back to an equivalent value objective for year zero. Looking at it another way, *if* the corporate value was already at its objective level for year 1, *then* shareholders could assume that it would grow so as to reach the objective level for year 5 in year 5. This thinking enabled ABC to introduce the concept of the 'value gap', the difference in value of a BU between its current equity value (calculated using the models described above and with the notional gearing concept) and its target value, when both were expressed as at the same point in time. The 'value gap' concept also applied at higher levels, such as regions or product groups, and at total corporation level. An alternative definition of the value gap, but only at total corporation level, was the difference between *current market capitalization* and the target value with the latter discounted to the current date.

> This thinking enabled ABC to introduce the concept of the 'value gap', the difference in value of a BU between its current equity value (calculated using the models described above and with the notional gearing concept) and its target value, when both were expressed as at the same point in time.

To deal with the 'perceived as fair' question, Strat-Pro proposed the concept of 'equal stretch'. By this they meant that, for each BU, the target value should be a uniform percentage of its current value. For reasons that will be explained shortly, it seemed that the uniform percentage, or 'stretch factor', would be about 140%. Thus, in Strat-Pro nomenclature, each BU's target value would, initially, be 140% of its current value and its value gap would be 40% of current value.

This proposal generated a lot of debate in ABC. It didn't seem fair that a business in a mature market should have the same stretch factor as one in a fast-growing, developing market. However, Mike Price and his colleagues pointed out that such differences should already be embodied within the plans that generated *current* value. Thus 'equal stretch' would *not* mean that all businesses had to grow at the same rate – though it did mean they would all have to find improvements to their current plans, worth about 40% of their current value. This was in line with the overall MFV principle of higher performance expectations. But possibly the clinching argument for 'equal stretch' was that introducing '*un*equal stretch' would involve even more debate and trials of strength between different factions.

Thus 'equal stretch' was adopted; but it soon became clear that there had to be exceptions. Within the ABC structure, there were numerous corporate and regional cost centres that, for most reporting purposes, were treated just like the operational BUs. Typically they had no revenues, few assets and costs that consisted mainly of salaries and wages; inevitably, their values were negative. Rather than increase these negatives, we agreed that these units' target values should be the same as their current values. Given that these targets were discounted back to the present, this effectively meant they had to make sufficient real savings to offset cost increases due to inflation.

ABC also had one or two investments in associated companies over which it had little influence; and also some subsidiaries whose sale had begun to be negotiated. These businesses' target values were set in the same way as for the cost centres. ABC also had a few newly founded businesses, in eastern Europe, Asia and Africa, that had projected losses for the five years and had negative current values. It was decided that their targets should be to *reduce* these negative values by whatever the uniform stretch factor implied.

These decisions, together with the current values of all the BUs and cost centres, provided just enough information to determine all the BU target values. Figure 8.4 shows how 'doubling' is reduced by dividend reinvestment, discounting a future target back to the present and not allowing cost centres to get worse, to a net uniform stretch factor of about 135%. This seemed high enough to drive markedly superior performance but not so high that it would demotivate those who might consider it out of reach.

There was one further practical problem. When VBM was being introduced, half a dozen new and important tasks – Activity Based Costing, Strategic Position Assessments, new reporting cycles, training personnel and so on – all seemed to be top priority. To cope with all this, the previous detailed planning process, in which each of about 50 BUs did its own plan, which was then

FIGURE 8.4

Doubling not as stretching as it seems ...

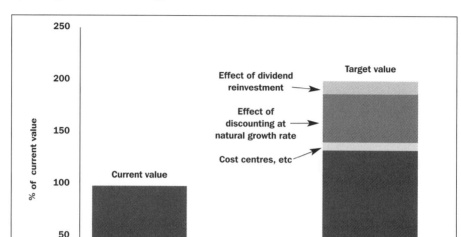

reviewed and modified, was streamlined. Instead, the top finance person in each of about ten regional entities was asked for a five-year forecast consisting of just a few rows of data. Some of them asked the BUs for which they were responsible to do their own forecasts, which were consolidated at regional level; others just did the regional forecasts themselves.

The practical consequence, as far as I was concerned, was that I was supposed to apply a uniform stretch factor to BU current values that could not be calculated from the data available! However, initially, we only needed target values for the five major BUs which, fortunately, aligned pretty closely with five of the regions. We were also able to determine target values for the rest of the corporation, with a split by main product groups. These targets were regarded as provisional while the directors responsible for the relevant businesses and product groups, and their finance staffs, considered the implications. Perhaps not surprisingly, they were uneasy that a structure of current and target values rested on a shaky forecast, by then about six months old. So it was agreed that this forecast could be updated to reflect more recent trading trends. One product group used this opportunity to make significant downward revisions; the others, where trading had remained more buoyant, left their forecasts unchanged. Since the total corporation target value – derived from a now-historical share price – was unchanged, this exercise had the effect of reducing

FIGURE 8.5
Current and target value chart

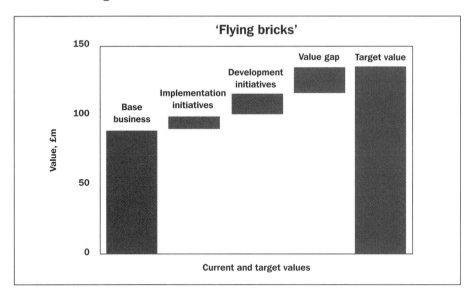

provisional targets for those with trading difficulties and raising them for the rest. The latter group then saw this as rewarding under-achievers and penalizing those who believed they could still meet their targets. In the end, the CEO resolved the situation by ruling that the revised target values, the correct result of an agreed process, should stand.

About a year later, when all BUs had done a new-style combined budget and plan, and had valued them with our ten-year or five-year model, we were in a better position to issue target values throughout the organization. There was, however, the question as to whether 'equal stretch' should apply to all (apart from the exceptions already noted) or only to those businesses that had not already been given target values. As changing the targets only one year into a five-year period would have sent out the wrong messages, the decision was in favour of the second approach. As it transpired, the uniform stretch factor now required from the updated current values was nearly the same as the 135% already issued. It was, in fact, decided to make it exactly the same and 'lose' the rounding error among the corporate adjustments to tax, WACC and K_e.

Every business was now in a position to prepare charts like the one shown in Figure 8.5. It became known as the 'Flying bricks chart' and was certainly useful in showing, at a glance, how a business's current value compared with its target.

This was not the end of the target-setting process. Since the budget/plan was only updated annually, current values could only be updated at similar intervals.

FIGURE 8.6
Budget/plan and target economic profit

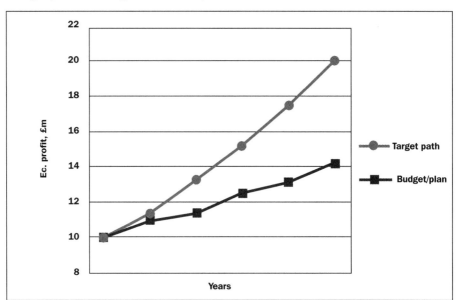

This was considered to be too long for managers accustomed to seeing sales, profit – and now EP – figures every month. What they wanted to know was whether their EP was 'on track' to achieve the target value or, if not, how far adrift it was. Strat-Pro had, at least in principle, a solution: the 'target EP track'.

Mike Price produced two main options for setting these target EP tracks. Each of them involved Excel 'Goal Seek' to find the appropriate value of a key variable. One of them was to find what percentage improvement, if applied year by year to the budget/plan EP, would lift the value to the target value. The other option was to calculate what constant annual EP growth rate, starting from the last complete year's actual EP, would lift the current value to the target value. The first option would accentuate any peaks and troughs in the budget/plan EP progression, so Mike and I decided in favour of the second approach, which would produce a smooth target EP track. A typical case is shown in Figure 8.6.

We planned to issue target EP tracks covering the years up to and including the last year of the five-year budget/plan. Either method would require an assumption as to the appropriate multiple of year 5 target EP that would represent the value of all the years beyond that date. Our instinct was to assume it was the same as implied by the current value. This had the important advantage – for me! – that the numerical values were already in the look-up table of the five-year valuation model. But was this simple solution theoretically sound? The multiples in the look-up table depended, in a rather indirect way, on the assumption as to 'fade' of EP per unit of volume. Although the target-setting process did not itself involve any assumptions as to volume, it seemed clear, from all the strategic reviews, that 'doubling of value' would depend on improving the product mix by cutting out low-margin lines, raising prices where the market would bear them, cutting costs wherever possible and increasing volume in a few areas. Thus the target EPs would, in most cases, imply higher figures than in the budget/plan for EP per unit. It followed that any 'fade' to a market average, by our assumed date 30 years hence, would, logically, be steeper. But how much steeper? As we have seen, the 'fade' assumptions were rather crude but not immensely important to final values. With these thoughts uppermost – and with few in the organization understanding this issue well enough to have any view – Mike and I decided that the multiples we already had would be accurate enough.

One or two questions remained to be resolved, however. One concerned exceptional costs, such as major restructuring. Clearly they had to be included in budgets/plans when calculating current values, but was it sensible to set a smooth target EP track if it was already planned that the track would be erratic? Our answer was to set smooth target tracks for 'underlying EP' (before exceptionals), calculated on the assumption that the target for such exceptionals should be the same as forecast.

Another problem was that, in some cases, the initial calculation of the target EP track might be below the budget/plan in the first year or two (even after adjustment for exceptionals). The solution was to set the target in line with budget/plan in such years and apply the 'constant annual growth' rule to the later years only. Finally, some pragmatic solutions were needed where the most recent actual EP was negative or such a small positive number that the 'goal seek' growth rate would have been over 100% p.a., if it could be found at all.

Maintenance of the process

Everything in this chapter so far relates to decisions made, and work done, in about the first 18 months of the MFV initiative. Although life became less hectic after that, I still had to deal with many practical questions. As any organization contemplating a similar initiative will probably have to answer such questions sooner or later, it seems worth addressing the more general ones here.

Acquisitions

Most large organizations will make several acquisitions or disposals in a five-year period. For an acquisition, Strat-Pro's basic rule was that the business's current value should increase by the value attributed to the acquisition and its target value should increase by the price paid for the acquired firm's equity. Thus the acquisition would, at least on the basis of information available at the time, create value equal to the difference between the acquisition case value and the purchase price. In terms of Figure 8.5, the base business would increase by the current value of the acquiree and the implementation and development initiative 'bricks' would increase by the value attributed to synergies – 'implementation' for those attributable to agreed integration plans and 'development' for any that required more investigation. The sum of these increases should be greater than the increase in the target value. There were, however, practical problems associated with this:

- Should the value created by the acquisition 'belong' to the central or regional department that negotiated it, or to the BU, or BUs, that had to implement it?

- How could the value and target adjustments be fairly split when two or more BUs were involved?

- If adjustments to the target EP track were calculated as explained above, they would almost always be lower than the incremental EPs promised in the acquisition case documents, which was clearly at variance with the concept of a target.

The solutions to these problems were necessarily pragmatic, on a case-by-case basis. Sometimes it was possible to set the adjustments to a BU's target EP track in line with the acquisition case (i.e. theoretically too high) and compensate by an adjustment to the target EP track of the cost centre responsible for negotiating the acquisition.

For most purposes, all calculations done at head office used data converted from various local currencies into dollars at the 'budget' rates fixed at the start of the year. It was agreed early in the VBM programme that each BU's value and EP targets should be in the local currency. Since the corporation's value target was derived from a fixed share price, this meant that, each year, conversion of BU targets at a new array of exchange rates resulted in a sort of head office exchange rate value gap – or a reduction thereof.

We discussed a number of questions that all began 'When, if ever, should we alter targets?' – and ended:

- if a BU's standard tax rate changes;

- if a BU's WACC changes;

- if a BU's performance is better than its target;

- if a BU's performance falls a long way below its target.

We concluded that the answers, in all these cases, should be: 'Never, unless there is a major, unforeseen change in the economic or business climate in the country concerned'. 'Never', of course, meant 'not within the currency of the five-year doubling objective'.

Thus, with very few exceptions, targets were not to be changed except for organization changes (both internal and acquisition or disposal). However, each year we needed to:

- restate the target values as at the current year, to keep them in line with about-to-be-updated current values – i.e. we needed to reverse one year of the discounting, done at the outset to discount target values for what was then five years hence, back to the present; and

- extend target EP tracks by one year so that they covered all the years of the new budget/plan.

This last requirement caused a lot of discussion. Three options were tabled, and all had significant pros and cons:

1. Do the calculations by reference to the assumptions for the year in question embodied within the residual multiple already calculated for each BU. Since, after the end of the planning period, real EP growth rates could never be more than the sum of historical population and per capita consumption growth (from the assumptions discussed earlier), they were typically only in the range 2% to 4% p.a. Even when inflation at an assumed 2% to 3% was added, the resulting nominal growth rate was far below the 15% implied by the governing objective. Thus it did not seem at all suitable as the basis for a target EP track.

2. Extend the target EP track using the constant annual growth rate that had already been established in the process of determining the target track. This method had the merit of simplicity and apparent consistency. However, for those (fairly numerous) BUs where the growth rate was over 20% p.a. it would represent adding an utterly impossible target for the new 'year 5' to follow an extremely challenging one.

3. Make an assumption as to what the corporation's governing objective would be for the years after the initial five years and extend the target EP track so

as to be consistent with it for each BU. Apart from agreeing on the key assumption as to the next objective, this method would involve a great deal of calculation and was also liable to be technically inconsistent with the *present* target values. However, it was the only one likely to avoid a severe jump – or drop – in target EP tracks as we passed from the last year of the first five-year cycle to the first year of the following one.

We agreed that the third of these options was the best, or the most likely to be accepted as fair and reasonable by the BUs and regions. This consideration was important for the VBM programme's continuing credibility. Thus we had to decide what the next corporate governing objective was likely to be nearly three years before announcement: the least contentious assumption, we thought, would be a repeat of the same, i.e. to double value again in the following five years. This definition, however, required us to predict what the share price would be in about three years' time, so we decided it was better to say 'to quadruple value in the ten years from the original start point'. As I recall, the first year we extended the target EP tracks, we just worked out what average growth rate would be needed across all BUs and applied it to each of them. The following year we were more sophisticated and, in effect, repeated the whole target-setting process in full, BU by BU, though only the target EPs for the new 'year 5' were issued as all the numbers rested on an assumed new objective.

Occasionally, someone in a BU or region would call me and say something like: 'Our proposed new budget/plan shows EPs worse than the target EP track but value better than target: why?' A reasonable question, I suppose. The answer, however, could be some combination of differences in initial assets, tax rates, WACC rates or – most awkwardly – the results of using the third option for extending target EP tracks rather than the technically correct first option.

> Occasionally, someone in a BU or region would call me and say something like: 'Our proposed new budget/plan shows EPs worse than the target EP track but value better than target: why?'

I did some preliminary work on what the target values would be under various other potential new governing objectives, but retired before any decision had to be taken. By then, the 11 September terrorist attacks had occurred and stock markets, which had already fallen, looked unlikely to recover quickly. The outlook was too uncertain for the board to commit itself to an absolute share price objective. I understand the new objective has been set in terms of achieving a TSR in the upper quartile of ABC's peers.

Bill Everett retired shortly before I did. In my last few months my new boss asked why we had such an array of valuation models: not only the 'ten-year' and 'five-year' ones I had devised but another for evaluating capital expenditure projects and various slightly different ones for acquisition projects. He might also have been concerned that, once I had gone, no one would know how to update the models. The solution was to use proprietary software for all evaluations. Partly as a result of advice from Andrew Black (his real name) and partly because one of the key finance staff at head office had used and liked it, Holt Evaluator seemed the best choice. It did, however, force us to look again at the old question of equivalence between our discounted EP methodology and the DCF method. While we were delighted to find that Evaluator guaranteed equivalence in all cases, we soon realized this was because of two simplifications (as we saw them):

- it used WACC, not K_e, as the rate for discounting EP; and
- it applied the capital charge to initial assets each year, and not our 12-month average.

This gave us a good reason to drop the awkward fiction that each BU was financed with 85% equity and 15% debt, with resultant confusion between BU enterprise and equity values. Instead, we adopted the much more convenient fiction that each BU was financed with 100% equity and any debt 'belonged' to head office, where we could make a further corporate gearing adjustment (remembering we already had tax and WACC adjustments). In theory, this decision would lead to an increase in each BU's WACC rate and consequent reduction in EP: this would not be popular, as EP had become the key performance measure. In practice, the change was hardly noticeable when the annual update of WACC rates (rounded to the nearest whole percentage) was done. In any case, by then the Hyperion system generated EP on both the old and the new rates so it was easy to see the effect of the change.

The use of Evaluator was not entirely straightforward as we soon realized we needed a customized 'front end' to link to ABC's chart of accounts and to pick up relevant data from the Hyperion system. We also discovered that, although there are several options for residual value calculations, our 'EP fade' method wasn't one of them. The nearest equivalent was fade of ROCE (Return on Capital Employed), which was all right for BUs with a manufacturing base but not the others. In the latter case, we decided to use the EBITDA multiple option, with the multiples chosen to come close to our previously calculated values. Consequently current BU values, as calculated in Evaluator, differed slightly, but not uniformly, from those that BUs had already calculated. The BUs were quick to point out that, unless target values were adjusted, the 'equal stretch' principle was being lost. Somewhat reluctantly, we agreed that target values should be altered on a pro rata basis to restore 'equal stretch'.

Conclusions

From almost any perspective, I believe the Managing for Value initiative must be judged a success. I say this despite the fact that ABC Corporation did not actually achieve its objective of doubling value in five years. It did, however, get closer than many thought possible. Admittedly, this may have been partly due to a general rise in P/E ratios but, even so, it represented a major advance on the previous staid performance.

> From almost any perspective, I believe the Managing for Value initiative must be judged a success.

Taking a longer-term view, I feel sure the changes in culture and systems will prove to be more important than whether the corporation doubled value. It now has in place a better organization structure and a new, more appropriate, Business Management Process – a term that was coined to embrace the more structured cycle of meetings, the integrated budgeting and longer range planning system, the standardized valuation methodology, the target-setting process, the clarity demanded by analysing value and so on. To say nothing of the more detailed value-based costing exercises that afforded clearer insights into which products, sales channels or geographic markets generated value and which caused value to be lost.

Strat-Pro's role in the initiative was crucial in the early months, although I feel it might have achieved the same results more easily with a little less dogma and a little more flexibility and understanding of ABC's established processes. It has a considerably smaller role now that a thorough training programme has percolated through the organization. As well as the technicalities of VBM, this programme has included modules encouraging adaptability, tenacity and responsibility; training in strategic capabilities, with clear links to the concept of development initiatives; and a teach-yourself financial training module. In summary, the whole MFV initiative was taken very seriously by almost everyone.

As was intended, people throughout the organization now aim higher in the belief that new opportunities to create value must be found and exploited. Business risk is now better understood and new 'risky' ideas will be fully evaluated and debated. If there is a downside to the MFV initiative, it is that increased focus on finding new and better products, working methods and so on may divert attention from ensuring that 'base business' continues to thrive. Also, the old problem of giving priority to meeting profit budget for the current year at the expense of investment for later years has not entirely gone away. ABC's 2002/3 share price fall, more or less in line with the market, has put significant strain on the credibility of internal valuations and goals. But with the MFV programme now thoroughly embedded in its culture and practice, the corporation should have an enduring competitive advantage – at least until its competitors implement similar programmes.

> If there is a downside to the MFV initiative, it is that increased focus on finding new and better products, working methods and so on may divert attention from ensuring that 'base business' continues to thrive.

Notes

1   David Gee recently retired from a senior finance position in the corporation he writes about: names, numbers and some nomenclature have been changed to protect commercial confidentiality but in all other respects this is a true personal account of the case.

2   A pseudonym (see note 1).

3   This was considered to be a true economic gain or loss not reflected in trading profit, and tax-free except in the unlikely event of disposal.

4   A pseudonym (see note 1).

9

MANAGEMENT CONSULTANTS AND MANAGING FOR SHAREHOLDER VALUE

Professor J.A. BARBOUR
University of Strathclyde, Graduate School of Business

Is MFV just another management fad?

What is a management consulting
perspective on MFV?

How have consultants leapt on the MFV gravy train?

How can companies help themselves to become
more value-based?

How can consultants serve clients more
effectively in this area?

The management consulting industry has a long history of finding novel ways of extracting fees from clients. The most far-fetched ideas and notions emanating from academics and self-styled gurus have been dressed up in marketing programmes involving new jargon, dramatic presentations and the obligatory book in an effort to catch the attention of gullible managers. Typically, the message on the bottle of snake oil is: 'We have discovered the secret of making businesses perform better. Become a disciple and do our bidding. Your business problems will disappear and you will have richer and more fulfilled lives.'

Some of the better-known gurus have included:

1 Deming and the Total Quality Management disciples, who tried to persuade us that quality was free;

2 Prahalad and Hamel, who thought that identifying and exploiting 'core competences' would somehow create competitive advantage;

3 Peters, whose *In Search of Excellence* held up alleged exemplars – both business and executives – for managers to admire and imitate;

4 Champney and Hammer, who dreamt up "Reengineering", which became an invidious excuse for restructuring business processes, normally involving significant downsizing accompanied by unfortunate consequences for all stakeholders.

Certain common themes appear to run through many of these initiatives:

1 There is often little or no robust intellectual underpinning for the proposals. Ease of marketing and future income from consulting fees and publishing seem to matter more than rigorous thought.

2 The business objective which managers are asked to strive for is often unstated, unclear or just plain wrong. What do these gurus want the business to maximize? Growth? Market share? Profitability? Stakeholder 'value'? Shareholder 'value'? All or some of the above in combination?

3 The terminology seems designed either to impress or confuse the audience. Management babble is widespread and – amazingly – many managers seem to have an insatiable appetite for this nonsense.

4 Managers are promised simple and obvious solutions to their problems. The answer has been staring them in the face for years but they just haven't seen it:

- 'be customer-led and all will be fine';
- 'be the market leader and you will succeed';
- 'the player with the highest quality wins'.

Of course, managers are smart enough to know that in reality their businesses are complicated. A simple cure will not fix the problems they wrestle with daily. And yet, time after time, seasoned hard-nosed managers fall for the easy and quick 'one size fits all' fix.

5 The gurus have no shame. When their books are found to be a less than helpful source of advice for managers, authors have responded not by going off-stage quietly to count their profits, but by producing even more books proposing different solutions to the problems of the corporate world.

Thankfully, most of these contradictory and confusing fads have either disappeared into oblivion or have become embedded – in greatly diminished and more realistic forms – within standard management practice. They have all failed in their implicit or explicit promise to produce sustainable and distinctive improvements in performance.

The questions I wish to address in this chapter are therefore:

1 Is managing for shareholder value (MFV) just another management fad?

> Is managing for shareholder value (MFV) just another management fad?

2 What is a management consulting perspective on MFV?

3 How have consultants created and leapt on the MFV gravy train?

4 How can clients help themselves to become more value-based?

5 How can consultants serve clients more effectively in this area?

Is MFV just another management fad?

My short answer is 'probably not' if we view MFV as a way of aligning the business with the clear objective of creating superior returns to shareholders over time.

As long as companies are owned by investors who are interested in their own prosperity; and so long as those investors find effective ways of motivating managers to improve performance, then managers will need to be focused on delivering returns to shareholders. They will need to learn and use the concepts, tools and skills of value creation – which is MFV.

What is a management consulting perspective on MFV?

MFV emerged from the academic world in the 1970s. Personal computers were being used to calculate discounted cash flow and economic returns to evaluate the attractiveness of individual projects – asking questions such as 'Will we make an adequate return if we invest in this new equipment?' A number of American academics working mainly in finance and business economics were wrestling with the idea of using these same principles and tools to estimate the value of businesses and of alternative strategies for those businesses.

Thus MFV had its roots in finance, and consultants spent their time worrying about how best to measure value creation and destruction. The calculation of the 'precise' cost of capital was a hot topic and we saw the start of the 'metric wars'. Should managers use economic profit or cash flows in valuations? Should we use equity capital or total capital? What adjustments need to be made to traditional balance sheets and profit and loss statements? Many managers – and many consultants – still believe that MFV is a financial toolkit. They are wrong. The financial dimension of MFV should be viewed as being a necessary but insufficient part of the subject.

Time passed and the question about MFV became 'If financial performance drives value, then what drives financial performance?' The answer was 'strategy' – normally defined in practice as the development of strategy. This provoked consultants to peddle strategic planning as the way to deliver superior performance for shareholders. So in the 1980s and early 1990s MFV broadened its scope to encompass strategic planning. 'Where and how should we compete?' were the key questions to be addressed. Unfortunately, managers – and consultants – who believe that MFV is mainly about better strategic planning processes are also wrong. Better strategies are – like value-based financial and operational metrics – important but insufficient parts of MFV. There is no point in having value-based strategies if we do not have managers with the skill and will to manage for value, i.e. to make the right decisions to implement the necessary changes effectively and efficiently.

> Better strategies are – like value-based financial and operational metrics – important but insufficient parts of MFV.

Further time passed and the most recent question for MFV has been 'If strategy drives financial performance and that drives value, then what drives strategy?' The answer to this has been 'people', and so MFV has expanded again to include thinking on:

- how to develop managers with the will and skill to manage for value;
- how to structure businesses to facilitate value-based decision-making;
- how to allocate roles and responsibilities to maximize the clarity of the accountability for managing the value of the firm; and
- how to deliver and use the information managers need to manage for value.

The key elements of a value-based business are shown in Figure 9.1. We will examine these in turn.

FIGURE 9.1
Elements of a value-based business

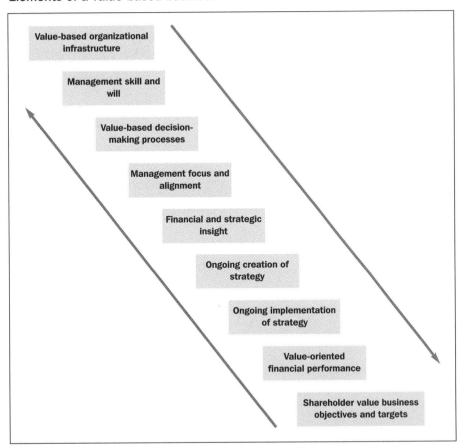

Shareholder value business objectives and targets

If a business wants to be value-based, then it needs to have objectives and targets that are closely related to value. These will drive management behaviour, guide management decisions and be at the heart of the business models created by managers. Value-based objectives are often expressed as total shareholder return (TSR) aspirations; typically set in relation to the TSR performance of a peer set of similar businesses. These aspirations need to be converted into year-on-year performance aspirations using value-oriented strategic and financial metrics such as profitable market share and economic profit. These aspirations need to be broken down and cascaded in meaningful ways to the various components of the business. These are the key performance indicators (KPIs) to be found in value-based management reports.

Many companies talk a lot about shareholder value to current and prospective investors; yet they confuse their own managers by proposing multiple (often competing) objectives that managers are supposed to use to guide major decisions. Their annual reports will contain a glowing statement from the chairman that sets out a long list of objectives the company apparently wants to achieve. Of course, much of this is window-dressing that fools no one, but the problem remains: how are managers supposed to take decisions in ways that somehow satisfy some or all of these worthy aims?

Perhaps the major difficulty encountered by consultants in this area of MFV is that the client's 'top team' states a shareholder value objective that is either ignored by – or not believed by – managers further down the organization. The acid test that the top team has to pass is often along the lines of: 'We believe that strategy alternative (a) delivers the most shareholder value – but strategy alternative (b) delivers more growth. Which are we going to implement?'

Value-oriented financial performance

Most practitioners in the field of MFV are now persuaded that the market value of businesses *over time* is driven by two key elements: delivered performance, as represented by the creation of free cash flows; and market expectations of future financial performance.

However, it is very common to meet senior executives who neither under-stand this nor – in some cases – believe it to be true. They fall into three broad camps:

1 Those who believe that earnings and earnings growth are the primary drivers of value. This means that businesses should be managed to maximize

earnings and earnings growth. These are noble objectives, but they are fundamentally flawed. The problems include:

- Earnings are based on accounting measures and conventions which are easy to manipulate, at least in the short term.
- They take no account of capital and its costs.
- Business risk is excluded.
- The time value of money is ignored.
- Management focus is often on delivering short-term earnings 'to please the City' (whoever that may be) at the expense of more fundamental and value-creating strategic initiatives.

2 Those who believe that return measures (such as ROI, ROE and ROCE) are the key drivers of market value. Therefore, managers should attempt to maximize returns. The good news is that they are starting to take at least some account of capital. The bad news is that they are ignoring growth. It is now clear to us that growth is even more important in driving value than was appreciated by many of the early adopters of MFV.

3 Those who believe that share prices are set by sentiment or magic. They are mystified or hypnotized by 'the City' and listen closely to the nonsense spouted by many of the analysts who follow companies and sectors.

So why do intelligent and seasoned managers persist with these flawed ideas? One reason might be found in the business education – or lack of it – of the leaders of many of our UK businesses. The average age of the directors of large UK-listed companies is now around 50, with the more senior posts being occupied – on average – by older individuals. When did they last have any significant education in business or management? If we assume that their functional training as accountants, engineers, marketers or whatever was over by the time they were 25, then they would have been exposed to the management thinking that was prevalent in the late 1970s and early 1980s, when we were all focused on earnings and earnings growth. A younger cadre would have been taught about the returns focus of the 1980s and early 1990s.

Another fundamental problem we have to address is that our existing management accounting procedures are designed to help with stewardship and reporting to regulatory bodies rather than to help managers take decisions. Management accounts (and many

Our existing management accounting procedures are designed to help with stewardship and reporting to regulatory bodies rather than to help managers take decisions.

management accountants) often focus on 'precision' at the expense of 'usefulness' and it is easy for managers to try to make value-based measures such as economic profit (EP) 'precise' rather than 'useful'. Indeed, it is surprisingly common to find that clients mistrust new financial measures such as EP. These ideas are somehow dangerous and need to be used with extreme care. Of course, these same managers often have an unjustified faith in the 'accuracy' of their traditional measures!

One common way of arguing against the use of value-based measures is to subject them to hurdles of perceived accuracy that are much higher than those imposed on more traditional numbers. Endless debates take place about if and how to allocate capital across the business in order to calculate EP or one of its variants. These same managers quite happily use earnings figures as though they were handed down from on high – perfect in definition and correct in every aspect.

Ongoing implementation of strategy

'Strategy creation is relatively easy, but strategy implementation is relatively difficult.' An obvious statement perhaps, but many managers – and many consultants – actually behave as though the opposite were true. Significant internal and external resources are allocated to 'strategy' – often seen as the realm of the highly educated, very bright, senior staff who interact with the top team using complex financial analysis and endless PowerPoint presentations. On the other hand 'implementation' can be delegated to less capable souls who grind away in the bowels of the business.

Effective implementation is all about three things:

1 the skills of project management which are not a strength of many line managers;

2 the resolve of management to do what they set out to do while being prepared to change direction as circumstances dictate; and

3 the use of value-based KPIs to measure progress in financial, strategic and operational terms.

The key question for management in implementation is: 'What are you going to do if your actual performance falls below that set out in the KPIs?' The typical response is to keep going while looking for opportunities to improve the situation. Resources continue to flow to the implementation as we try to figure out what has happened and what needs to be done. The truth is often that either we are implementing the wrong strategy or we have not implemented as well as we wanted to – or both. A more robust response to failure is to immediately suspend the flow of resources to the project until we understand exactly why we are failing.

Ongoing creation of strategy

Two broad and complementary models of strategy appear to be widely used. One is the 'strategy' approach, in which the whole of the business is reviewed in a strategy development exercise, often 'supported' by teams of consultants. Timing is often dictated by the calendar: it will be said that 'our strategic planning process starts in September, it lasts for a long time and we finalize the strategy and agree the budgets in February'. In many businesses this 'strategy' process has become truly incredible. It doesn't work and everyone knows it, but no one is prepared to grasp the nettle and do something about it. Instead, managers do the best they can: they manage using the budget. Unfortunately, this is normally introspective and backward-looking. Competitors and customers don't figure largely in most budget exercises and therefore the company ends up allocating resources to the wrong uses.

The other model is the 'strategic' approach, which views strategy as being the output of a continuous stream of management decisions that define the customers to be served, how they will be served, the costs that will be incurred by the business in serving customers, how the business will be structured, how and how much employees will be paid and so on.

In my experience, many businesses and consultants get the balance wrong in the use of these two approaches. They focus unduly on 'strategy' and insufficiently on 'strategic'. The downside of the 'strategic' approach is that the business has to improve the decision-making capabilities of all managers who take decisions which could have a major impact on the value of the business. This involves cascading both capability and information, and delegating more willingly to lower levels in the business. Easy to say but harder to do.

Financial and strategic insights

'What you don't see or understand you can do nothing about.' Managers need to have a robust understanding of both *where* and *why* they and their competitors create and destroy value. Strategy and finance need to be viewed as two complementary perspectives on the value creation or destruction

> Managers need to have a robust understanding of both *where* and *why* they and their competitors create and destroy value.

potential of the business. Many businesses view financial performance as being – in the main – an output of strategic vision. A far better viewpoint is to consider finance as being both an input into – and an output of – the ongoing strategic decision-making process.

Failing to understand these two key drivers of value encourages managers to focus their efforts and resources in completely the wrong areas. A typical example of this is where parts of the business that destroy value are grown at the expense of other areas that create value.

Managers are often surprised, or even shocked, when they see for the first time the where and why of value creation and destruction in their business. Favoured product lines are revealed to be value destroyers while other products are seen to create all the value. Old management prejudices are questioned, past decisions are shown to be wrong, management priorities need to be redefined and new customer opportunities are revealed. This can be difficult medicine for managers to swallow; there is always a danger that they will react with denial or emotional rejection.

> Managers are often surprised, or even shocked, when they see for the first time the where and why of value creation and destruction in their business.

Management focus and alignment

I believe that a significant proportion – and I mean something like 50% or more – of management time and effort is wasted in many companies. By this I mean that 50% of total time and effort has no impact on the value of the business. Managers who don't understand the drivers of value in the business fall prey to all sorts of temptations that soak up their energy, especially the pursuit of unprofitable growth. They insist on throwing scarce resources at activities and initiatives that have no positive impact on the value of their business. An easy test is to find out how many large projects are running in a business at any one time, or to review the agendas of board meetings. Too many projects under way, or board agendas that seem to bear little relation to the drivers of the company's value, are pretty good indicators of a management team with poor focus.

Value-based decision-making processes

The decisions that managers take determine the value of their businesses. And yet decision-making as an activity is often taken for granted in business. Like driving or sex, managers are somehow supposed to be 'good' at it. Value-based businesses pay attention to both the decision-making processes they use and to the decision-making capabilities of individual managers. Take a look at the major proposals that reach the board in a typical company. If you find that they vary widely in format, content and – most importantly – quality, then you are likely to be in the presence of sloppy decision-making. Managers often

> Decision-making as an activity is often taken for granted in business. Like driving or sex, managers are somehow supposed to be 'good' at it.

complain that decision-making takes too long in their businesses. The truth is that the timing of decision-making is often haphazard, driven by some arbitrary bureaucratic timescale such as the pre-set dates for board meetings. Some decisions are indeed taken too slowly – but others can be taken too quickly. Timing needs to be a more explicit choice informed by the issue being addressed and the current condition of the business. Many managers seem to want to take a small number of 'big' decisions, perhaps in the belief that this demonstrates strong management or clear leadership. Value-based businesses figure out the right timing for decisions in advance and prefer to take lots of small decisions – adjusting direction and pace as they go and striving for consensus among the key decision-makers.

Management skill and will

Recent research by INSEAD has revealed that companies which were successful in becoming more value-based paid a lot of attention to management education and training. We know that – in general – 'value-based managers are made, not born', and yet many companies appear to ignore the development of the general managers who sit at the heart of value creation. It is often the case that functional capabilities are developed and then managers are heaved into the general management role with little preparation or support.

> If managers are rewarded for achieving targets that are not well aligned with value, then the wrong behaviour and the wrong decisions are likely to be encouraged.

The other key dimension here is 'will' – the willingness to manage for value and to take decisions that drive the value of the business. If managers are rewarded for achieving targets that are not well aligned with value, then the wrong behaviour and the wrong decisions are likely to be encouraged.

Value-based organizational infrastructure

Some companies are structured so that it is clear who is accountable for managing the value of the businesses and for taking the key decisions that drive value. Most are not – accountabilities are unclear; roles and responsibilities are overlapping and vague.

Some companies provide managers with the information about their customers, their competitors and their own performance – information that is needed to identify and resolve the largest value creation opportunities facing the business. Most do not; managers 'fly blind' using outdated or inadequate information.

Bringing it all together

Which companies are most likely to create superior returns for shareholders? The message here is that companies need to ensure that their various elements are aligned with value in a coordinated way. There is little point in using complex value-based financial metrics if you don't change how managers think about strategy and how they take decisions. Equally, there is little point in dreaming up new strategies (even with the help of consultants) if the objective of the business is not aligned well with value, or if you don't change the focus and capabilities of managers so that improvements can be sustained in the future. Nor is there much point in trying to engage the workforce in the 'let's work better together' exercises beloved of HR directors if managers continue to focus on the wrong priorities, pursue the wrong strategies, use inadequate strategic and financial metrics or chase the wrong objectives.

Businesses that want to become more value-based normally need to make a number of changes in different areas in a coordinated and synchronized way. This can be off-putting to managers looking for the 'quick fix' solution promised by the snake-oil salesmen described at the start of this chapter.

How have consultants leapt on the MFV gravy train?

We can put the consultants who purport to work on MFV into three main categories:

1. *Generalist management consulting firms that have some kind of MFV offer in their catalogue.* These firms offer a wide range of services that managers at different levels and in different parts of client businesses might conceivably want. They typically use the partner-leverage model, where the offer is delivered to clients using teams of consultants ranging from experienced partners through to analysts fresh from university. Examples would be McKinsey and PwC.

2. *Specialist firms that provide either a 'holistic' MFV offer or who specialize in specific narrow aspects of MFV.* 'Holistic' specialists split into two main groups: traditional partner leverage-based firms and 'boutiques' (such as my own firm, Corporate Value Improvement Ltd), who believe that the partner-leverage model is fundamentally flawed because it works in favour of the consultants (or at least the owners of the consulting firm) and against clients' best interests. These firms typically use seasoned experts in MFV who work closely with client personnel on a 'coaching with content' basis. 'Narrow' participants include firms, such as Stern Stewart, which concentrate on financial measurement and value-based management reward programmes.

3. *'Implementers' – who offer a sound understanding of the dynamics of shareholder value and back this up with the ability to undertake major elements of the implementation on behalf of the client, often by outsourcing key activities.* Here we see the arrival of the major IT-empowered and asset-driven firms such as Accenture. They talk the language of shareholder value but they have the additional advantage of being able to actually deliver many of the changes needed by management to achieve superior shareholder returns. They are ready to take over major activities such as IT, HR or call centres in order to improve service at lower economic costs. They have enough money to put their own skin in the game, which is appealing to many clients. They are likely to challenge the traditional 'strategy' consultancies, who will need either to form alliances with the big players or to graft new – and very significant – capabilities onto their current practices.

How can companies help themselves to become more value-based?

Experience has taught me the following lessons:

1. *There has to be a clear and compelling reason for wanting to improve performance for shareholders.* What can trigger a move to become more value-based? A common reason is pressure on senior management from non-executives or major shareholders to deliver better performance. The board's role in this area is critical; recent developments in corporate governance may drive boards to be more demanding of their executive colleagues. Another trigger can be the arrival of a new CEO. An MFV programme is an ideal way for a new leader to get under the skin of the business as well as to demonstrate strong leadership. A final reason is that many management option schemes are 'under water'; managers therefore either try to have a scheme recast to soften targets or – more honestly – try to improve performance in order to earn bonuses.

2. *The change has to be owned and driven by the top team.* The top team needs to 'lead by doing' if a company is to move successfully towards being more value-based. This means the team must get involved personally, lead pieces of work and be accountable for delivery.

John Sunderland of Cadbury Schweppes is an outstanding example of 'leading by doing'. He took a clear lead in the programme of change at Cadbury Schweppes. This included 'finding a thousand different ways of saying the same thing to the organization', in order to continually reinforce the message that the governing objective was to maximize shareholder value over time. The challenge here is to find ways of expressing the message in terms that are meaningful for different levels and in different parts of the business. This has to be balanced against many managers' desire to subject the business to glossy communication campaigns. It is easy to get these wrong, developing and encouraging cynicism rather than harnessing support for the programme. Unfortunately, many managers 'lead by telling' in the naïve belief that people will obey their orders rather than interpret priorities and set directions based on the acts of the leader.

If the top team members have real reservations about the need to become value-based – or about their personal or corporate ability to undertake the changes required – then they should not launch an MFV programme. It will fail, money and time will be wasted and credibility will be lost. Their replacements will make the business more value-based!

3. *Management education has to be a high priority at all levels and it should start at the top.* The skills, concepts and techniques of managing for value are still not taught widely or well by business schools. Indeed, a number of the core concepts used in managing for value seem to fly directly in the face of traditional management thought. If the top team is to lead the charge to become more value-based, it also needs to lead in developing its own competence and understanding, both as a group and as individuals. A key element of the implementation of MFV at Lloyds Bank – led by Sir Brian Pitman, one of the great value-creating chief executives – was a number of intensive education sessions for the board of directors.

4. *Management will have to set and keep to priorities. Some current initiatives will need to stop or be delayed.* One of the key concepts of MFV

is that managers should focus their time, efforts and resources on the highest value opportunities and issues that face the business – normally a small number of priorities: five or six, say, in a typical large business. Unfortunately, by setting the priorities to be worked on we simultaneously define the initiatives that must be delegated, suspended or abandoned. This is easy to say but apparently hard to do. Managers may be reluctant to stop ongoing projects because they will be perceived as wasting already spent resources or as inconsistent or wavering in their decisions and actions. Clearly there can be emotional attachments to work that may have been under way for some time. But the hard question remains: why devote scarce resources to projects that will have little impact on the value of the business while – at the same time – there is insufficient capacity to carry out the high value-at-stake work effectively?

5. *Changes in management reward schemes to align them with shareholder value can be expected and they should be implemented early in the programme.* The advice given to clients used to be 'Don't change how you reward people until they become familiar with the tools and techniques of MFV'. I now believe that changing how people get paid is a good way to gain their attention and tell them what is important. So bonus schemes should be changed early on to use value-based measures at the appropriate level, such as TSR performance for senior executives and EP for more junior managers.

6. *IT systems may need to be altered significantly to provide the information managers need to manage for value.* Many MFV implementations start off using spreadsheets to model value creation and destruction. Capital allocation – needed to calculate EP – is done off-line from the core financial systems that often struggle to produce the required information. This is a good way to keep junior consultants occupied for long periods, but it is not suitable for managing an ongoing business. Prospective adopters of MFV need to get their financial and IT resources lined up early on so that systems can be changed at the right time.

7. *Decision-making will need to become a core competence.* Our decisions drive the value of the businesses we run; yet little attention is paid to decision-making in many companies. Experience has shown that enormous benefits can normally be gained by using more systematic and fact-based approaches to making decisions. A key part of this improvement is to encourage and permit the most senior decision-makers to become activist. By this I mean get them involved at various stages of the work needed to develop a value-based decision for a high value-at-stake issue. This partly

redefines the role of the top team: they are now expected to get more actively involved in resolving the major issues facing the business and to spend less time sitting in judgement over the work of others. For many senior managers this is a blessed relief. It takes advantage of their core skills and knowledge of the business in a most positive way.

8. *The top team needs to have an insatiable appetite for profitable growth, i.e. growth in which returns exceed the cost of capital.* Warren Buffett warns managers and investors to beware of the 'institutional imperative' – the unjustified search for growth at any cost. Unprofitable growth, i.e. when returns over time are less than the cost of capital, is a major and unnecessary source of value destruction in many companies; yet many managers find it difficult to identify and eradicate bad growth. In these same businesses there are often wonderful opportunities for profitable growth which cannot be grasped because scarce resources are being squandered in the wrong areas. In the heyday of Boots plc, value-based analysis revealed that its core business – Boots the Chemist – was an opportunity for significant profitable growth. Unfortunately, it lay in the shadow of so-called 'growth' businesses within the Boots group, such as Boots Pharmaceuticals, that soaked up the lion's share of corporate resources and management attention. When resources were redirected to Boots the Chemist the business responded by delivering outstanding shareholder returns for nearly a decade. We know that growth is a key driver of investor sentiment and expectations. However, many consultancies have failed to appreciate the real power of this growth. Some have been criticized – rightly – by clients for paying too much attention to reducing unprofitable growth and cutting costs rather than finding ways of growing the business profitably. Perhaps this poor focus has been driven by the wishes of the finance functions who have sponsored MFV in many companies; or perhaps it is just that junior consultants are more easily used in the hunt for cost reduction.

9. *There has to be a finely struck balance between analysis, management judgement and action.* There is no doubt that many management decisions would be improved by the more extensive use of the right information. Understanding the where and why of value creation and destruction for products, customer segments and customers would enable managers to take better and more value-based decisions. But it also possible to fall into an analytical trap, to believe that the realities of complex business environments can be reduced to a few spreadsheet models owned and driven by consultants. Clients need to find a balance between analytical rigour and management judgement, between 'boiling the ocean' of facts and using the experience of competent managers.

How can consultants serve clients more effectively in this area?

I believe that traditional 'partner-leverage' strategy consultancies are in gradual decline. Many of them have shed consultants and are trying to reinvent themselves by repackaging the same old capabilities in different guises.

They are falling away because clients have realized that these consulting models cannot deliver the required impact on business performance, and that this type of input is neither essential nor good value for money.

Why? One reason is that the average member of a typical partner-leverage consultant team has had very limited exposure to working in a line role; and has been given hardly any time to acquire the skills and capabilities needed to be an effective consultant. It is hardly surprising, therefore, that they struggle to influence managers, give credible advice or justify their fees. Clients now have their own MBAs who can combine technical capability with in-depth knowledge of the business. They don't need junior consultants to build spreadsheet models and to give them the latest management babble.

I believe that consultants who want to survive and prosper are going to have to reappraise their own business and consulting models to emphasize:

- driving real learning and capability into the client;

- working more closely with internal client specialists instead of fielding large teams of inexperienced consultants;

- adopting a general manager perspective on client problems and opportunities. This will be difficult for traditional firms because their main sources of recruits – business schools and universities – are not geared up to deliver general managers. Recruits from these sources have little or no general management experience and at best a modest understanding of how businesses really operate in practice;

- Using a 'strategic' rather than a 'strategy' perspective. In other words, to see their role as being to improve client performance by making sustained improvements in the decision-making capabilities of client personnel at different levels rather than carrying out text-book strategy studies.

It seems to me that the winning consultancies – as measured by client impact and by their own profitability and growth – are liable to be the specialist boutiques and the 'implementers'. These firms can attend to the real needs of clients and can deliver deep knowledge of managing for value, underpinned by implementation capability, in cost-effective ways.

10

ACHIEVING VALUABLE GROWTH THROUGH M&A

BOARDROOM LESSONS FOR THE ACQUISITION GAME[1]

MARK L. SIROWER
Boston Consulting Group and New York University

The synergy trap – why acquisitions are a unique investment

Shareholder returns from the merger boom

Becoming the 'always on' company (Board practice no. 1)

Reviewing the PMI board pack (Board practice no. 2)

Testing investor communications (Board practice no. 3)

A final checklist

In some mergers there truly are major synergies – though often times the acquirer pays too much to obtain them – but at other times the cost and revenue benefits that are projected prove illusory. Of one thing, however, be certain: if a CEO is enthused about a particularly foolish acquisition, both his internal staff and his outside advisors will come up with whatever projections are needed to justify his stance. Only in fairy tales are emperors told that they are naked.

Warren Buffett, 1997

Not a red dime is needed, in fact we'll save money; and if we ever needed money our investment banker is sitting two seats to the left, ha ha ha...

Bernie Ebbers at press conference for WorldCom acquisition of MCI, 1997

The 1990s and early 2000s will go down as perhaps one of the most important periods in industrial history. Ten years ago, we could not have begun to comprehend the redistribution of global assets witnessed in the largest merger wave ever. In 1999 and 2000 alone over 70,000 acquisitions were announced globally with a combined value of over $6.7 trillion – dwarfing the great merger wave of the 1980s.[2]

With the steep declines in the S&P, and particularly the Nasdaq market, the available currency for deals has dropped significantly. Mistakes that were covered up by a rising market are now visible for all to see. Perhaps most important, company directors now understand that they will be held accountable by shareholders, especially for 'bet the company' decisions. This new spotlight on officers and directors is great news for investors, because two decades of research on M&A performance confirm that CEOs often give investors good reason to *sell* shares on announcement of a major transaction.

For example, following a loss of nearly 17% of the market cap of a food company on the announcement of its largest acquisition, the chairman of the company declared, 'My objective is to be a billion dollar company by 2002'. Perhaps he should have added, 'no matter how much shareholder value we lose in the process'. Unfortunately, this kind of M&A 'logic' is the norm rather than the exception.

Figure 10.1 plots the shape of the recent merger wave: rapidly increasing activity followed by a steep decline. One critical inference from this is that merger waves occur when companies that haven't previously done deals start doing them, or when active acquirers start doing more or larger deals. Thus, an important implication of an M&A wave is that the environment is packed with *inexperience* – either inexperience with any kind of deal or inexperience with the new pace and size of transactions. Too often, major transactions are completed as a reaction to the deal environment rather than to a carefully thought through business case.

FIGURE 10.1

The recent wave of global mega-mergers – announced deals over $1 billion

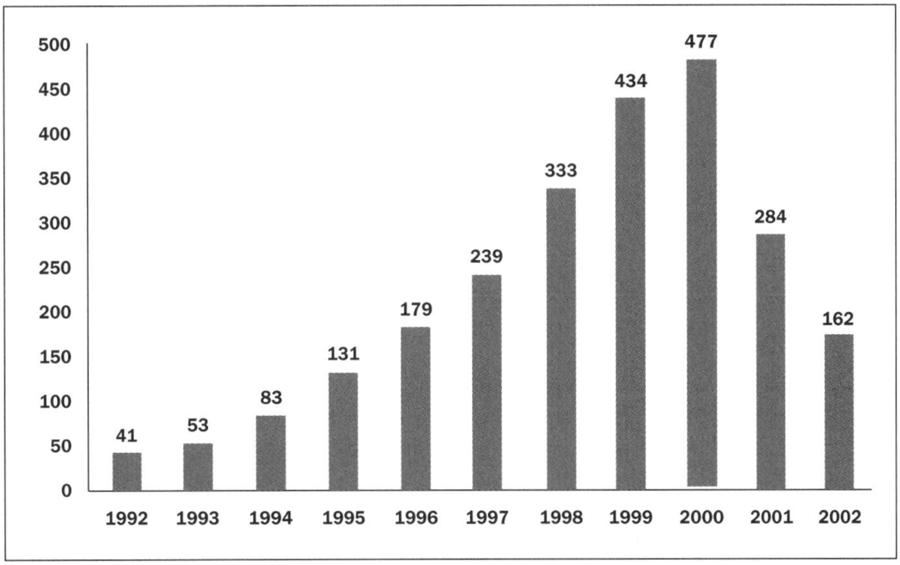

The board owes the fundamental duties of loyalty and care to its shareholders. The duty of loyalty is that a director must not self-deal at the expense of the shareholders. The duty of care calls for directors to act as a prudent person would and on an informed basis with due deliberation before making or approving a decision. There are few, if any, strategies that carry with them as much immediate and ongoing risk to shareholders as a major acquisition. In this chapter, I present important and prudent practices for boards regarding these 'bet the company' commitments of shareholder capital.

We now know enough about the economics of acquisitions to call for a standard of prudence with regard to how boards must represent shareholders in these highly risky decisions. There are simply too many great companies that have grown successfully using M&A – GE, Wells Fargo, IBM, ADP, etc. – to ignore the breakdown in governance that occurs in poorly informed boards.

Much attention has been given to the Enron, WorldCom, Adelphia, Tyco and Global Crossing scandals that resulted in the landmark Sarbanes-Oxley legislation. And for good reason: boards must ensure that appropriate procedures are in place to prevent criminal activity by management and produce reliable disclosures to shareholders regarding the financial state of a company. Unfortunately, far less coverage has been given to losses from poorly

Far less coverage has been given to losses from poorly informed acquisition decisions that, in the aggregate, have been at least as damaging to the investors of the acquiring companies.

informed acquisition decisions (e.g., Conseco/Green Tree, Hercules/Betz Dearborn, Mattel/Learning Co., etc.) that, in the aggregate, have been at least as damaging to the investors of the acquiring companies. These deals represent capital investment decisions that are many times larger than typical capital investment decisions for which systems, structures and procedures are in place – and could not have occurred without board approval.

Even in the current environment, an acquiring board's fiduciary duty of care can be satisfied by having an investment banker issue a fairness opinion stating that the price being paid is fair. Trouble is, I have never seen a fairness opinion state that an offering price represents overpayment – and yet we know that at least 50% of these fairness opinions are likely to be wrong. Boards of superior performers do not rely on fairness opinions to make informed acquisition decisions. *An investment bank can provide important information about what a company has to pay to complete a deal, but not necessarily what it should pay.*

And as the Enron *et al.* scandals so vividly demonstrated, shareholders are not nameless and faceless, but are often a company's own employees. This is an especially important problem for acquisitions. When a deal is met with a drop in the acquirer's share price of 5%, 10% or more, not only do employees – the folks who will have to make the deal work – lose a significant portion of their pension assets, but morale suffers accordingly, even before the critical task of deal integration begins.

The following are five fundamental premises that guide my thinking for this chapter and should be touchstones for senior management and boards when considering M&A as a component of a successful growth strategy.

1. Successful acquisitions must *both* enable a company to beat competitors *and* reward investors.

2. Successful corporate growth processes must enable a company to find good opportunities and avoid bad ones *at the same time*.

3. Prepared acquirers (what I call 'always on' companies) are not necessarily active acquirers.

4. A good post-merger integration (PMI) will not save a bad transaction but a bad PMI can ruin a good (i.e. strategically sound and realistically priced) one.

5. Investors are vigilant and smart – that is, they can smell a poorly considered transaction right from announcement.

I first review why acquisitions are a unique investment – and why investors are naturally sceptical. Next, I then discuss a major study that examined shareholder returns of acquirers during the merger boom of 1995–2001. I then discuss three critical practices that informed directors must understand and can use to fulfil their fiduciary duty of care in M&A decisions. Finally, I close with a simple checklist that every board should take senior management through before approving major transactions.

The synergy trap – why acquisitions are a unique investment

It is often claimed that 'getting a deal done is a lot easier than making it work'. The implication is that the key to a successful transaction lies in the hard work after the deal is closed. In fact, it is the economics of a transaction that drives the performance needs of the integration effort. And, unfortunately, most major transactions that ultimately fail are predictably dead on arrival no matter how they are managed after the deal is done. Successful post-merger integration depends on a well-founded business case and an operating model for how that case will actually generate value before a deal is even announced.

Since the early 1980s, in about two-thirds of all acquisitions, the acquirer's stock price has fallen immediately after the deal is announced. As I will show, in most cases that drop is just a precursor of worse to come as the company's subsequent performance confirms the market's initial negative expectations. The market's routinely negative response to M&A announcements reflects investors' scepticism about the likelihood that the acquirer will be able to maintain both the original values of the businesses in question and achieve the synergies required to justify the premium. And the larger the premium, the worse the share price performance. But why is the market so sceptical? Why do acquiring companies have such a difficult time creating value for their shareholders?

> Since the early 1980s, in about two-thirds of all acquisitions, the acquirer's stock price has fallen immediately after the deal is announced.

First is the fact that acquisitions, although a fast route to growth, require full payment up front. By contrast, investments in research and development, capacity expansion, or marketing campaigns are made in stages over time. In acquisitions, the financial clock starts ticking on the entire capital investment right from the beginning. Investors want to see compelling evidence that timely performance gains will materialize, particularly when a premium is being paid. Otherwise, a company's shares will lose value before any integration takes place.

Second, even without paying an acquisition premium, the stock prices of both the acquirer and target already reflect significant performance improvements – I call this the *base case*. The capitalized current level of operating performance with no assumed improvement accounts for less than 40% of the typical company's stock price.[3] The rest of the stock price is based entirely on expected performance improvements. Synergy can only occur when there are operating improvements above this base-case trajectory. Viewed in this light, the typical 30–40% acquisition premium for synergy raises the bar even higher – a lot higher – for required improvements. The bottom line: acquirers can lose a great deal more than the premium by not protecting the profitable growth expectations already built into their shares and those of the target.

Third, synergies don't come for free. Whether they are revenue synergies or cost synergies, there is almost always a financial cost associated with achieving them. I call this the *synergy matching principle*. An acquisition target cannot be credibly valued without considering the amount and timing of both benefits and related costs. The wrong time to consider severance outlays, additional capital investments, etc. is after a target company has been valued. These 'unexpected' costs will later translate into shareholder losses.

In other cases, acquisitions disappoint because competitors can easily replicate the benefits of the deal. Competitors do not stand idly by while an acquirer attempts to generate synergies at their expense. Arguably, unless an acquisition confers a sustainable competitive advantage, it should not command any premium at all. Indeed, acquisitions sometimes increase a company's vulnerability to competitive attack because the demands of integration can divert attention away from competitors. Acquisitions also create an opportunity for competitors to poach talent while organizational uncertainty is high. I have seen cases where competitors have held job fairs at local airport hotels and begun interviewing key executives in both merging companies immediately following announcement.

Finally, it is difficult and extremely expensive to unwind a merger that goes wrong, particularly after significant integration activity takes place. Managers, with their credibility at stake, may compound the problem by throwing good money after bad in the fleeting hope that more time and money will prove them right.

All too often, the purchase price of an acquisition is driven by the pricing of other 'comparable' acquisitions rather than by a rigorous assessment of where, when and how management can drive real performance gains. A simple tool I have found useful with acquirer boards for assessing the relative magnitude of synergy risk is a straightforward calculation that I call *shareholder value at risk* (SVAR). SVAR is simply the premium paid for the acquisition divided by the market value of the acquiring company before the announcement is made. Think of it as a 'bet your company' index, which shows how much of your company's value is at risk if no post-acquisition synergies are realized. This index also can be calculated as the premium percentage multiplied by the market value of the seller relative to the buyer. The greater the premium percentage paid to sellers and the greater their market value relative to the acquiring company, the higher the SVAR. Of course, as I've discussed, it's possible for acquirers to lose even more than their premium. In these cases, SVAR underestimates risk and is therefore a conservative measure of risk.

> A simple tool I have found useful with acquirer boards for assessing the relative magnitude of synergy risk is a straightforward calculation: I call it 'shareholder value at risk' (SVAR).

Table 10.1 shows how an acquirer's SVAR for an all-cash deal varies both with the relative size of the acquisition and the percentage premium paid. The table also shows how SVAR for an acquirer is different for a stock deal. Why would

TABLE 10.1
Acquirer SVAR% in all-cash versus all-stock deals

		Ratio of stand-alone value of seller to stand-alone value of acquirer			
		0.25	0.50	0.75	1.00
		All-cash deal			
	30	7.5	15	22.5	30
Premium (%)	**40**	10	20	30	40
	50	12.5	25	37.5	50
	60	15	30	45	60
		All-stock deal*			
	30	5.6	11.3	16.9	22.5
Premium (%)	**40**	7.5	15	22.5	30
	50	9.4	18.8	28.1	37.5
	60	11.3	22.5	33.8	45

*Acquirer owns 75% of the combined company.

Source: Adapted from Rappaport, Alfred and Sirower, Mark L. (1999) 'Cash or Stock: The Trade-offs for Buyers and Sellers in Mergers and Acquisitions', *Harvard Business Review*, November/December.

this be different? The main distinction between cash and stock transactions is this: In cash transactions, acquiring shareholders take on the entire risk that the expected synergy value embedded in the acquisition premium will not materialize. In stock transactions, that risk is shared with selling shareholders. More precisely, in stock transactions, the synergy risk is shared in proportion to the percentage of the combined company the acquiring and selling shareholders each will own. To calculate an acquirer's SVAR for a fixed-exchange ratio stock deal, you must multiply the all-cash SVAR by the percentage that the acquirer will own in the combined company. I assume for the all-stock example in Figure 10.1 that the acquirer shareholders will own 75% of the combined company and the selling shareholders will own 25% of the combined company.

Little wonder then that acquirers found shares such an attractive method of payment in the recent merger boom. But there is a big catch – remember, investors are smart. While technically SVAR is reduced, stock deals send two important signals to investors. First, the best time to issue new shares is when they are overvalued. Thus, there is a classic asymmetric information problem where the seller must question the motives of the buyer. Second, if an acquirer management team were truly confident about getting the projected synergies, why would they want to share the future benefits by paying with stock? In other words, paying with stock is a signal of lower confidence in the deal than if the acquirer paid with cash. Moreover, cash deals typically require debt financing which requires both confidence and discipline to meet the interest payments. When acquirers pay with stock – that is, use equity financing – they often lull themselves into acting like somehow equity is free and forget about its required return (the cost of capital). Ironically, the same CEOs who publicly declare their company's share price to be too low will cheerfully issue large amounts of stock at that 'too low' price to pay for their acquisitions. In the next section, I present a study of deals from the 1990s merger boom with some interesting results on the returns to acquirers using cash versus stock as a method of payment.

Shareholder returns from the merger boom

Before I began the study, I was intrigued by a comment made by Carly Fiorina, CEO of Hewlett-Packard Co, regarding the near 20% drop in the price of HP's shares on the day of announcement of its acquisition of Compaq Corp. Ms Fiorina claimed in a *BusinessWeek* interview: 'You don't make this kind of move, and judge its success, by the short-term stock price.'[4]

Well, that is certainly a testable proposition. Together with a colleague,

Mark Golovcsenko, I examined more than 1,000 deals valued at least $500 million announced between 1 July 1995 and 31 August 2001.[5] We first excluded those deals where the acquirer's share price could not be tracked on a major US stock exchange. Then, using the rationale that a deal had to be of material relative size, we excluded those deals in which the value of the seller was less than 15% of that of the acquirer. Last, we culled those deals in which the acquirer subsequently announced another significant acquisition within a year. What remained were 302 deals, for which the average acquirer market capitalization was $14.2 billion and average seller market cap (five days before announcement) was $5.5 billion. The average market cap of sellers relative to their acquirers was nearly 50% – so these were very significant deals.

To measure performance, we calculated total shareholder return (stock price appreciation plus dividends) to the acquirer at the announcement of the deal (one week before to one week after) and one year later.[6] We examined not only absolute return, but also a relative total shareholder return (RTSR) relative to both the broader market (S&P 500) and the acquirer's industry peers (within the S&P 500). The key results for our sample of 302 deals using RTSR to industry peers are as follows:[7]

1. *On average, acquirers underperform their industry peers.* Average returns to acquirers around deal announcement are minus 4.1% with 64% of deals viewed poorly and 36% viewed positively by the market – a familiar result. One year later average returns are still minus 4.3% and 61% of acquirers lag their industry peers.

2. *Initial reactions are persistent and indicative of future returns.* One year later, the portfolio of deals that begin poorly (minus 9.2%) maintained almost the same negative return (minus 9%). The portfolio of deals that began positively (5.7%) maintained a strong positive return (4.9%). A closer look shows that 67% of the initially negative deals were still negative and 50% of the positives were still positive a year after announcement.

3. *Deals that begin in the right direction – and deliver – overwhelmingly outperform deals that begin poorly and stay that way.* In the year following announcement, acquirers whose deals were met initially with a negative investor reaction, and continued to be perceived negatively, posted an average return of minus 24.9%; whereas acquirers whose deals initially received, and continued to receive, a favourable response, returned an average of 33.1% – a difference of 58 percentage points!

4. *Price matters.* The average premium paid for targets across the whole sample was nearly 36% with an average premium of 38.4% paid by the

initially negative group and 30% by the positive group. One year later, virtually the same finding is intact. Regardless of initial reaction, those buyers that are ahead of their peers one year after announcement paid on average 31% premiums; those buyers lagging their peers paid 39% premiums. Most striking, the average premium paid by the persistent negative performers was 40.5% whereas the persistent positive performers paid an average premium of only 25.8%.

5. *Cash deals outperform stock deals.* Cash deals, while less common (12% of all deals), markedly outperform stock swaps. At announcement, the returns relative to peers of cash deals beat all-stock deals by 4% (minus 1.0% versus minus 5%). One year later, the gap widened to 8.3%: cash deals beat their peers by 0.3% while stock deals lag their peers by minus 8.0%. This finding reaffirms the widely reported result on the underperformance of stock deals. Further, poorly received stock deals are the most persistent performers with 73% of them still negative a year later (having a minus 26.8% return).

6. *Sellers are the biggest beneficiaries of M&A transactions.* While buyers lose on average, shareholders of selling companies earned an average 20% return from the week before the deals to the week after.

7. *M&A transactions create value at the macroeconomic level.* Mergers create value for the economy. While the shareholders of buyers most often lose value, the shareholders of sellers most often gain value. In the aggregate, there is value creation of 1% at announcement when looking at the combined market cap changes of both buyer and seller. In our sample, stock deals had negative combined value creation of minus 0.5%, while cash deals yielded a return of nearly 7%.

Table 10.2 illustrates the general pattern of returns to acquirers. These are important findings and are no accident. Investor reactions are powerful forecasts of the future based on previous expectations and the new information given by the company about the economic wisdom of the transaction. Acquirers that truly deliver or show evidence of their ability to honour their promises do extremely well over time; acquirers that deliver on the negative expectations do extremely poorly over time.[8] Thus, investor reactions set a critical tone that the company – and its employees – must live with while it attempts to make a deal work. The often-heard statement that initial market reactions are meaningless, or just short-term, is on balance a myth. Boards should exercise caution when they are presented with a proposal where management expects investors to get hurt at announcement.

I now discuss three practices that should be part of every board's arsenal for

TABLE 10.2

Returns from the merger boom

		No. of deals	Announce-ment return	1 year return	Premium
RTSR (Peers)	Persistent positive	52	–	33.1%	25.8%
	Initial positive	103	5.7%	4.9%	30.7%
	Full sample	302	–4.1%	–4.3%	35.7%
	Initial negative	199	–9.2%	–9.0%	38.4%
	Persistent negative	133	–	–24.9%	40.5%

RTSR (Peers) axis: 40, 30, 20, 10, 0, –10, –20, –30

Announcement period (Day –5, +5)   1 year

a prudent consideration of an acquisition proposal from senior management. First is ensuring that the deal under consideration has come from a credible strategic process. Second is insisting that the board package include not only the strategy and fairness opinion materials, but also key issues regarding the operating model that sets the direction for how the integration will be managed. Third is formulating the questions regarding what will be communicated to investors and employees – critical questions that test whether investors are likely to sell the acquirer's shares or be encouraged to buy them.

Becoming the 'always on' company (Board practice no. 1)

In the Introduction I alluded to the one of the fundamental gaps to which acquisition failure can be attributed – the typical lack of experience of senior management in using significant transactions as a component of a company's growth strategy.

This inexperience translates into little or no strategic M&A process – that is, a gaping hole between the long-run strategy of the company and how the company screens potential transactions. Too often the board has little time to peel back the strategic logic of a transaction and instead is just presented with a deal as a *fait accompli*. Potential deals do not get on the board meeting agenda until they are subject for approval. Successful boards will insist that acquisitions stem from a proactive, well-defined corporate development process.

Most acquirers are merely reacting to deals happening around them and the opportunities that land at their doorstep – that's precisely what drives a merger wave. And would-be acquirers are easy prey for the merger myths that emerge during waves and help support reactive thinking (see 'Great merger myths' below). In most cases, there is little linkage between strategic planning and deal-making that will benefit the company and its investors.

In other words, instead of emerging from a thoughtful, proactive strategy, far too many transactions begin as reactive, one-off decisions. Rather than continually considering the total universe of options, as successful LBO firms do, executives tend to focus exclusively on the deal at hand. Viewed in isolation that deal might look attractive, but if it were to be compared to other potential M&A candidates, it might seem less than a perfect fit. Compare it to marrying the first seemingly compatible person you ever took out on a date: it could work – but the odds are it won't.

The danger for companies is that by becoming overly enamoured of a deal simply because it comes along and seems like a good opportunity, management may ignore negative information that emerges even during a thorough evaluation of the candidate. It works like this: an opportunity presents itself and nothing else is on the table. The acquirer then develops a compelling story to support the deal and its required price. The deal gets done, despite warning signs that it may not work, because of overly optimistic assumptions built into the numbers or the lack of a credible plan to deliver results. When results fall below expectations, 'cultural' factors (often poorly defined) take the blame.

What's worse, when unprepared companies trap themselves into reacting to and looking at potential acquisitions that happen to come their way, they waste tremendous time and resources that could have been devoted to finding more suitable opportunities in the first place. That's because management must conduct extensive due diligence for each merger opportunity that presents itself, despite the fact that many of them should not have even made it to the table. And while even the best-intentioned due diligence will help avoid bad deals, it won't help find the right opportunities.

> While even the best-intentioned due diligence will help avoid bad deals, it won't help find the right opportunities.

It is no coincidence that the most successful international acquirers are also the most disciplined. Before making a deal, such experienced acquirers satisfy themselves that their strategic alternatives and acquisition opportunities have been carefully explored and their potential for creating value quantified. They understand which of their existing businesses should be developed organically, which should be sold, and which would benefit from growth through acquisition.

An important awakening for boards occurs when they realize the power of choice a company creates for itself when it is strategically prepared to consider potential acquisitions. Prepared companies are not necessarily active – they don't need to be. In my experience, prepared companies, which I call 'always on' companies, have gone through a strategic process that has allowed them to develop a short watch list of acquisition opportunities. This allows them to be patient. Companies that had well-documented watch lists were in a great position to buy when market valuations dropped dramatically after the stock market bubble.

> An important awakening for boards occurs when they realize the power of choice a company creates for itself when it is strategically prepared to consider potential acquisitions.

From reactive to 'always on'

To find true value-creating acquisitions, acquirers must do more than simply avoid economically unsound deals. That means being able to spot false positives and false negatives. False positives are opportunities that are accepted when they should have been rejected. False negatives are opportunities that are rejected when they should have been accepted. When a company reacts to a single opportunity, it has implicitly screened out a universe of other opportunities, driving up the risk of false negatives (missed opportunities). Compounding this problem is the fact that reactors will also have a more difficult time dismissing dubious opportunities when they lack other options.

Most of the work on transaction risk has focused on minimizing false positives (opportunities that should have been rejected) by promoting better due diligence or by raising integration issues early in the evaluation process for a single deal under consideration. Largely overlooked is how false positives and false negatives might be avoided at the same time by using a systematic process for opportunity selection.

Such a process would mean that before considering *any* acquisition opportunity, senior management must agree on the direction of the business, strategic gaps and profitable growth opportunities. They must assess the company's competitive strengths and weaknesses, as well as top management's aspirations. Most boards spend very little time talking about where they want their business to be over the long term. A common frustration among directors is that they spend a lot of time talking about current and recent past issues, a problem compounded by the demands of the recent Sarbanes-Oxley legislation.

> Before considering *any* acquisition opportunity, senior management must agree on the direction of the business, strategic gaps and profitable growth opportunities.

These short-term issues are important, but keep the board from setting a clear vision and strategy for the future – where they want to be in five to ten years' time? What are the major issues that will determine the success of this business in the future? Where is growth going to come from?

That immediately takes the board into the question of organic growth or acquisition. There is no substitute for the board regularly visiting that subject and getting documentation from management. If this is done, then the context for acquisition and the logic for acquisition will be well established. It helps define the initial screen that management will use to search for acquisition opportunities. If an acquisition does show up out of the blue, then at least there will be context against which it can be evaluated.

A master list of acquisition opportunities should then be constructed that casts a wide net and covers the strategic gaps and opportunities that management has identified. *A director might simply ask to see this list.* Once a high-level screen has been set up, management can develop detailed filters that narrow the list of potential acquisition candidates. Designing these filters forces executives to refine their strategic priorities. Applying these filters screens out inappropriate opportunities. Such a systematic process for selecting opportunities helps companies minimize their transaction risk by preventing illogical opportunities from even making it to the table for consideration.

By following this process, management will debate and identify the key strategic issues that will enable it to generate a short watch list of the most promising acquisition candidates. Through detailed discussions, issues will be raised, including pricing, due diligence and PMI (Post-merger Integration), that affect the likelihood of success of different deals. In the end management will have a much better view of its competitive environment and the true priorities of the businesses. As this process continues, the senior team – and the board – will have a clear framework of business growth needs and will be able to respond intelligently to new opportunities that may subsequently emerge. As an IBM senior corporate development executive put it, 'The more you look, the more you find; the more you look, the more you learn; the more you look, the more you test your strategies.'

In the later stages of this screening process, management should consider post-merger integration issues as a screening tool so that a real PMI plan will be in place well before any deals are announced. Here is where potential transition risks such as culture clashes, long-term labour contracts, tax issues, facility locations, distribution gaps and management depth can be used to differentiate deals and identify those opportunities most likely to realize value. It is next to impossible to complete a truly sophisticated financial analysis of synergy potential – including probability estimates and timing of expected synergies – without evaluating integration risks. Finally, the process will assist management in developing and communicating sensible, credible acquisition stories to the board, investors and employees.

By implementing this rigorous selection process, companies can readily consider the relative merits of emerging targets versus other investment opportunities. For example, at General Electric, one of the world's most successful acquirers, acquisition search and selection is done at the division level by the same managers who will be responsible for implementing the deal, and whose compensation is linked to its performance. Rather than reacting to single-deal opportunities as most boards are forced to do, GE has developed pre-approved screening filters that division managers use long before GE directors are asked to approve a specific transaction.

It is important to note that it is virtually impossible for an investment banker to do this effectively away from management because management is essentially making strategic decisions in designing filters. And when a strategic search is done right, a banker should not be able to bring management a significant transaction that the company has not already considered. Management will be able to retrace why a company that is available for sale is not on their watch list. Putting this process in place requires significant internal resources and certainly can be expensive – but not having it virtually guarantees deals will not be strategic.

An informed board can assess whether a deal has emerged logically from a strategy previously accepted, or whether it is entirely an opportunistic event. The easiest way to avoid merely being the last hurdle on the CEO's path to announcing a major transaction (with full support of his investment bankers of course) is to insist that a clear M&A process is in place well before any opportunities are presented to the board.

Thus the board's role is not merely to ensure that a deal is backed by strategic logic – that can be done for practically any deal. The board should require management to describe a logical process similar to what I have described. A successful corporate development process must not only screen out sure losers, but also shine a bright light on the best ones, and transform them into superior shareholder returns. The board plays a vital role in setting the context in which this process can work effectively.

The great merger myths supporting reactive behaviour

Merger waves bring with them powerful myths that help support many reactive and unfortunate decisions. The following is an all-star line-up from the last couple of decades. Board members in particular should hold shareholders' pockets tightly when hearing any of the following:

■ *'Initial market reactions don't matter, we're in this for the long term. Besides, the stock price of acquirers always goes down on announcement of a deal.'* Well, not on *good* ones. Negative market reactions are bad news – they are the investors' perceptions of what the company has communicated to the marketplace. The evidence is that these initial reactions are the best predictors of long-term performance.

■ *'The financials looked fine on paper but we didn't manage the cultures right.'* This excuse for past deals gone bad has become so powerful that 'culture' is now being blamed for everything that goes wrong. The truth is that many deals that ultimately fail were *predictably* failures – that is the financials were never 'fine'. It is extremely rare that a good post-merger integration can rescue a bad acquisition. The idea that deal success or failure rests on how it is integrated supports the reactive behaviour of just getting the deal done and then attempting to make it work.

■ *'Good deals must be accretive to earnings.'* There is no correlation between accretion/dilution and the stock market's assessment of deals. Stock price is EPS times P/E ratio. The P/E ratio is a proxy for expectation of long-term profitable growth. It is common to see EPS increase but P/E decrease. Although EPS is no longer affected by accounting treatment (pooling versus purchase), we are in a very serious situation if accounting treatments can actually drive company-shaping decisions.

■ *'If we don't do this deal we will be the last man standing without a dancing partner.'* When an acquirer is reacting to one deal with no other options in place, this can also be stated as 'you can't overpay for a strategic deal'. Committing capital to an acquisition through fear of nothing left to buy is never a good bet for your shareholders. This logic is a signal to all of a lack of preparation.

■ *'It will cost us much more money and time to build it from scratch.'* That may be true, but it might not be a smart part of a business to be in the first place. Since all the money gets paid up front in an acquisition, there are no options to slow or stop funding as is the case for organic growth projects.

Reviewing the PMI board pack (Board practice no. 2)

Having ensured that a potential acquisition has emerged from a true strategic process, the board should now be in a good position to assess whether management has a real plan in place to translate the business case into value.

While boards have become much better at pressure-testing the economic rationale and synergy claims made by the CEO, board packages on proposed deals seldom contain any real information on how a deal will actually be integrated. What's more, the recent mantra of many PMI 'experts' to move decisively in the first hundred days, pay attention to culture, and communicate-communicate-communicate offer little tangible advice to directors who are attempting to act prudently before approving what hopefully are value-creating acquisition decisions.

In this section I describe a PMI 'board pack' that boards should demand so that they can exercise their fiduciary duty of care to their shareholders. As Citigroup chairman and CEO Sanford Weill recently commented, 'Mergers fail because the people who do them are not really on top of the details … It's like putting an engine in a car. If you don't connect it right, the car is not going to move.' This is precisely what worries investors when deals are announced: can the acquirer actually deliver on its promises? Because that initial market reaction will set a tone for what the organization will have to live with for years to come, it is vital for senior management to bring a credible story to the market.

Directors must feel confident that the claims of management are supported by a specific plan *before* approving a deal. The up-front payment for a transaction requires this plan. While the role of culture in PMI has received tremendous attention for years, it is my experience that when the key up-front PMI issues are ignored or mismanaged, it is easy – and often incorrect – to blame 'culture' for almost everything that goes wrong. The right PMI process and structure will motivate timely senior management decisions, stabilize the businesses, reduce employee uncertainty, drive collaboration and quick wins, set targets and establish a tracking mechanism that recognizes the promises the company has made to investors. Large PMI's bring with them as many as 10,000 non-routine activities that must be completed in a compressed time frame while in the public eye.

This board pack should especially help boards avoid the scenario, so often played out in poorly planned acquisitions, in which directors tell the CEO, 'You mean you didn't think about these issues before you started slamming the two companies together?' Unfortunately, by that time the board can no longer protect its shareholders.

The five elements of the PMI board pack

The board is in a unique position to ensure not only that a proposed transaction makes sense strategically and financially but that the groundwork has been laid to deliver the promised results. By making specific demands of senior management, directors can have a tremendous influence on the outcome. Before a deal is approved by the board and announced publicly, the following five key elements must be detailed:

1. **PMI process calendar** showing phasing of activities;
2. **key top-level shaping decisions** to be made up front;
3. **tailored integration approach** that is clearly articulated;
4. **structure, teams and resourcing** to deliver the PMI;
5. **business plan** that delivers the performance promises for the deal.

PMI process calendar and phasing of activities

A successful PMI does not begin or get done in the first hundred days after closing. It is a structured series of events that begins long before and continues long after the deal closes. The board should have a good view of the phasing of these activities along with a timetable of what is to follow. In recent disastrous transactions, such as Conseco/Green Tree and Mattel/Learning Co., the CEOs have stated for the record that there was little in the way of PMI planning. The respective boards could have easily seen the problems that were to come. In fact, by the time directors even consider an M&A proposal, the PMI process should already be well under way.

Figure 10.2 is an outline of the key phases and activities. These four phases, from up-front planning through implementation, run sequentially but may be advanced or extended:

The *up-front planning and direction setting* phase begins around the same time management is conducting due diligence and valuation work. In hostile transactions, this phase will have to be completed only with publicly available information on the target. During this phase, senior management determines the integration approach and makes key decisions on timing, team structures and roles, resource allocation and performance targets. These elements, which are described later, must be in place before the deal is announced.

The *data gathering and analysis* phase may begin and end well ahead of regulatory approval and deal closure. Integration task forces will collect information on the current operations of the two organizations, then share and compare them to identify key differences and similarities. Clear guidelines must be established, with the help of legal counsel, for what data can and cannot be shared between the two companies prior to closing. While there are constraints on what data can be shared pre-closing, in many cases this is not a major constraint on integration planning since the key data to be shared are focused on organization structure, process and cost-base details that can usually be shared without compromising competition.

> Clear guidelines must be established, with the help of legal counsel, for what data can and cannot be shared between the two companies prior to closing.

In the *design and decision-making* phase, integration teams focus on resolving differences between the two companies. This phase may start before or after closing, depending on the speed of regulatory approval, but it cannot end before the deal is closed. In this critical phase, which will begin to shape the new company, teams gain a deeper understanding of each company's history, culture, strategies and decisions. This understanding should emerge as options for the new company are developed, evaluated and debated. The recommendations developed in this phase need to deliver the target synergies.

The *implementation* phase starts at deal closing and continues until all key integration steps are taken. At this point, a management priority is leading the transition from an integration team structure to the new line organization. This must include rigorous integration tracking that maintains high visibility of synergy commitments and accountability for the actions needed to deliver them.

FIGURE 10.2
Integration process phasing and activities

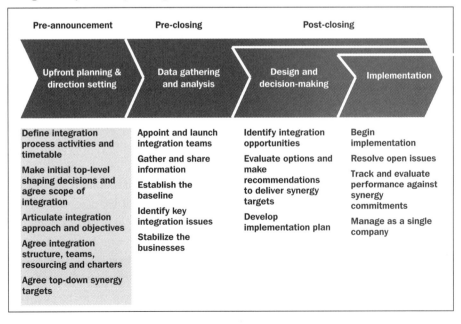

Key top-level shaping decisions

At the outset, several key decisions need to be made – or deliberately postponed – by the senior team for the PMI to move forward. These shaping decisions focus on integration scope and high-level organizational issues. They include what parts of the two companies are being integrated, who will be the CEO and his direct reports and initial details of the organizational structure of the new business. The extent and nature of these upfront decisions will depend on the situation, and on the designate CEO's preference for central versus delegated decision-making. However, these decisions are not easily delegated to an integration decision-making structure. In mergers (versus acquisitions) some of these decisions will be a critical part of the negotiation.

For example, in a recent pharmaceutical merger the new CEO and his team were designated during the negotiation process and announced with the deal itself. Immediately thereafter, the CEO-designate made key organizational structure and personnel decisions that were necessary for the integration teams to progress with their work. These decisions could not be delegated. For example, the scope of responsibility of each of the CEO's direct reports needed to be clarified sufficiently to resolve asymmetries between the two merging companies. One such asymmetry involved Investor Relations. In one company Investor Relations reported to the CFO, while in the other company it reported to Corporate Affairs. The decision was for Investor Relations to report to the CFO.

Some key decisions may have to be deliberately postponed. In a recent financial services merger, for example, the issue of how to merge the two branch networks was postponed for some time beyond the initial integration process. This was because of significant strategic branding issues that needed time to resolve, and because of data-protection laws that would constrain the sharing of customer data.

Tailored integration approach

Few issues pervade organizational life in a post-merger integration more than uncertainty. If this uncertainty is not managed well it will become destructive and almost surely undermine the process. All mergers and acquisitions are different. It is thus crucial that the new senior team agree on a clear, tailored approach to the PMI and clearly communicate this to the two organizations early in the process. This approach will include speed of the PMI, tone (best of both versus acquirer dominates), how decisions are made (e.g. who is involved, decision criteria), and how, when and to whom information will be communicated.

In effect, expectations are being set for the new organization. The senior team must make sure the approach is logical given the economic rationale of the transaction and that their subsequent actions are consistent with the expectations they set for their organization. In times of tension, management and employees will need to feel confident that the senior team is 'on the same page'. Mistakes in approach can lead to PMI failures that will likely be blamed on 'culture clash'. By exercising careful oversight, the board can pressure-test the approach and help management avoid this pitfall.

Very few large transactions can be characterized entirely as acquisitions or mergers of equals. This is particularly true of large, global mergers that may require a tailored approach by geography. For example, in the merger of two global entertainment companies it was clear from the start that they had very different strategies and resources in each of their respective geographies. On the one hand, the acquirer sourced most of its content from the USA while the international operations were primarily sales and marketing operations. The target, on the other hand, derived its content from many different countries. Local operations enjoyed considerable autonomy and networked to share content. Both companies were roughly equal in size globally. But the acquirer was slightly stronger in the USA, while the target was significantly stronger in every other geography. The approach was more like a 'reverse takeover' in non-USA geographies, but with sharply reduced autonomy from corporate relative to what had been before. In the USA it was closer to a merger of equals that involved corporate as well as operating units. As a result, the challenges to be faced in the USA were much more complex than in other geographies, and the bulk of the integration effort was focused there. In sum, the merger felt very different in different geographies and this was reflected in the varied levels of resources required to support the PMI effort.

Structure, teams and resourcing

After key decisions are made and the approach to the integration is clear, a discrete integration structure, separate from running the individual businesses, is needed to manage the PMI. Senior management cannot be fully involved in the thousands of decisions, large and small, that must be made. Therefore, empowered PMI teams must be created with clear roles, responsibilities and reporting relationships to make clear recommendations for top management to ratify (see text accompanying Figure 10.3, 'Typical PMI management structure'). These teams facilitate the structured collection of information on the companies and create early working relationships between the companies that will make possible some early successes. Teams within a PMI structure also drive the bottom-up approach that, combined with a tight calendar, forces senior management to make/ratify tough decisions and maintain momentum in the process.

Resourcing the PMI teams must also be considered carefully by senior management. It is not unusual for 10% or more of senior and middle management to be heavily involved in the PMI process. Because these managers should be the most talented people from either organization, who and how much time will be required must be clear so that focus is not lost in keeping the ongoing businesses competitive during the PMI.

In short, the board should understand this structure, the key executives within the structure and the likely timing and level of human resources needed to drive the integration process – consistent with the chosen integration approach.

Typical PMI management structure

FIGURE 10.3
Post-merger integration management

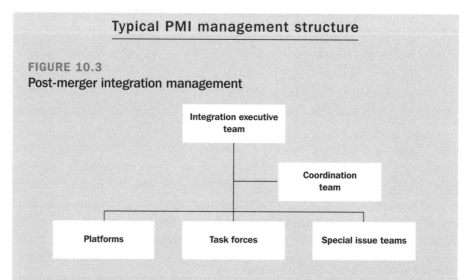

- The **Integration executive team** leads the overall process, sets direction and priorities, approves targets and timelines, makes executive decisions, provides resources, and approves recommendations of the task forces. It typically consists of the most senior management from both companies, not all of whom will play a part in the new company.

- The **Coordination team** drives and manages the integration process, helps identify and resolve issues that cut across task forces, supports target development, coordinates and tracks the progress of the teams and acts as staff to the Integration executive team. This team typically comprises a select group of high-calibre young executives who are all likely to play a key role in the future company. Ideally, this team includes representation from both companies, and includes managers who are second- or third-line reports to the CEO.

- The **Platforms** advise task forces in key functional areas such as HR (e.g. appointments and selection), finance (e.g. synergy tracking), communications, and information technology. The platforms develop guidelines and mechanisms for the task forces to operate consistently during the PMI and include key functional specialists from the two companies.
- The **Task forces** are responsible for developing and delivering integration recommendations and plans for how the new organization will operate consistent with delivering synergy targets. They must cover all relevant parts of the business (e.g. manufacturing, marketing, R&D, etc.) and are typically organized both geographically and functionally. Task force recommendations are reviewed by the Integration executive team.
- **Special issues teams** develop options and recommendations in key areas that interface with other task forces, and need representation from more than one task force to resolve. Examples include decisions about head office location, and major cross-functional processes such as new product development and the R&D-marketing interface.

Once the structure has been created, formally agreed team charters are a way of ensuring that the integration teams are focusing on the right issues and not duplicating the efforts of other teams. Agreeing team charters up front, with the integration executive team, that clarifies which decisions, in fact, are being delegated and to which teams.

The business plan

Before a deal is publicly announced, senior management must devise a credible business plan for the new entity that spells out the synergy targets, goals and one-off costs of the integration effort. The board should understand these broad targets and how management expects to achieve them. It should be clear to the board that these synergy targets – cost savings or revenue enhancements – exceed a baseline of what the two firms were expected to achieve if the merger had never taken place. The detail of the business plan will evolve as the PMI moves forward from initial top-down synergy targets through to final synergy commitments built into internal budgets and plans.

Very often, synergies are not developed with sufficient rigour and may be buried in financial plans with little clarity or visibility. This makes it virtually impossible to know 6 to 12 months later whether the synergies have actually been achieved. To give performance targets more visibility, it is may be helpful for the board to see some additional integration measures and milestones, such as headcount changes, facility closings and new product launches, so that the board can later assess the progress of the integration effort. Creating these integration-tracking mechanisms helps to cement responsibility for delivery of synergies in the new line organization.

The business plan is both content and process. The integration process involves refining and gaining commitment to the business plan. The board must see not only a broad plan, but a process for testing, adjusting and then keeping score against the plan during the implementation phase.

A successful PMI organization is really a 'turbo-charged decision-making machine'. The right PMI structure preserves management focus on the ongoing businesses while supporting a discrete process – for building the new organization – that can accommodate new information and unexpected events. Requiring management to supply the five key elements of the board pack may also help boards distinguish between deals that are ego-driven from those that are truly value-driven. In a sense, the PMI pack is a temperature check on the high-level assumptions made by management regarding the new strategy and expected synergies, and whether the CEO truly believes the new firm can deliver. This credibility may be worth billions to shareholders as deals are announced to the market.

> Requiring management to supply the five key elements of the board pack may also help boards distinguish between deals that are ego-driven from those that are truly value-driven.

Testing investor communications (Board practice no. 3)

Too often, M&A communications expose a lack of preparation by senior management, and investors react accordingly. This early reaction of investors is, as I have shown, an excellent indication of eventual success or failure of the deal. While much has been written about the secrets of successful transactions, little has been said about the communications required to encourage investors to purchase – rather than sell – an acquirer's shares after a deal is announced. Deal-makers and students of deal-making alike have treated M&A communications as an afterthought.

This is a huge mistake, for several reasons. First, well-conceived M&A communications during due diligence can serve as a litmus test for the prospective acquirer in thinking through whether the transaction is a good idea in the first place, and whether it will give investors more reasons to buy than to sell. Another reason is that investors performing their own due diligence use the information contained in press releases, investor presentations, conference calls and interviews. Also, employees, customers and other vital constituencies scrutinize communications materials for signals on how the deal will affect them. Consequently, communications strategy can make the difference between success and failure on everything from securing shareholder approval to meshing the cultures of two distinct organizations.

M&A communication must signal that senior management understands fully what it is proposing and promising. Before directors approve a potential acquisition they should feel confident that the reaction of investors to the deal announcement will be positive. Thus boards should review the press release and the investor presentation, which combined must be able to satisfactorily answer three questions:

1. Is there a credible story with clear targets that can be communicated and accomplished by the acquirer, and monitored over time by investors?

The story – the strategic logic – must address why the company can beat existing expectations, as reflected in the pre-announcement share price, and do so in ways not easily replicated by competitors. This logic must be accompanied by reasonable operating targets that can easily be understood and monitored. Forecasting overly optimistic gains from would-be 'synergies' without explaining how or when they will be realized sends a red flag to investors. It's better to say nothing than to make predictions that can't be achieved. When management fails this first crucial test, it comes across as seriously misguided.

For example, Conseco Inc. attempted to make a case that its acquisition of Green Tree Financial Corp. was 'strategic' by asserting that Green Tree had a successful track record and that the deal was not driven by cost savings. In contrast, when The Mead Corp. and Westvaco Corp. announced their merger, they itemized $325 million in cost savings, released a timetable for achieving the savings, and during the regulatory period, each company posted frequent updates on its website.

Experienced acquirers can also run afoul of investors by predicting benefits for one type of deal based on the success of other, completely different transactions. For example, prior to Newell Co.'s announcement of its $5.6 billion acquisition of Rubbermaid Inc., Newell had a successful 30-year track record in making small, single-product acquisitions. Trouble was, the Rubbermaid deal was 50 times larger, on average, and vastly more complex than any of its earlier transactions. The result: on announcement, Newell shareholders lost $1 billion – precisely the amount of the acquisition premium – and its shares plunged by one half in the first year of the merger.

2. Does the story remove uncertainty and give direction to the organization so that employees can effectively deliver?

Uncertainty is one of the unavoidable facts of life in M&A. But major M&A announcements that inject unnecessary uncertainty are extremely disruptive, and compound the already disruptive effects of post-merger integration. Such announcements will not only cause employees to question the deal's logic, but will also prompt many of them to aggressively consider other career options.

The new management team and key reporting relationships must be in place when the deal is announced to avoid a leadership vacuum that can jeopardize the integration of the two companies. Facility closings that require major relocations and headcount reductions must be carefully communicated. Employees must be told quickly and honestly how they will be affected.

In September 2001, when H-P announced plans to acquire Compaq, the companies said that they would achieve $2.5 billion in cost savings, largely by cutting 15,000 employees over a two-year period – which was over and above the combined reductions of about 11,000 employees that had already been announced by the two companies. This was not received well with employees, in addition to creating a headhunter's paradise. The uncertainties implied therein contributed to the 19% drop in H-P shares on announcement, and a continued decline, as the highly publicized battle between H-P and H-P heir Walter Hewlett heated up in the press.

In contrast, when Reed Elsevier plc announced its $6.5 billion acquisition of Harcourt General Inc. in October 2000, its investor presentation clearly spelled out the strategic rationale, along with plans for selling or integrating each of Harcourt's business units. Reed Elsevier effectively shaped investor and employee expectations for the new organization, and shareholders responded by bidding up its share price by 10% on announcement.

3. Does the story link post-merger integration plans to the economics of the transaction?

Acquisitions often involve the payment of a significant premium to the shareholders of the selling company. Unfortunately, the message communicated to investors does not always square with the performance required to justify the price. Even when management offers credible answers to the preceding two questions, investors will mark down the acquirer's share price to reflect the deal's 'true value' if the synergy numbers do not justify the premium.

Nothing is more likely to cause investors to sell their shares than a deal that cannot justify the value being given to another company's shareholders. Failure of the acquirer to provide critical information might cause it to lose even more value than the premium because of the signals this sends to investors – that the company might be trying to cover up other internal problems.

Besides creating unnecessary uncertainties, the H-P announcement failed this key test as well. Although H-P projected cost savings of $2.5 billion, it said these synergies would not be fully realized for two years, during which time combined revenues would also decline by as much as 10%.

An egregious case was Prudential plc's bid for US insurer American General Corp. Prudential offered roughly a $5 billion premium for American General (all stock) but stated there would only be $130 million of annual synergies. If we capitalize the $130 million at a 10% cost of capital, the synergies have a present value of only $1.3 billion. Investors are smart – Prudential's share value dropped by more than $3.5 billion right on the announcement of the bid, drastically lowering the value of the offer and allowing AIG to emerge as the winning bidder.

Not only will a negative market reaction jeopardize the success of the merger, but it will also distract managers from ongoing business activities. After Conseco got a chilly reception to its plan to acquire Green Tree, Conseco's CEO Steve Hilbert declared that the company would not make other acquisitions while it digested Green Tree – in effect, shutting down the growth strategy that had led to 15 years of superior shareholder returns and causing dramatic declines in its share price.

The theme that emerges in poor investor communications – and in deals that are unlikely to be good for investors – is a distrust of investors. This distrust is generally associated with the failure by senior management to reconcile the performance that is being promised with the benefits that realistically can be achieved.

A good 'story' is just the beginning. As evidence from the recent wave of mergers convincingly demonstrates, investors will eventually see through a flimsy story if acquirers don't deliver. The decision to merge or acquire is very often a bet-the-company decision, and it's a bet that any company aspiring to superior performance cannot afford to lose. Boards should be well informed about the answers to the three communications questions. If not, then it will not surprise anyone that investors have not been rewarded for the deal the board has approved.

Getting it right: PepsiCo's acquisition of Quaker

While many companies bungle their M&A communications, those that get it right stand to reap big rewards for their shareholders – starting on the day of the announcement and over time. A good example is PepsiCo Inc.'s formal announcement of its $13.4 billion acquisition of The Quaker Oats Co. in December 2001.

PepsiCo had to overcome significant communications problems before that deal could be consummated. Reports had been floating in the market for weeks about a not-so-private auction of Quaker, with The Coca-Cola Co. and Groupe Danone the other suitors. After PepsiCo offered to pay a 20% premium for Quaker, it exercised unusual discipline by not raising its bid, even in the face of competing offers. PepsiCo's announcement was received very positively by investors – its shares rose over 6% in the days after the announcement and have continued to outperform the shares of its peers over time.

PepsiCo got off to a good start with a detailed press release and investor presentation, supported by a lengthy analyst/investor call and a webcast. It also sent letters to employees, customers and bottlers to address the concerns of these various constituencies. Not only did PepsiCo promise that the transaction would be accretive to earnings in the first full year after closing, it went so far as to express expected results in terms of return on invested capital (ROIC), saying it would increase by 600 basis points over five years. While sophisticated investors understand this language, it is rarely seen in merger press releases. Additional detailed materials outlining the deal's synergies were also available on the company website.

PepsiCo's investor presentation had three key hallmarks. They were:

1. *Establishment of the base cases.* At the outset, PepsiCo spelled out to investors what the company had already promised concerning revenue, operating profit (EBIT), EPS and ROIC growth. Thus, the case for improvements – the synergies – could then be clearly expressed as increases in profitable growth.

2. *Trackable and defendable synergy forecasts.* PepsiCo described in detail where it realistically expected synergies, differentiating these expected gains from those it anticipated but did not include in the investor model. The investor presentation compared the revenue, EBIT, EPS and ROIC growth rates it expected for the integrated company with PepsiCo and Quaker as stand-alone entities. The presentation described but didn't include any assumptions about the benefits of selling Quaker Oats' Gatorade beverage line through the Pepsi network. Rather, emphasis was given to the benefits that Gatorade brought to PepsiCo's Tropicana business. The presentation erred on the side of modest cost savings assumptions. A total of $230 million of synergies was identified and expressed in terms of their respective contributions to operating profit: $45 million from increased Tropicana revenues; $34 million from Quaker snacks sold through the Frito-Lay system; $60 million from procurement savings; $65 million from cost savings derived from

selling, general and administration expense, logistics and hot fill (beverage temperature when packaged) manufacturing; and $26 million saved by eliminating corporate redundancies. It was clear what investors and employees could expect in every major part of the business. They could easily see how the deal would produce improvements in operating profit, more efficient use of capital and reductions in tax rates – more than justifying the modest 20% acquisition premium of about $2.2 billion.

3. *Clarity of leadership and reporting relationships.* PepsiCo announced that Steve Reinemund would become the new chairman and CEO, Indra Nooyi would become president and retain her CFO responsibilities, and Roger Enrico and Bob Morrison (former CEO of Quaker) would become vice chairmen and report to Reinemund.

The management team articulated clearly how it planned to integrate Quaker Oats and all of its brands into Pepsi and how capabilities from both companies would be leveraged to achieve additional growth. Moreover, Roger Enrico, Pepsi's outgoing chairman, stressed frequently that management used conservative estimates for cost savings and revenue synergies. Despite senior-level management changes at the top of the company, virtually every constituency understood how it would be affected by the transaction.

The December conference call announcing the deal generated a positive initial perception that persisted because of the process that followed the deal closing on 2 August 2002. At that time, PepsiCo released, in Excel format, the restated financial statements for the combination and reviewed all the changes that had occurred since the original presentation. It also hosted a full-day investor conference reviewing the synergies and growth opportunities. Because of the clarity PepsiCo achieved during the closing process, the company actually increased the value of anticipated synergies to $400 million from $230 million.

Using well-prepared documents, a very successful investor conference call, and careful follow-through at closing, PepsiCo was able to paint a rich strategic and financial portrait of the transaction and the effects on the company.

A final checklist

At the end of the day, the key issue that boards must assess is the following: *how will this deal affect our stock price and why?* The time to stress-test the merger strategy, integration and communications plans of the senior team is not after the deal is announced. In this chapter I have outlined what an ordinary prudent person (or director) in similar circumstances should understand before approving a major acquisition proposal by senior management. These are the basics for satisfying the duty of care for a proactive and informed board.

Because everyone loves checklists, the following is a basic bare-minimum list of issues that any board can go through with their CEO on a proposed deal. Think of it as a final racing diagnostic:

- Is there evidence this deal emerged from a clear strategic process?
- How is this deal consistent with our long-term objectives for customers, markets and products/technologies?
- What are the stand-alone expectations of acquirer and target?
- Where will performance gains emerge as a result of the merger?
- Are the projected performance gains in line with the premium being paid?
- Which competitors are likely to be affected by the deal?
- How will those and other competitors likely respond?
- What are the milestones in a 12–24-month implementation plan?
- What added investments will be required to support the plan?
- Who are the key managers responsible for implementing the plan?
- Which pieces of either company are good candidates for sell-off or split-off?
- Why is this deal better than alternative investments?

Given the poor track record behind most major acquisitions and the stakes involved, boards must ensure that senior management can credibly defend and promote these capital investment decisions that can have a material impact on shareholders. And for boards of selling companies that are being offered stock, the same questions must be answered. Consider the poor MCI shareholders whose board encouraged them to take WorldCom stock rather than the $34 billion in cash being offered by GTE – really!

There is a real challenge here for boards – well beyond the procedural requirements of Sarbanes-Oxley. Boards of companies with superior performance have already stepped up to this challenge of not only safeguarding their shareholders' interests but also working with senior management to create value in corporate growth strategies.

Taking a cue from Warren Buffett's quote at the start of this chapter, the board must be able to tell the emperor when he (or his court) is naked. This is why shareholders elect a board of directors.

Notes

1 I wish to thank Loretta Denner, Mark Golovcsenko, Richard Stark, Vikas Taneja and Phillip Zweig for many helpful hours of discussion and important contributions to this chapter.

2 Source: Thomson Financial.

3 This has been widely reported; for example, research by Stephen O'Byrne of Shareholder Value Advisors.

4 'Making the Case for Combining,' Interview with Carly Fiorina, *BusinessWeek*, 17 September 2001.

5 Mark Golovcsenko is a corporate finance expert and project leader at The Boston Consulting Group in New York.

6 While one year may seem a short period in which to judge success or failure, the first year is critical to deliver performance promises because it signals the credibility of those promises. Moreover, there is a growing body of research that shows that initial market reactions are a very good predictor of the acquirer's operating performance over subsequent years. See for example, Sirower, Mark L., and O'Byrne, Stephen (1998) 'The Measurement of Post-Acquisition Performance. Toward a Value-Based Benchmarking Methodology', *Journal of Applied Corporate Finance*, Summer.

7 Results were very similar using RTSR with S&P 500 return as the benchmark.

8 It is interesting to note that the initial market reactions of both the persistent positive and persistent negative portfolios (5.6% and minus 10.3% respectively) were later discovered to have been nearly the same as the overall initial positive and negative portfolios. Thus, the subsequent performance of the persistent performers is largely a function of acquirers confirming – through rapid delivery (or the lack thereof) or convincing signals to that effect – the initial perceptions of investors.

11

LINKING CAPITAL ALLOCATION TO INDIVIDUAL CAPITAL EXPENDITURE DECISIONS

ERIK OTTOSSON and FREDRIK WEISSENRIEDER
Anelda AB

The CEO terminated the discussion regarding the disappointing outcome of a large capital expenditure project by stating 'No manager makes bad investment decisions on purpose! Why waste valuable management time discussing past mistakes?' The meeting was over.

His remarks go to the very heart of the problem with capital expenditure decisions. Good managers are forward-looking and fight hard to make good decisions.[1] Unfortunately any decision-making process will result in 'mistakes' and in the average company, by definition half of all investment decisions will turn out to have an outcome below the cost of capital. Managers in most organizations are reluctant to accept this and learn from past mistakes. Instead they remember only the successful ventures, overestimating their own achievements and their company's performance – and repeat their mistakes.

Managers focus on cash flows and discounted values when making decisions regarding capital expenditure. But to evaluate actual outcome, instead of monitoring realized cash flows, they measure accounting profit. Systematic errors in the company's book return measures provide misleading financial information, and managers are at a loss trying to understand whether or not they are improving company performance.

By evaluating the outcome using accounting profit, rationing of capital and focus on rapid payback, senior management can also be perceived by divisional management to be short-sighted, constraining the company's ability to maintain its long-term competitiveness. Management sends mixed messages to the organization when on the one hand it communicates the importance of a value focus for decision-making but on the other hand has a short-term focus when making decisions and basing follow-up on the short-term development of accounting profits.

An improved feedback loop is necessary. Decision-making can be improved if there is a substantially stronger link in financial management control between decision-making, financial reporting and incentives.

Dramatic moves in share prices and collapsing stock markets should not come as a surprise. Why should investors be able to value a company if its management, with access to internal information, is unable to evaluate the actual performance of its own investment decisions?

Funds available for capital expenditure are heavily determined by how investors judge the attractiveness of an industry. This will vary over time and the 'invisible hand' will force funds to flow from mature industries to industries with perceived higher growth potential. Is the market efficient in this respect? In the 1990s there seemed to be inexhaustible funds available for IT, telecoms and media investments while companies in capital-intensive industries such as steel, automotive, paper and chemicals were pushed to increase dividends to support share prices. Even before the evident excesses of the 'bubble economy', a major Harvard study[2] concluded that US systems for allocating capital within and across companies were failing.

> Even before the evident excesses of the 'bubble economy', a major Harvard study concluded that US systems for allocating capital within and across companies were failing.

Successful adaptation of a management control system to supervise the investment process does have a value, but it is difficult to set up a good enough system. In this chapter, we will try to illustrate how individual capital expenditure decisions are part of a large screening process that includes decision-makers and stakeholders all the way from the capital market down to the shop floor. The approval of an individual capital expenditure is only the final step in a much larger capital allocation process. This capital allocation process is often malfunctioning; in the following sections we will attribute this to:

- a piecemeal decision-making process focused on individual projects and capital rationing;

- investments in new businesses and technology creating new value are not differentiated from investments in existing businesses and technology to defend existing value;

- the information regarding business profitability in the follow-up is misleading, and the feedback loop is broken.

We also present some potential improvements in connection to these.

An example of a typical capital expenditure decision

A paper mill's management requests funds for a new press section[3] in Paper Machine 1 in a US newsprint paper mill with a yearly production capacity of 250 ktons of newsprint. The request is approved by the company board. The decision is announced in the following press release:

> The board of directors of Paper International Inc has decided to invest €30m to install a new press section in paper machine 1 at the District Bay Paper Mill. The project will improve paper quality and increase yearly production capacity with 40 ktons of newsprint. ... [The plant manager states] 'The District Bay mill is one of the most profitable paper mills in the USA. We will deliver this project in an excellent way, focusing on cost efficiency and safety. Our customers can look forward to continued reliable deliveries of top quality paper.'

In the evening the District Bay Paper Mill management, the project team and the suppliers enjoy a celebration dinner. Finally, the long awaited project has been approved. Within 12 months the project is successfully delivered. The market is strong, sales and profits are in line with expectations.

The question is: was this a good or bad investment decision? Can we tell? In this chapter we will put the decision into a context, trying to describe key issues and indicate areas where the capital allocation process could be improved.

Capital rationing and accounting profitability drives investment decisions

In capital budgeting a cut-off rate for investment projects is often described as the main decision criterion. Projects with returns above the 'hurdle rate' are approved and projects with returns below are rejected. It has been argued[4] that the level of the hurdle rate has no impact on the proportion of requests with high net present value (NPV). We argue that capital rationing and perceived divisional profitability are the determining criteria in the capital budgeting process in large corporations and that the prevailing practice of funding individual capital expenditure projects, combined with a focus on counting profit, leads to short-termism and unintended under-investment at the divisional level.

In most large companies, a list of 'necessary capital expenditure projects' is filtered through the organization layers in a screening process in the capital planning cycle. The position on such a list and total funds available determine whether a project is going to be approved. Once senior management and divisional management have agreed on the list of budgeted projects, the formal investment decision with NPVs, IRRs (internal rates of return) and so on is in most cases only a formality.

An increased cut-off rate is likely to result in an increased proportion of maintaining investments,[5] since these are more likely to pass the hurdle rate, as we will show later. This will result in prolonged asset lives and postponed technology shifts.

The most important way to affect capital expenditure decisions is thus to change the perceived level of funds available, since this will have a direct impact on the list of planned capital expenditure projects. When the company board decides on a new dividend policy, a share buy-back or a changed debt-equity target, it is, in fact, impacting the entire capital expenditure process.

In some companies senior management communicates externally a committed target level of capital expenditure, often related to depreciation, that the company will not exceed. This smoothes out capital expenditure, since management will be reluctant to exceed the target in any year. The effect on the 'wish list' is that large projects will lose out to smaller capital expenditure projects that can be more readily fitted into a smooth investment pattern. In many cases this is unintentional and based on misunderstandings between investors, senior management and divisional management. Each level wrongly misinterprets the signals from the level above.

A study[6] of large divisionalized UK companies concluded:

> The parents claimed that they were concerned with the (long-term) strategic plan, while the divisions believed that the parents' prime concern was (short term) divisional profitability. ... It may partly arise from misunderstandings and misperceptions ... the parents seem to be unaware of the pressures they are generating.

In the study, quick pay-back preference and rationing by parents were rated by divisional management as the most important factors impairing investment decisions.

The reverse situation can be equally dangerous. If senior management feels that investors only value growth and that internal and/or external funding is abundant, the risk of over-investment is obvious. It is vital for senior management to appreciate fully the need for a realistic balance between R&D – technology – and investment strategy and financial targets regarding growth, debt/equity and dividend policy. The CEO of Gillette, Jim Kilts, in a pamphlet titled *Escaping the Circle of Doom*, claimed that businesses get themselves into trouble by setting unrealistic targets and then, in attempting to meet these targets, making bad decisions.[7] After joining Gillette in 2001, Kilts dramatically reduced Gillette's top-line growth targets to 3–5%, from double-digit growth during the 1990s.

In the early stages of the planning process the list with capital expenditure projects is referred to as the 'wish list'. After several iterations the list is eventually narrowed down to become the list of budgeted projects. In a large company the 'wish list' can consist of several thousand items – not always ranked by estimated project returns, since most of the projects are 'necessary' in order to keep production efficiency and product quality.

In the case of the District Bay investment, plant managers had already in 1995 put the new press section on their wish list, but capital was tightly rationed by head office and the project was not allowed to be included in the group capital expenditure plan. The reason was pressure from investors on the whole industry to increase dividends after a period of over-investment in the 1980s.

The press section project become part of the group capital expenditure plan in 1999 and was finally approved in 2001. At this point in time it was difficult to postpone the decision any longer, since key customers had started to complain about paper quality. Without the investment there was a clear danger that the whole business would be lost.

The number of capital expenditure projects finally executed in a specific year will be determined by total investment funds and internal resources available for project execution. A latent investment need is built up if total funds available are low. The challenge for company management is to ensure that prioritized units get sufficient funding to finance new technology and growth. This will inevitably lead to a shortage of funds for other units. The projects on these units' 'wish lists' that did not make the final cut in the capital expenditure planning process will be postponed. This shortage of funds for these units will lead to loss of competitiveness and they will eventually either face a larger modernization programme or they will be closed.

The capital allocation process must ensure that the internal process of 'creative destruction' is managed in an efficient way. Unintended short-termism in the capital allocation process can lead to a bias against larger capital expenditures and technology shifts, resulting in lost competitiveness. This misuse of capital has a large cost attached to it. The average company should expect no less than 10% of the annual investment budget to be lost in this inefficient investment process. Companies that are not able to manage the internal prioritization will be faced with increased pressure from the capital markets and will not survive without major change.

> Unintended short-termism in the capital allocation process can lead to a bias against larger capital expenditures and technology shifts, resulting in lost competitiveness.

The challenge is to understand how individual decisions fit in to the overall strategy and investment strategy. It must be understood that the profitability or NPV of the individual investment cannot be the decision criterion.

We argue that the internal capital allocation process could be improved if management framed the 'wish list' so that long-term chains of related investments are evaluated as part of the strategy process and that senior management start to 'walk the shareholder value talk' internally with explicit commitment to long-term value creation rather than evaluating divisional management performance on the basis of accounting profitability. This view is supported by the findings in a recent study[8] of value-based management (VBM) implementations. Successful VBM companies had made explicit commitment to value creation and had also moved away from funding discrete projects and towards approving and funding complete strategies stretching out several years.

The importance of linking technology cycles to investment evaluation

Many companies, especially those in capital-intensive industries, make a large investment followed later on by many smaller ones during the entire life of the large initial investment. This will result in cycles in the level of capital expenditure, cycles often driven by new technology becoming available. In reality, this is a complex situation where a large amount of smaller investments to maintain existing production facilities are made at the same time as large investments in new technology.

In the financial information all this is summarized into one capital expenditure number for the period. Today the financial information available regarding capital expenditures does not give sufficient information either to management or investors. More qualitative information regarding capital expenditure and technology status is needed to help managers and investors to value companies and balance dividend payouts against long-term investment needs and opportunities. There are examples from recent years of companies providing investors with additional information regarding the purpose of their investments. The Swedish company, SCA,[9] is such an example. In its cash flow statement, SCA specifies capital expenditures necessary to maintain current competitiveness versus 'strategic investments' made to grow future cash flow.

> More qualitative information regarding capital expenditure and technology status is needed to help managers and investors to value companies and balance dividend payouts against long-term investment needs and opportunities.

Without an overview of the large 'strategic investments' – historic, present and future ones – it becomes impossible to evaluate individual investments. It is also easy to underestimate the necessary investment spending to defend existing sales and cash surplus, with serious implications for managers and investors using free cash flow models to value companies and business cases.

In industries in the early stages of a technology life cycle, long-term investment needs are often underestimated. With ordinary project returns, companies can easily achieve sales growth of 5 to 10% per annum by only investing at depreciation level. Managers fail to see that most of the investments made are pure expansions and the remaining part is only minor maintaining investments. The inevitable investment costs that eventually will be needed to meet competition when future technology shifts occur are disregarded and long-term growth potential and profitability vastly overestimated. The result of this optimism can easily be the approval of too many growth investments, creating over-capacity in the market or the overpricing of acquisition targets.

The disastrous race for 3G investment in the European telecoms industry is an example. 3G might have an enormous value if considered as a pure growth investment, a value that might have mesmerized managers, investors and politicians. A large technology shift does however not necessarily imply the creation of *new* value; instead, existing value is often merely replaced.

If 3G instead is perceived as partly a replacement investment, the risks involved in taking on huge new debt to finance the 3G venture become obvious. The 'creation' of 3G implies a large-scale 'destruction' of the existing telecoms business. Revenues related to 2G and fixed telephony are threatened since they compete for the same customer base. The revenues from today's business are likely to deteriorate unless massive investments to improve 2G are made. In both cases the cash flow from today's business available to service the 3G debt will be limited.

Companies often neglect the need to put any investment decision into its context, with a too short planning horizon in the capital allocation process. Instead the process should be framed so that the value of alternative chains of linked investment decisions and technology life cycles can be considered. It could be argued that investors and managers have acted in too short-sighted a fashion for some companies, putting too much value on the growth phase of the new technologies (e.g. 3G) and neglecting the sooner or later inevitable deterioration of both existing and new technology (2G and 3G).

Using DCF valuations of free cash flows, where the terminal value inevitably is a large part of the value, is very dangerous in this situation. Investors and managers value the 'investment business case' and feel confident that zero free cash flow growth in the terminal value is conservative. However, in this way investors and managers rarely put a negative value on the deterioration of the base case. The risk is that the full value of the new technology is considered, but the 'destroyed' value in the base case is not included.

As Barwise *et al.* had already stated in 1989,[10]

> unless the base case is realistic, the incremental cash flows – the difference between the 'with' and 'without' scenarios – will mislead. Often companies implicitly assume that the base case is simply a continuing of the status quo, but this assumption ignores market trends and competitor behavior.

To avoid the pitfalls of over-optimistic base cases in free cash flow valuations, valuations based on the discounting of residual earnings could be used. Properly used models such as CFROI™, CVA®[11] or EVA®[12] are less likely to produce 'castles in the sky' since the terminal values in these models only include excess profits over the cost of capital and in most cases should, assuming a competitive situation, fade to zero over time.

Companies must be better at linking their own investment strategies to technology cycles and articulate the inevitable shifts in free cash flows that will occur. Today we are in a situation where stock market psychology, the use of free cash flow valuation and excess volatility in share prices is mirrored inside the company as volatile capital expenditure cycles of over- and under-investment. The effect is higher costs for new technology, since suppliers are burdened with costs for inefficient resource utilization.

To improve decision-making, managers must stop evaluating individual investments in isolation. Instead most investment decisions should be understood as one single step in an investment strategy where the decision in question is dependent on investments already made as well as the long-term strategy of future investment and vice versa. What investment structure will enable individual investments to be aligned more closely to strategies?

A framework for structuring investment decisions

In this section we will in more detail discuss how capital expenditure decisions can be structured. Figure 11.1 describes a case where an expansion investment of 30 is made in year zero (the case is kept simple to allow for a discussion on principles). The expected life of this investment is ten years, and the present value of the investment is 45, which is larger than the investment sum. The NPV of the investment in year zero is hence +15.

The company will of course have to make several smaller investments in

FIGURE 11.1
Example of an expansion investment

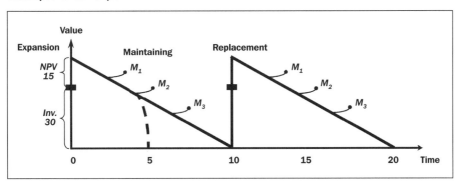

order to reach the ten years. These smaller investments can be said to maintain the value created in year zero – which is why we call them maintaining investments here – and should hence be included as negative cash flows in the present value of 45. They do not add new value as expansion investments do; they defend value already created by previously made investments (here the expansion investment of 30). The profitability and value creation of the project will therefore be overstated if these maintaining investments are not included as a cost in evaluating the initial expansion investment.

After ten years the company decides to defend its existing revenues and long-term market position – that is, to make a replacement investment. Replacement investments are often wrongly perceived as expansion investments by management. Instead, the main effect is that existing customer base and revenues are maintained long term by the introduction of up-to-date production technology and quantity.

From this we can conclude the following:

- *Strategic expansion investments* are the ones that create new cash flow and new value (if successful).

- *Major strategic replacement investments* repeat the same type of cash flow and value that expansion investments create. The replacement investments maintain/defend existing sales and customer base.

- *Maintaining investments* maintain/defend the intended life and value of the expansion and replacement investments.

Hence, three substantially different types of investments exist, conceptually. Financial management control/reporting can be improved if the characteristics of these three types of investments are systematically considered.

What are the consequences if financial management does not differentiate between maintaining investments and strategic investments in expansion or replacement? We will discuss two serious issues with a negative impact on the quality of investment decisions.

Maintaining investments appear to have a high value (IRR/NPV)

Many experience the situation where the profitability (measured as IRR) of smaller investments (Ms as they are called in Figure 11.1) appear a lot higher than the value of the larger expansion or major replacement investments. This is to be expected but cannot be left at that. The reason can be found in the different types of values that are calculated.

Picture this simplified daily-life situation. If you buy a car, it can be viewed as an expansion investment for you personally (if you did not have one before). The Net Present Value of doing this in relation to the magnitude of the investment is often quite low considering how expensive cars are. Nevertheless, you buy it and you have hopefully added some value to your life. After four years the starter motor breaks down. Now you face the issue of whether you should fix it or not. Let's say you have two alternatives to evaluate:

- What is the value of the car if I repair it?
- What is the value of the car if I don't repair it?

The Net Present Value of repairing the car is the value of the first question minus the second minus the cost of the repair. This calculated value tends in most cases to be substantial in relation to the cost of a new starter motor. In fact, the IRR can sometimes be enormous. But now to the crucial question: Have you added this value to your life? No, you have merely – at a cost – avoided a loss of this value. Hence, the value or IRR that has been calculated here has little to do with the overall benefit of your having a car.

Again, for the expansion investment we calculate a value we create, while for the maintaining investments we calculate the value we defend. Those investments are most often listed together in companies' investment plans. Which investments then appear as the ones the company should prioritize, assuming what is a reality to most companies, that capital is a scarce resource? Well, the smaller ones will come out from the process as the more profitable and 'value creating'. It goes without saying, but a company that does not differentiate between those types of investments is likely to lose in relative competitiveness: they will focus on fixing starter motors instead of on larger technology and/or product shifts and expansion. They will focus their resources on ageing operations with acute investment needs instead of on opportunities and larger technology shifts. It is often easy to postpone expansion investments since they often do not 'have to be done' – especially if combined with a perceived low return in relation to the ones that have to be done. For instance, you often do not have to buy another car, although you might want to and it might add further value to your life, but you have to fix a starter motor when it breaks down. We are not

> The different types of values that different types of investments generate must be understood.

implying that the one is more important than the other, but caution is called for;

the different types of values that different types of investments generate must be understood.

Maintaining investments will also distort understanding of the ongoing profitability in a business. Nine out of ten maintaining investment decisions will show IRRs well above 20% since they simply tell how much money will be lost if these investments are not made. Why should managers and board members be expected to understand that an IRR of 18% on a strategic investment might be of much larger long-term value to the company than maintaining an investment's IRR of 35%?

In most companies the process for capital expenditure decisions includes formal board meetings with proper preparation and documentation. Depending on the industry, the individual amount of maintaining investment decisions can be substantial: most companies evaluate these investments using the same process as for evaluating the strategic ones. This creates a sense of management control, but is actually counter-productive. The number of maintaining investments is often ten times the number of strategic investments, consuming valuable management time and distorting the perception of business profitability.

By definition maintaining investments have a high return, and the decision about them is actually not a question of yes or no but only of when. Handling all types of capital expenditure in the same process is not efficient. Senior managements are wasting time deciding issues that they cannot influence in any meaningful way. Instead they should focus on the evaluation of strategic investments and delegate the responsibility for maintaining investments to divisional or local management.

Misleading financial information impacts capital allocation decisions

It is evident that accounting profitability impacts investors and senior management when they allocate capital. It is unfortunate, then, that accounting profitability is misleading – a problem that had already been recognized in the academic field some 40 years ago. Accounting profitability (ROI/ROCE) cannot measure 'discounted cash flow rate of return' or 'true yield'.[13] Ezra Solomon concluded as early as 1967 that ROI is a dangerous measure:

> One must be wary of comparing current book-yields in one division, or company, with book-yields of other divisions, companies or industries. Even a comparison of

current book-yields against book-yields earned in the past by the same entity can be dangerous. ... It is probably better to use adjusted book-yields even if the adjustments are imprecise, than to use unadjusted book-yields figures which we do know are subject to error.

Look at Figure 11.1 again and imagine that you are managing a business with that investment pattern. Assume that eight years have passed and that over the last years you have received a number of maintaining investment proposals showing IRRs of 20–40%. ROCE has been close to 20% in the last years and is expected to improve in the budget. Will you consider your business to be profitable knowing that your cost of capital is roughly 10%? Probably yes. You are likely to act as a manager running a profitable and value creating business. What you miss is that you might be running a long-term value-destroying business, which requires you as a manager to act quite differently.

On a grander scale, systematic errors in the accounting profitability information also impact on analysts' and investors' perception of company and industry profitability. The following statement is from the front page of a recent research report from one of the big US investment firms: 'The global company is number 1 or number 2 in all its markets ... ROCE is reasonable in the USA ... however, the European acquisition depresses ROCE.'

Figure 11.2 illustrates the development of book return of an individual investment with constant sales and cash surplus (with an assumption of 2% inflation). As assets are depreciated and profits inflated, book return grows exponentially. Much, but definitely not all (and to what extent will remain unknown) of this effect is smoothed out at group level. It is only smoothed out

FIGURE 11.2
Development of book return of an investment with constant sales and cash surplus (inflation 2%)

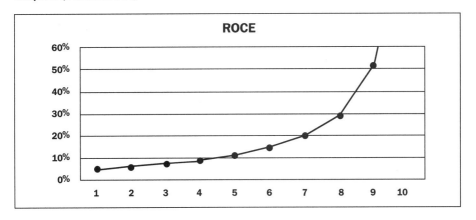

to a small degree at business unit level; the profitability information is hence dangerous. At the point in time when it is necessary to plan for modernization of the plant, depreciated assets results in high returns.

The following statement regarding the District Bay Paper investment decision illustrates the point: 'The average 25% Return on Capital Employed of the District Bay plant in recent years makes the projected return of 18% in the capital expenditure request look conservative.' The statement was part of the discussion at the District Bay Paper board of directors when the investment was approved.

Without reliable information regarding the historic profitability of a business, it becomes difficult to judge the likelihood of returns in an investment request – are we being realistic or not? The problem is amplified if managers' compensation is tied to book return. Managers are not held accountable for the outcome of their investment decisions since the decisions are based on cash flows; but follow-up and compensation is tied to reported earnings and book return.

It is widely recognized that the feedback loop is broken. The IRR of smaller investments or ROCE for the company do not at all indicate the profitability or value creation of the overall business. Managers' decisions regarding capital expenditures are influenced by biased information. Accounting profitability and incremental investments' IRRs must be disqualified from being a part of the answer to the question, 'How are we doing?'

> How can investors judge whether higher book returns are a result of good performance, good decisions or if they are pure accounting errors?

How can investors judge whether lower book returns are a result of poor performance, poor investment decisions or if they are pure accounting errors? How can investors judge whether higher book returns are a result of good performance, good decisions or if they are pure accounting errors?

Perceived industry profitability is also a driver of investment fund flow. Active owners are pushing management in traditional industries to reduce investment levels and increase equity payouts. However, high book returns are no longer seen by some institutional investors as a valid argument. Given the impact that return on book values has on investors' and managers' perception of company performance, it is surprising that these fundamental errors in accounting prevail.

It is high time the standard-setting bodies started addressing the issue. Under the US Sarbanes-Oxley Act,[14] CEOs have to sign that their accounting statements give a fair view of the company. Can managements readily do this when it is evident that the information in their financial statements cannot be related to 'true yield', and investors are potentially misled by an over- or under-estimated accounting profitability?

Companies must also address these issues. There are methods such as CVA®[15] or CFROI®[16] readily available today that circumvent the main biases in accounting profitability. These include (for example) corrections for inflation effects, distortions by linear depreciation. With modern information technology, more accurate information can easily be made available to managers and investors.

Creating a fair self-image is an important factor towards making better decisions and it is vital to make sure the perception of current profitability is correct when allocating capital. Cash-flow-based profitability measures should be used also for follow-up, not only for evaluation of investment decisions. This is likely to notably improve the feedback loop – both decisions and follow-up are based on the same logic: discounted cash flow.

Investment strategies instead of a piecemeal investment process

In most companies the capital allocation process is mainly a screening process with a three- to five-year time horizon. The aim is to eventually narrow down an initial 'wish list' to a list of planned capital expenditures for the coming year. However, the time frame in the screening process usually results in a failure to detect relations between investments and overall profitability and value creation. Major expansion or replacement investments are made in equipment with a useful life longer than the time frame considered. What is perceived as individual investment decisions are often actually a part of a chain of economically dependent investments going back into history and into the future. This can often be a 'brick wall' of investments, where management unintentionally is locked into value-destroying strategies: again and again it has decided on a long series of 'profitable' investments where the end result is long-term value destruction. As we have discovered, this can go on for years without being revealed.

In Figure 11.3 we have used the CVA investment mapping method to map a paper mill's major assets with regard to how much annual cash flow each asset needs to generate to reach an NPV of zero (the Y-axis) and life (the X-axis). This gives us a map of the strategic assets in this plant. We can see each

FIGURE 11.3

A simple investment map of a paper mill showing strategic assets and when they are expected to be replaced under a certain market scenario

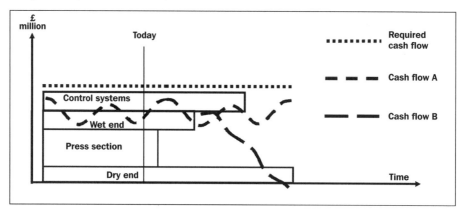

individual asset's required cash flow placed in time relative to the other assets and also compare it to with actually generated cash flow.

The mill was built a number of years ago as a greenfield paper mill. The analysis at that time of that decision showed that the decision was value-creating. However, today we can look back at a number of years and conclude that it turned out worse than planned; the greenfield investment is generating a cash flow that is not sufficient to meet what is required for value creation. The accounting-based financial reporting, however, has failed to recognize this and the reported accounting profitability is above the cost of capital. This should come as no surprise, since accounting-based financial reporting is not intended to recognize whether or not the outcome of a cash flow is in line with the required cash flow given by past decisions.

We can see in the figure that we have an emerging reinvestment need in the press section. The cash flow is expected to continue on an acceptable level if the press section is replaced ('cash flow A'). The alternative to this is to continue to maintain the current press section – but the quality and quantity losses will become an increasing problem for both the paper mill and its customers. Hence, the cash flow for that alternative ('cash flow B') is expected to fall rapidly due to increased costs and falling sales. The value of the investment, when we look at this individual decision, is the present value of line A minus the present value of line B minus the investment sum. The more urgent it is to make the investment, the faster line B will fall and increase the value of this individual decision. The decision to go through with the investment will most likely be taken – a typical example of reactive[17] decision-making.

Time will go by and the next investment request, for the wet end, will be brought forward with similar arguments as the ones for the press section. A similar type of analysis will be made for this investment, i.e. that investing is better than not investing – and a classic double-counting of cash flow A takes place. The same conclusion will be drawn for the next investment and the next and the next for years to come. It is important to recognize that each one of the individual investment decisions has a positive NPV. Management is making the financially 'correct' decisions in this respect.

What the traditional individual NPV investment analysis, or any other analysis normally made in situations like this, fails to show is that the paper mill in itself does not make enough money – the initial investment in the mill turned out to be a failure. Even cash flow A is below the required cash flow over time! One effect of this can be that companies over time put large amounts of money into value-destroying businesses. It should not be a surprise since investments are dealt with on an individual basis in combination with profitability information from account statements. Also in this situation, with poor overall profitability, individual investments, such as the investment in the new press section, have a positive NPV from 'A minus B' calculations. One result of this is that we do not treat units as they deserve – truly profitable and truly unprofitable units deserve often fundamentally different treatments.

Figure 11.3 tells us, then, that calculations on individual investments alone should be avoided. Looking at chains of potential investments will result in better individual decisions. What happens with the decisions for the wet end and the control system if we postpone the press section decision? There is always something around the corner that should be considered in the analysis.

Many capital-intensive businesses have emerged to what they are today by making individual investment analyses. These build an asset base which has brick-wall style profile. Companies, or parts of companies, are often locked into this 'brick wall' state, visualized in Figure 11.4. The brick wall state means that major assets are replaced with some reactive frequency.

The limited funding available for investments and the internal competition on the wish list makes it difficult to avoid the 'brick wall'. The NPV and IRR of a late and therefore more urgent replacement of an individual press section will often be much higher than the NPV and IRR of a larger investment (the difference between cash flow A and cash flow B will become larger and larger as the investment is postponed). The mill will in this case have a low incentive to do things differently. Continuing a 'brick wall' with cash flow at the level described in Figure 11.4 will over time result in value destruction. Without evaluating chains of investments with methods such as CVA (Investment Mapping), it is

FIGURE 11.4

A typical value-destroying going concern business where each individual investment decision shows positive NPV

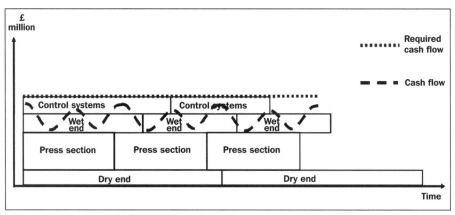

very difficult for a company to get out of such value-destroying 'brick wall' investment patterns.

We can conclude that the internal competition on the wish list will drive operations to request funds for more or less urgent 'have to do' investments in many companies. It is also important to realize that companies investing according to the 'brick wall' pattern are doing this at the expense of larger investments in technology shifts. Resolving the brick wall might increase the volatility of investment sums relative to the quite smooth investment levels that characterize the brick wall.

> It is important to realize that companies investing according to the 'brick wall' pattern are doing this at the expense of larger investments in technology shifts, since available funding is in practice more or less restricted over time for companies in mature industries.

Each individual step in a brick wall might be financially correct according to the individual analysis, but over time the road might turn out to be a dead end. Instead, before every investment decision managers should make sure that they have a map showing them the potential crossroads where they could change direction.

The mill could instead try to avoid the brick wall and behave proactively by identifying in advance the options in time when major technology shifts, plant closures and so on could potentially add value. An example of this is presented in Figure 11.5, where the lives of some major assets (the control system and the press section) are extended and some (the wet end and the dry end) are shortened. Here the mill has assumed a market scenario with a set of factors such as future price levels, technology shifts and so on, and developed the most

FIGURE 11.5

An alternative investment strategy for a value-destroying business – options are created by avoiding the "brickwall" structure

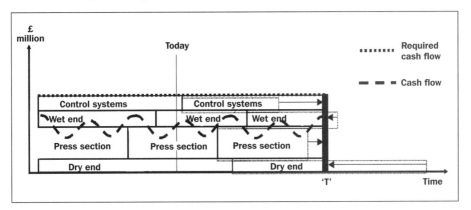

value-creating strategy for that scenario. The mill assumes that some assets can extend their life by (for instance) increased maintenance. This requires a long-term strategy for replacements since these analyses often span entire technology life cycles.

Will a replacement of the entire mill at time T, with a future relationship between the cash flow and the required cash flow similar to the previous historic relationship, be justified? No, since the overall NPV will be negative. Individual investments in a brick wall structure, with the same poor level of cash flow, will most often get the go-ahead (they will individually have a positive NPV in the 'A minus B' double-counting of benefits calculation), but not if all assets are replaced simultaneously! In that situation, it is necessary to invest in a new and competitive technology if a replacement investment is to reach a positive NPV.

Decision-makers have a limited ability to make strategic choices when the business is locked into a 'brick wall' decision structure. The flexibility for decision makers will increase with identified potential replacement occasions.[18] We believe that one consequence of this must be that managers involved in the capital allocation process must recognize that a tighter link between R&D and technology strategy, technology shifts and the timing of reinvestment decisions is needed.

The feedback loop will be improved, since follow-up will be made using the same logic. Cash flow and value can be used both for valuation, decision-making and follow-up. The answer to the question, 'how are we doing?' will now not be found in accounting but instead in this value-focused logic. The organization can be rewarded based on whether strategic decisions create value or not.

Summary

Existing processes for capital allocation often malfunction. The reason for this is that the piecemeal decision-making process focused on individual projects and capital rationing leads to unwarranted short-sightedness. The problems are accentuated by misleading accounting profitability information. We believe that there is a lot of money to be gained by companies that take a grip of this issue. The positive impact of improved accountability when managers get consistent feedback should not be underestimated.

Decision-makers can use long-term focused tools such as CVA Investment Mapping to understand the context in which individual decisions are taken. With today's IT systems, managers can proactively simulate the impact on value of various investment strategies, link investment strategies to individual decisions and consistently follow cash flow profitability in the financial reporting at relevant management levels.

A financial feedback loop is necessary for learning and accountability.

The CEO in the very beginning of this chapter is both right and wrong. Yes, managers actually do their very best when they evaluate investments. No, we should not only look into the future. We have to learn from experience. A financial feedback loop is necessary for learning and accountability.

Notes

1   Clearly there exist managers with a personal agenda that does not put value creation as a priority. However, anyone seriously addressing these topics will eventually conclude that the vast majority of managers are trying to do their best and that most decisions are made in good faith.

2   Porter, Michael E. (1992) 'Capital Disadvantage: America's Failing Capital Investment System', *Harvard Business Review*, September–October.

3   In a paper machine, the press section forces water out of the paper. Typically press sections are replaced after 10–15 years, improved technology enabling production increases by 10–20%.

4   Brealey and Myers (1984) *Principles of Corporate Finance*, second edition. McGraw-Hill, p. 244.

5   A maintaining investment in this chapter is an investment made to maintain, or defend, the life or value of a previously made investment. This should not

be confused with the more common technical word 'maintenance' investment.

6 Barton, H., Brown, D., Marsh, P. and Willey, K. (1992) 'Does Top Management Add Value to Investment Decisions?' *Long Range Planning*, Vol. 25, October.

7 'How Gillette Got Its Edge Back', *Fortune*, 25 December 2002.

8 Hazpeslagh, P., Noda, T., Boulos, F. *et al.* (2002) 'Managing for Value: It's Not Just About the Numbers', *Harvard Business Review*, July–August.

9 Annual Report 2002 SCA; www.sca.com; SCA Investor Report no. 3 (2003).

10 Barwise, P., Marsh, P.R. and Wensley, R. (1989) 'Must Finance and Strategy Clash?', *Harvard Business Review*, September–October.

11 Registered trade mark by Anelda.

12 Registered trade mark by Stern Stewart & Co.

13 Solomon, E. and Laya, J. (1967) 'Measurement of Company Profitability: Some Systematic Errors in the Accounting Rate of Return', in Robichek, A.A. (ed.) (1967) *Financial Research and Management Decisions.* John Wiley.

14 On Sarbanes-Oxley, see Chapters 2, 5 and 7.

15 Ottosson, E. and Weissenrieder, F. (1996) 'CVA – A New Method for Measuring Financial Performance', Gothenburg School of Economics, www.ssrn.com.www.ssrn.com. CVA Investment Mapping is a tool for finding, visualizing, analysing and communicating investment strategies.

16 Madden, Bartley J. (1999) *CFROI Valuation: A Total System Approach to Valuing the Firm.* Butterworth-Heinemann

17 'Reactive' in the sense that the mill's management reacts to an emerging individual reinvestment need and initiates an investment decision process.

18 This approach is similar to models based on option theory.

INDEX